HUMAN VALUES IN EDUCATION

By the Same Author

- ★ Current Trends and Problems of Progressive Education
- ★ A Search for Human Values
- ★ Creativity and Values—Educational Perspectives
- ★ New Education Policy—A New Era in Education
- ★ Mulya Parak Shiksha
- ★ Manav Mulyon Ki Khoj
- ★ Cross-Cultural Communication: World Perspective
- ★ Neo-Humanism and Human Values
- ★ Humanistic Tradition of India
- ★ Encyclopaedic Survey of Oriental Thought, Vols. I-III
- ★ Women Education: Through the Ages

About the Author

Dr. N.L. Gupta (*b.* 1940) is the first scholar to obtain a Ph.D. from two different faculties of Nagpur University. He has a series of Postgraduate degrees and many firsts at his credit. He is the first candidate to submit a thesis for D.Litt. in R.S. University Raipur. He is the first writer to get subsidy for a Hindi book *Berar Ke Sufi Shayar* from Governor of Maharashtra, which is oftly quoted by Urdu scholars. Recently he has been awarded by Maharashtra Hindi Granth Academy for the best work on Literary criticism styled as "Nav-Manavatavadi Chintan" (Neo-humanistic Thought).

Dr. Gupta is a prolific writer. Besides many research papers, he has 41 books in both Hindi and English at his credit. Dr. Gupta's writings have a very broad spectrum of themes which include Literature, History, Culture, Education, Sociology, Philosophy, Theology and so on. He is considered to be the authority on 'Value Education' on which he has contributed as many as six books with different angles. Latest in the series was *Education and Values in the Mahabharata, Mulya Parak Shiksha* of about 400 pages published from Ajmer, has been profusely quoted by the scholars.

Presently Dr. Gupta is working as Assistant Commissioner, Kendriya Vidyalaya Sangathan, Bhopal, Madhya Pradesh.

HUMAN VALUES IN EDUCATION

N.L. GUPTA
Assistant Commissioner
Kendriya Vidyalaya Sangathan, Bhopal (M.P.)

CONCEPT PUBLISHING COMPANY, NEW DELHI-110059

ISBN 81-7022-847-6 (HB)
ISBN 81-7022-973-1 (PB)

First Published 2000
Reprinted 2002

Published and Printed by

Ashok Kumar Mittal
Concept Publishing Company
A/15-16, Commercial Block, Mohan Garden
New Delhi-110059 (India)
Phones: 091–11–5351460, 5351794
Fax: 091–11–5357103
E-mail: publishing@conceptpub.com

PREFACE

Education of late has become a highly explosive subject to evoke general criticism. In theory, Education is supposed to be a powerful instrument of change and progressive improvement of human behaviour, but in actual practice, it is doing very little to cultivate moral and spiritual values in our youths and to promote national consciousness in the country. The gulf between the content and purposes of education continues to be as wide as before despite several attempts in the past to reform the system and strengthen our new democracy.

The instances of deteriorating standards of human conduct and neglect of social concern are quite numerous in the recent history of our country in all walks of national life, and the prevailing crisis of character has stirred nation-wide interest of people for a critical appraisal of the school practices and our educational programme. The quality of teachers and teaching schools and school products has now become a subject of the deepest national concern.

In the aforesaid context of the National situation, the formal and informal agencies of Education—School and Home in particular—assume the position of supreme significance. It is the schools and homes where the primary attitudes and values towards social relationships and personal conduct get fixed and carried all through life. Unless the values we cherish are clearly defined and strongly and assiduously developed by all the agencies of Education, any educational system, no matter how elaborate or expensive, will fail in its purpose. A vigorous programme of value-oriented education, therefore, is the need of the hour.

In the terminology of Indian History of Education the term 'Value' has not been well-set yet; because the theme of 'Value Education' was initially acknowledged in the form of 'Religious Education' or 'Moral Education'. 'Value Education' is more wider, practicable and adaptable than the former two; as no specific faith or religion is reflected through ethical, moral, social, cultural or spiritual values. Here each and every faith or religion has a contribution to make without revealing its identity. It is only at comparative level when we may endorse that value-tenets in U.S.A. are influenced by Christianity or Indian value-tenets have their seeds in Hinduism, Buddhism, Jainism, Islam, etc. In this regard Indian phenomena is uniquely different as compared to the socio-cultural phenomena of the advanced countries like U.K. or U.S.A. For any one it will be a futile endeavour to search Indianness in Hinduism, Islam or Buddhism. It is historically acknowledged truth that true 'discovery of India' lies in the continuous analysis and synthesis of various faiths of Indian origin in particular and others also to some extent because the essence of these faiths is deeply rooted in our composite culture. In spite of this, our constitution stands for secularism. Arena of education is also covered by the spirit of secularism through Articles 28 and 30 of the Constitution. The beauty of our secularism lies not in negation of other faiths but respecting equally other faiths, religions and culture.

The idea of multi-faith school is being successfully translated into practice in U.K. According to one of the surveys, all high schools in Britain are multi-faith in the sense of being pluralist in belief and values. Through value education in our pluralistic society, the theme of multi-faith can be materialized without specifying the identity of faith or religion.

All cherished aims of any nation have been realized through the classrooms only. Butler Act of 1944 in U.K. had a nice line written on top: "What Our Schools Are, The Race Shall Be." It is but natural to have great expectations from our classrooms. Our teachers and students very often fall short of our expectations because their personalities are developed mostly intellectually by assimilating and vomitting of the information ('knowledge') and not by acquisition of moral and spiritual values. International Commission on Education has rightly pointed out that our education basically suffers from "the gap between its content and the living experience of its pupils, between the system of values that it preaches and the goals set up by society, between its ancient curricula and the modernity of science".

The changing character of curricula is such that students find themselves grossly involved to cope up with the gradually growing burden of the curriculum. Parental expectations are also found to be very high. The expectations from the individual teacher and the institution at large are of most idealistic nature. While talking to the teacher of their wards, one may easily find the parent sharing his or her own experiences of school days and ideal character and personality of their teacher. By narrating all these, they expect the same from the teachers of their ward. Perhaps for a while they forget that the present educational system is a sub-system of the prevailing social system, a part of the whole. When their expectations are not fulfilled, they become frustrated and start criticizing the teachers and institution without analyzing the whole phenomena and going to the roots of the problem.

Never before the job of teacher's and parents was so challenging as it is today. An educationist has rightly observed:

> "The erosion of values is now a national phenomenon, so complex and gigantic that a more balanced school curriculum, new learning materials and competent teachers alone can do very little. The task of national development is massive and urgent and no worthwhile achievement is possible without an upsurge of ethical values, of cleanliness of public life instead of the prevailing cynicism and corruption, and genuine practice of moral and spiritual values by all sections of our people."

The anxiety and concern reflected in the concluding paragraph of the report on Religious and Moral Education Committee which was submitted in December 1959 is still more pertinent and relevant as far as the need of 'Value Education' is concerned in the present system of education. A part of the paragraph is as under.

> "We are bound to say that the many ills that our world of education and our society as a whole is suffering today, resulting in widespread disturbance and dislocation of life, are mainly due to the gradual disappearance of the hold of the basic principles of religion on the hearts of the people. The old bonds that kept men together, are fast loosening, and the various new ideologies that are coming to us, and which we are outwardly accepting without inwardly digesting their meanings, are increasingly worsening the situation. The only cure, it seems to us, is in the deliberate inculcation of moral and spiritual values from the earliest years of our lives. If we lose these, we shall be a nation without a soul; and our attempts to imitate the outer forms of other lands, without understanding their inner meaning, or psychologically attuning ourselves to them, would only result in chaos and confusion, the first signs of which are already very distinctly visible on the horizon."

The author of these lines was greatly inspired to write the present volume because of certain experiences. The author happened to attend one of the lectures on 'values' organized by National Institute of Educational Planning and Administration, New Delhi. This inspired him to resolve to write on this very theme.

There was High Level Seminar on 'Moral Education' held at Shimla on 27-28th May, 1981.

The Seminar put forth many revolutionary recommendations. One of them is that "there is a need for producing literature especially designed for the value-orientation of education. The Seminar further recommended special teacher—orientation programmes to train teachers in the effective methods of development of values among students and teachers. Perhaps in persuasion of this recommendation many workshops on 'Value Education' were organized by Kendriya Vidyalaya Sangathan, New Delhi, an autonomous body under the Ministry of Human Resource Development. The author had an opportunity to direct one of these workshops. The desired impact of the workshop on participant teachers further made my determination firm to finalize the format of the book.

This book is written in the hope that inculcation of moral, ethical, social, cultural and spiritual values among the students of schools and colleges will gain some impetus in the context of new 'Educational Challenge'. I believe, all those, who are concerned in one way or the other with the secondary or higher education will get their ideas on the topics synthesized through this volume. General readers specially interested in Indian culture and education will also find many thought-provoking threads in this book.

Besides five appendices there are in all fourteen chapters in the book. The headlines of the chapters run as under:

1. Value-System: Perception and Perspectives.
2. Concept of Values and Culture.
3. Tenets and Teachings.
4. Values and Value Education.
5. Listing and Classification of Values.
6. Modernity *vs.* Value Crisis: A Challenge.
7. How to Inculcate Values.
8. Co-curricular Activities and Value Education.
9. How to Make History Teaching Value-Oriented.
10. Education in Values Through Language-Teaching.
11. Prospects of Value-Education.
12. Towards United and Secular India.
13. Value Education and Women.
14. Prospects of Value Education.

These titles of the chapters are self-explanatory. Besides these fourteen chapters, there are five appendices appended to the book. It is hoped that these appendices will be useful for all those, who are interested in various aspects of value and value-orientation of the younger generation. These appendices are—Value-sheets, code of conduct for students, code of ethics for teachers, inculcation of values through story-telling and bibliography.

Union Government has published mimeographed two volume document entitled as "Challenge of Education—A Policy Perspective," which has been debated at length. In the draft proposal it has been aptly visualized that the new policy should be instrumental in rejuvenating and updating the existing national system and design of education so as to make it respond more fully to the needs and aspirations of the people and to enable the country to meet the difficult and demanding challenges of the 21st century. The new NEP should make its own real contribution to bring about a social transformation, integrate and unite the people of India and modernize society, *while preserving what is authentically and abidingly Indian in our cultural heritage* and enhance efficiency and productivity in all sectors, industrial, agricultural as well as the service sector.

In the new NEP, the following national goals are set:

(i) A United, Secular India;
(ii) A Modern Nation;
(iii) A Productive People; and
(iv) A Humane and Caring Society.

If judiciously planned and successfully implemented, Value Education can prove to be very vital and effective in realizing goal No. (i) and (iv) particularly. Therefore, the Commission has rightly recommended that Value Education should find important place in the school curriculum in the policy statement, it has been suggested that "The basic and essential values underlying our Constitution (Preamble) as well as those contained in the four national goals referred to above should form the basic syllabus for value education, which should find an important place in school curriculum and be given the necessary attention and time". In the light of this fact the present book bears great relevance especially when there is an acute need for literature designed for value-orientation.

The author could not trace any book on Value Education with an Indian perspective except two booklets published by NCERT and one report on the value-orientation of teachers published by the Ministry of Education and Culture. This is like a start. The author will consider his labour fruitful if it will serve the purpose it is designed for and inspire the learned friends to come forward with innovative works on Value Education. The author is fully aware of his own limitations and that of this work also. He will be glad to have free and frank suggestions or even criticism, if any, so that it may come out in more perfect form in the next edition.

I must thank all those known and unknown authors, whom I have quoted here and there. Lastly, I should record my thanks and appreciation for Shri Ashok Mittal (Concept Publishing Co.) who could bring out the book with a nice get-up.

Kendriya Vidyalaya Sangathan Dr. N.L. GUPTA
E-15, Staff Quarters,
Opp. Maida Mills
Bhopal-462 011

CONTENTS

1

VALUE SYSTEM: PERCEPTIONS AND PERSPECTIVES

In common usage, the verb 'to value' means either to like (prize, hold dear) or to apprise (esteem, hold to be of worth). Thus, for example we ordinarily speak indifferent of valuing a worthless trinket which is reminiscent of a loved one, of valuing a bank-account, of valuing a character of a friend and of valuing a work of art. Though these two types of activities are different from each other each has been affirmed as the correct meaning of the phrase "I value". In fact values are indefinable; but they are not unintelligible. The criteria of truth are studied by epistemology; of ethical value, by ethics; of beauty, by aesthetics. Y.B. Keats says: "Truth is beauty and beauty is truth." But he does not explain how they are identical with each other. Herbert identifies good with beauty. Proportion, harmony, or symmetry constitutes beauty. Disproportion, disharmony or a symmetry is ugliness. Wollaston identifies good with truth and regards a right action as an assertion of truth, and a wrong action, as an assertion of falsehood. But these views are exaggeration. G.E. Moore regards 'good' as simple and indefinable. A.C. Ewing also is of the same view. It cannot be analysed into simpler elements. It can be defined by pointing out instances. It is known directly.[1]

Truth, Good and Beauty

The Truth, Good and Beauty—these three intrinsic values are directly linked with intellect, will and feeling respectively, *i.e.*, *jnana, karma* and *bhakti*, which have been arch value oftly reflected in the art and literature of tne East. Cognition, affection and volition are interrelated to one another, and form an organic unity of the mind. Therefore, it is believed that truth, beauty and good have an essential unity which is rather difficult to define adequately. Here we are recalled of

Schliermacher's saying that *Quantity of knowledge is not quantity of piety.* Similarly we can say that the one which is beautiful is not supposed to be necessarily good also. Some objects or ideas are good enough instrumentally; but not so intrinsically. Three main ways (*margas*) of Indian life are closely associated with the trio—*Satyam* (truth), *Shivam* (good), *Sundaram* (beauty). Right from the Vedic period four main values of life have been highlighted, *viz.*, *Purusharthas.* They are *dharma* (righteousness), *Artha* (wealth), *Kama* (enjoyment) and *Moksha* (salvation). As per ethical merit of the East wealth and enjoyment should invariably have the support of righteousness that is called "*dharmavirudha kamo*" (enjoyment unopposed to righteousness). The principles of enjoyment are given or sanctioned by the ethics of the land. Enjoyment has to be canalised according to ethical laws of the society and religion.

According to Jadunath Sinha: "There is one element common to truth, beauty and good. They contain an element of order. Truth is the harmony of ideas and judgements with facts and relations of facts in the environment. Ideal consistency and factual consistency constitute truth. Beauty is harmony of form with matter, unity in variety of contents, symmetry in rhythm. Good is harmony of reason with sensibility, order among desires, harmonious functioning of different capacities. In this respect, truth, beauty and good, which are intrinsic values, are allied to one another, still truth, beauty, and good are unique and irreducible values".[2]

Objectivity and Relativity of Values

The truth of the religious world-view is largely the question of the objectivity of human value. The objectivity of values is most obvious in the case of Truth. It is almost a universal conviction that Truth is, in its very nature, objective. In knowledge we pass beyond the World of Universal Truth. By the way of endorsing our value-judgement we say that a thing is true or false. On the basis of the age-old mystic experiences of the saints and mystics of the East as well as West we pronounce that God is good. In one of the Psalms (117) of the Bible it is prayed:

> Give thanks to the Lord for he is good,
>   for his love has no end.
> Let the sons of Israel say
>   'His love has no end'.

Let the sons of Aaron say
'His love has no end'.
Let those who fear the Lord say
'His love has no end'.[3]

In Hindu philosophy there is oft-quoted attribute for God—'*Sat, Chit, Anand*' (true, conscious, blissful). Establishing a sort of inseparableness between 'God' and 'Good' some philosopher has rightly said that 'God' is nothing but an abbreviation of 'Good'. For Mahatma Gandhi "Truth was God and God was Truth." This sort of identity was the main source of his strength. He had unflinching faith in God. It may be art, architecture, sculpture or literature, in every sphere we come across a deep and dense touch of spiritual values. For Leo Tolstoy (1828-1910), "art is the communication of emotions experienced by a person, by means of lines, colours, sounds, movements, or form of words, to others who may experience, and be infected with the same emotions. The stronger the infection the better is the art. The appraisement of emotions is made by the religious perception of the age. Truth communicates love for God, love for man and brotherhood, which unite all men. It communicates these simple emotions to a mass of men. The progress of the humanity towards perfection."[4] There is no gainsaying the fact that 'love' is a very vital force for unifying the peoples of different cultures and sub-cultures. Chaitanya Mahaprabhu, a great saint poet and apostle of love divine, rightly says: "I pray not wealth, I pray not honours, I pray not for pleasure, or even for the joys of poetry. I only pray that during all my life I may have love: that I may have love to love these." The love may be worldly or towards the God—in both the forms it is worth having.[5] Jalaluddin Rumi, a noted Arabian mystic, maintains that worldly love is the ladder for attaining the divine bliss. Rumi says:

"O Thou Whose Soul is free 'We' and 'I'
O Thou who are the essence of the spirit in men and women
When men and women become one, Thou art that One
When the units are wiped out, too, Thou art that Unity."[6]

There is an important maxim about values that "values are not taught but caught." Examples and models play much more effective role than precepts. With the objective point of view five values are noteworthy. These have rightly been said eternal values or spiritual treasures, quite capable of ensuring happiness and harmony in life. When actions are right, peace reigns and one's mind is free from traces of violence. Out of these five eternal values, according to Sathya Sai Baba, love is the sustenance for all the other four values. He maintains that:

> Love as thought is Truth,
> Love as action is Right Conduct,
> Love as feeling is Peace,
> Love as understanding is Non-violence.[7]

These four fundamental values are generally practised and propagated in educational institutions. Here it will not be out of place to put forth a few more quotes of Sathya Sai, which are in euphemistic form and hence interesting and didactic also in character:

> Politics without principles,
> Education without character,
> Science without humanity,
> Commerce without morality.[8]

are not only useless, but positively dangerous.

> The end of knowledge is wisdom,
> The end of culture is perfection,
> The end of wisdom is freedom,
> The end of education is character.[9]

In his *Shukraniti*, Shukracharya maintains that every country and society has its own central value system inherent in its own culture which forms the cultural tenets of that country or society. He has included it as one of the thirty lores enumerated by him. This last lore (*vidya*) is termed as *Deshadidharma* (basic religion of the country).[10] By this, perhaps he meant only thinking process of the country, which is not disturbed by the ravages of time. This thinking process is the real foundation-stone for the culture of that country, on which the culture is built up and gradually refined. The customs and manners are found to be different in different countries for many socio-geographical reasons. Different climates and different modes of agriculture and craftsmanship naturally engender diversity in the ways of life. It is not difficult to perceive the apparent difference in food, clothes and sanitary habits in the tropical regions and arctic regions. In spite of the fact that the values are relative, peoples display different types of behaviour towards different matters. Harry S. Brondy has rightly observed: "They behave as if the relativity theory were true in unimportant matters, and as if it were false in matters that count. That the Russian Communists should prefer vodka to corn whisky is understandable and tolerable to most Americans. That freedom of speech is not preferable to a controlled press is much harder for Americans to understand and therefore to tolerate. The more deeply we cherish a value, the more it permeates our character, the harder it is to think of it as relative to our own taste, culture, upbringing."[11]

According to Will Durant, certain customs like monogamy or polygamy, endogamy or exogamy, abstention from murder within the tribe, and willingness to kill outside it, come to be looked upon as vital to the common good; they develop into "categorical imperatives"—commands not to be questioned—and are defended by passionate prohibitions, exhortations and excommunication. Conventions are customs which are more preached than practised. They are duties which we require of our neighbours.[12] Moral codes vary from time to time and place to place in a very astonishing manner. St. Augustine was disturbed by the polygamy of Abraham, but rightly pointed out that it was not "immoral" for the ancient Jews to pay the expenses of several wives, since it was the custom of the time. Moreover, it was the demand of the age of war because it was blessed with many children. Therefore, polygamy became a virtue in that age among the Jews. Ancient Kings of India and China also practised it as custom without any inhibition. There were few exceptions also like Rama, a hero of *Ramayana*.

Recalling the instances of relativity of morals Will Durant says: "Orientals cover the head to show respect, Occidentals bare it. A Japanese woman (though this, like so many truths, may be no longer true) pays no attention to the nudity of a workman, and yet she can be as modest as Priscilla Dean. It was 'obscene' (literally, 'on the stage' referring to the Aristophanic looseness of ancient comedy) for an Arab woman to show her face, or a Chinese woman her foot; either concealment aroused imagination and desire, and served the good of the race. The Melanesians buried alive their sick and their old and thought it a kindly way of disposing of their waste. In China, says Lubbock, "a coffin is (was?) regarded as an appropriate present for an aged relative, especially if he were in poor health."[13]

In Hartmann's Monumental Ethics we find a unique amalgam of two very diverse approaches, Platonic objectivism and the Kantian stress on the person. As in Scheler, here too we have a hierarchical view of values; the higher values are dependent on the lower and yet the latter are autonomous in their own field. It is for this reason that no theistic conclusion can be derived from our moral experience.

Scriptural Value System and Operational Value System

In order to analyse the value system of any cultural group scriptural value system is very important as most of the organized societies claim to derive their ultimate values from scriptures. All the values enshrined in the scriptures are not practical or operative at all the time. As per the aspirations of the people and demand of the time we find change in the scriptural values. F.L.K. Hsu[14] calls them 'conceived' values to differentiate them from the operational values. According to Will Durant[15] morals in etymology and history derive from customs (*mores*) and as such they adhere to customs or conventions only. It is needless to say that the source of these customs and conventions are our scriptures concerned.

Max Weber and K. William Kapp have done notable work on the impact of religious ideas on the economic development. Both of these scholars represent the same tradition. The ideas which were germinally present in Max Weber have been cultured by K.W. Kapp into a full-blown thesis. F.W. Kapp first mentions Weber's view on the link between the Protestant Reformation and the emergence of the 'capitalist' spirit with approval[16] and then accepts Max Weber's approach on the similar issue of the relationship between Hindu values and economic development.[17] In other words we can say that the traditional formulated by Max Weber is elaborated by K.W. Kapp.

Max Weber felt that the process of rationalisation in terms of organization, management, etc. occurred only in Western civilisation. Therefore, he argued that the underdeveloped countries failed to develop economically because those rationalising tendencies which he associated with the economic transformation of the West did not appear in these countries. He developed an analogous explanation for the non-appearance of this tendency in other cultures; just as the Protestant ethic had promoted it in the West, the prevailing religious values of other cultures prevented its appearance in those cultures. Max Weber considered the value system of Hinduism as perfectly reflecting its social system. In other words, he regarded the scriptural value system of Hinduism as fully operational and inextricably intertwined with its social system. In particular he considered the Hindu concepts of *Karma* and *Dharma*[18] as an obstacle in the growth of rational tendency.

In his essay titled as "Protestant Ethic and the Spirit of Capitalism" he has clearly concluded that Hindu religious ideas, especially those of *Karma* and *Dharma* as providing the value basis of economic traditionalism and hence to be negatively associated with the prospect of economic development.[19]

Weber and Kapp have analysed the following value concepts with specific reference to the economic development in India:

1. *Parloka*—the other world.
2. *Tyaga*—renunciation.
3. *Maya*—the view that the world is an illusion.
4. *Moksha*—salvation, freedom from the bondage of repeated reincarnations.
5. *Aparigraha*—non-possession.
6. *Yuga*—the belief that the universe undergoes predetermined cycle of four ages of immense durations, and that at the moment it has entered the '*Kaliyuga*' or the worst of the four ages.
7. *Sanatana Dharma*—the concept that Hinduism is an unchanging eternal law or religion.
8. *Karma*—the law of cosmic causation under the influence of which every action must produce a corresponding result for the doer in one or several incarnations.
9. *Dharma*—religion; law; the concept that an individual should perform his duty and fulfil his obligations.
10. *Varna and Jati*—terms broadly embodying the concept of the caste system. Varna literally means colour. Hinduism recognises four Varnas: Brahmana, Kshatriya, Vaishya and Shudra—the priestly class, the warrior class, the mercantile class and the lowest.
11. *Ahimsa*—non-violence.
12. *Jnana*—knowledge.

K.W. Kapp and other like-minded economists hold that these values had a negative effect on the economic development of India. Kapp has vigorously attacked the concept of *tyaga* (renunciation) as extremely inimical to economic development. In *Bhagavadgita* renunciation has been mentioned as one of the potent sources of God-realisation. Lord Krishna says: "Even living the life of a householder, man can realise God through the practice of renunciation. Indeed, 'renunciation' is the principal means for attaining God."[20] In *Bhagavadgita* itself renunciation has been divided into seven classes:

1. Total renunciation of prohibited acts.
2. Renunciation of acts performed for satisfaction of worldly desires.

3. Total renunciation of worldly thirst.
4. Renunciation of the habit of extracting service from others with a selfish motive.
5. Total renunciation of indolence and desire for fruit in the performance of all duties.
6. Total renunciation of the sense of meum and attachment with all worldly objects and activities.
7. Total renunciation of subtle desires and egotism with regard to the world, the body and all actions.

K.W. Kapp is very critical of the III and VI type of renunciation. The renunciation of thirst, as well as the renunciation of the desire for fruit, with regard to all objects and activities, have been described above as third and sixth types of renunciation. But even after such renunciation the sense of meum and attachment for them are left as residues; just as even though Bharata, through practice of *bhajan* and meditation and observation of *Satsanga* (good company), had renounced all thirst and desire for fruit with regard to all objects and activities, his sense of meum and attachment for the deer and protection of the deer remained.

Various Definitions of Values

Some philosophers maintain that values or ideals are in the nature of *Ought*, not in the nature of *Is*. They always transcend the real and objective, and are incapable of complete realisation. They are neither foreseen by any mind, human or divine, nor planned by any mind. They are known when they appear. Rickert holds that values or *Oughts* are prior to being, which do not exist either actually or ideally, which are not existents, and which are not related to consciousness. Values are neither existents nor thinkable.

Rickert's view seems to be unsounded. Values as pure norms, absolute *Ought*, unrelated to consciousness and existence, are unthinkable. Plato's ideas exist in the incondescendental world beyond time and space. They are thinkable by reason (nous). But Rickert's values or oughts are neither existent in time and space not beyond them nor thinkable. So they are unthinkable and useless as a philosophical concept.

W.M. Urban regards values as real entities intrinsic to the structure of reality and gives an ontological status to them. He believes in the realism of values as the realist believes in the ontological existence of nature. He recognises the existential dependence of the real on the valuable.

There is a serious objection to this theory. If values are already intrinsic to reality, then there is no real distinction between the actual and the ideal, existence and value, "what is" and "what ought to be." What is, what ought to be, and what will be would derive from what ought to be. If value is intrinsic to all existence, there is no disvalue or evil in it. But evil is too real and positive to be denied.[21]

Nicolai Hartmann regards values as 'essences' as distinguished from 'existents' and 'qualities'! Values are real, but not existents. Things or acts embody values which are essences. Values are real as essences, but do not exist. They are unchanging, and may be said to subsist. They are not sensed in the same way as odours are. They are known by direct apprehension through 'the sense of value'. Knowledge of values is a priority and not dependent upon experience in the ordinary sense. They are known immediately, whether they are recognised or not. But they are not qualities, like colour, but essences. They give meaning to existence; they are similar to the *a priori* forms of experience according to Kant. Values are unchanging, while things which embody them are changing and variable. But Hartmann regards them as independent not merely of existence, but also as independent of the mind; whereas, Kant regarded the *a priori* forms of experience as of the mind. Values of Hartmann are similar to the ideal of Plato. They arc not 'existents', but 'subsistents', real and unchanging.[22]

Hartmann explains the objectivity of values and the subjectivity of value judgements. But what is the relation of value to existence? Just as it was difficult for Plato to relate the ideas in the transcendental world or eternal archetypes to the sensible individuals in the world of shadows, so it is difficult for Hartmann to relate values to existence. It is also difficult to place values in the existent objects as Aristotle placed forms in the objects. Further, intuition or direct apprehension of values by the sense of value is not recognised by the majority of contemporary thinkers, though Ross, Ewing and others recognise a form of intuition.

Munsterberg maintains that logical, aesthétic, moral and religious values reside in the Super-Ego or Pure Will. They satisfy the over-individual, Pure Will. They do not reside in the individual wills; nor are they based on their satisfaction. They do not depend upon pleasure of individual minds. They are ultra-personal ends of the Super-Ego for the satisfaction and progressive development of its Pure Will. Munsterberg gives an ontological status to logical, aesthetic, ethical and religious values. They reside in the Super-Ego as over-individual ends or ideals, which are gradually realised by its Pure Will. The Super-Ego is Pure Will. It is like the Absolute Ego or Moral Will of Fichte.

Munsterberg's concept of values is more adequate than Rickert's absolute Oughts, transcending thought and existence. They are not subjective creations of the individual minds. They do not depend on their pleasure or pain or hedonic feeling. They are over-individual and ultra-personal. So far Munsterberg's concept of values is satisfactory. But their foundation is Super-Ego or Pure Will, devoid of thought and feeling. It is like the blind universal will of Schopenhauer, unenlightened by reason, and unconsciously realising its ends. The ends are not ends, if they are unconsciously persued. The Super-Ego should be conceived to be rational and conscious. The ends are immanent in it. They are consciously pursued and realised by the Super-Ego or Absolute Spirit for its supreme delight.

Royce rightly holds that the Absolute is the fulfilment of all values, which is infinite self-consciousness, will, and love. Pringle Pattison also regards the absolute as the eternal embodiment of Truth, Good and Beauty which is not pure will only, as Munsterberg thinks. Theistic Idealism holds that values are the supreme ends foreseen, planned, desired, and willed by God, the cosmic Mind, and gradually realised through the world. This concept of values is most satisfactory.

Some modern philosophers hold that moral and aesthetic values are products of creative evolution, which is a process of realisation. Truth, beauty, good, justice, righteousness, love are the 'eternal values', the ends in themselves, which determine the means of their realisation. The various steps in the evolutionary process are indispensable to the ends. The means and the process of achievement are controlled and guided by the ends of values themselves. The ends, ideals, or values are regulating powers, final and alluring causes rather than efficient causes.

This conception of values appeals to the modern mind with a bent for naturalism. But it is far from satisfactory. Values or ideals without relation to a mind are inconceivable and meaningless. Values are values for consciousness. Values as ends in themselves, unrelated to, and unthought of, by a mind, and yet directing and guiding the process of their gradual realisation as alluring rather than efficient causes, are not conceivable. Direction is always conscious. Ends or ideas are always conceived by a mind. They are related to consciousness; they are consciously realised by a mind. It is rational to conceive of the supreme norms, ideals or values as realised in the Absolute or God, which are gradually realised in the spatiotemporal order and the social order. The Absolute is the embodiment of Truth, Good and Beauty. God or the Holy is the Absolute. Values are rooted in Reality. They are not mere transcendent Oughts or subjective creations.

Perry, a Neo-Realist, regards values as an object of interest. An object, real or imaginary, acquires values, if someone is interested in it. A desert is without value, until someone is interested in it positively or negatively. When a wanderer finds it lonely and terrifying, it acquires a value for him. Or when it is harnessed to human needs, it acquires a value.

This doctrine is not satisfactory, since it makes value subjective. A person is not interested in justice and other moral values. Therefore, they cease to be values for him. Then, a person is interested in an object for some reason, *i.e.*, it serves a purpose. Interest depends upon a purpose.

Some modern realists (*e.g.*, Alexander) maintain that values are 'emergents'. They emerge in the course of emergent evolution. Alexander thinks that even Deity will emerge in the course of emergent evolution. He regards truth, goodness, and beauty, tertiary qualities, or values as the products of interaction of the mind and reality. He considers them to be subjective and objective both. Alexander says, "They imply amalgamation of the object with the human appreciation of it. Truth does not consist of mere propositions but of propositions as believed; beauty is felt; and good is the satisfaction of persons." Some modern realists hold that values are 'subsistents' not existents. They do not exist in time and space. They subsist in themselves above space and time. Some contemporary realists regard God as 'the totality of values'. These new fanged notions have the value of novelty, but they do not satisfy the philosophical impulse. 'Emergent values' or values as 'subsistents' are as unsatisfactory as values conceived as pure norms or transcendent oughts like Plato's Ideas.

Pragmatists regard truth, good, and beauty as relatives to human needs. Truth is workability, practical efficiency, or utility. It is not distinct from good. Truth is what we ought to believe, or what works in life, or what satisfies our emotion or what produces harmony in life. All good are productive of desirable consequences in life. They are instrumental; they are good as means. There are no intrinsic goods which are good in themselves. Health, education, business and other cultural and social values are good because of their valuable consequences. Belief in God and immortality, two important articles of religion, have a healthy influence on life and so have pragmatic utility. They cannot be rejected as fictions if the imagination is engendered by human emotions and passions. But their ultimate validity cannot be guaranteed. The will-to-believe is the cause of many beliefs. Faith is justified by its practical utility.

Logical positivists maintain that judgements of value regarding truth, good, and beauty are not universal judgements because they do not refer to objects which are verifiable by experience. They are mere commands, wishes or exclamations. Value propositions are not assertions, but merely emotive expressions and social commands.

Pragmatic theory makes values subjective, relative and mind-dependent. Logical positivism also makes values entirely subjective and ephemeral. These views are not philosophically sound.

Philosophically speaking values are those standards or a code for moral behaviour conditioned by one's cultural tenets and guarded by conscience, according to which human being is supposed to conduct himself and shape his life patterns by integrating his beliefs, ideas and attitudes to realise cherished ideals and aims of life. The 'good' of many or all should be taken as sole criterion for values. Psychologically in the context of instructional objectives 'valuing' falls under 'Affective Domain'. Affective domain has five major categories—receiving (attending), responding, valuing, organization and characterisation by value or value complex. The third category 'valuing' includes the individual's commitment to a certain goal, idea or belief. The fourth category builds up a value-system that includes his behaviour. The last category in this taxonomy is characterisation by value or value complex. At this stage of development, the individual acts assiduously and consistently in accordance with the values he has internalised.[23]

In fact, value lacks universal definition. According to Rokeach "values are beliefs about how one ought or ought not to behave, or about some state of existence worth or not worth attaining. Values are abstract ideals, positive or negative, that represent a person's belief about ideal modes of conduct and ideal terminal goals."[24] A value is a standard we use to influence the values, attitudes and actions of others; it is like a yardstick we use to guide the actions, attitudes, comparisons, evaluations, and justifications of ourselves and others.[25]

Types of Values

Economic Values: An object has economic value if it commands a money price. It is a commonplace that we do not value money or material things for their own sake, but rather for the enjoyments they make possible. Economic value is instrumental rather than intrinsic, although the miser may get a genuine and perhaps unique satisfaction from the mere handling of his money.

Health, Bodily, and Recreational Values: Under this heading we shall include the values of health or physical well-being, play, and all the satisfactions that come from the gratification of bodily needs, such as hunger, thirst, rest and sex.

Social Values: The satisfactions we get from friendship, love, family, and membership in groups are to be included in the social values.

Moral Values: These are the satisfactions and dissatisfactions that accrue to the individual in the course of his attempts to make right choices.

Aesthetic Values: Perceived objects to which the adjectives beautiful and ugly are relevant give rise in the observer the kind of experience we call aesthetic.

Intellectual Values: We prize or get satisfaction from attaining truth in any of its forms. We say that an object or action has intellectual value if it in some way helps or hinders the finding of truth.

Religious Values: If an object by virtue of its relation to the divine can be called holy or sacred, it is said to have a religious value, and the experience of such objects as sacred or divine is called a religious experience.

Each value area has a subjective and an objective aspect. Sometimes we speak of the value as meaning the individual's experience of satisfaction and sometimes value refers to some property or quality of the object or of an act. This is so because value is a relation between an organism and an object, although we cannot ever be sure just how much each contributes to the transaction.

Intrinsic and Instrumental Aspects

A distinction is commonly made between valuing and evaluating. Valuing refers to the fact that we are actually prizing something; evaluation is a judgement which asserts that what we prized really was or was not worth prizing. Valuing is the intrinsic phase of value experience.

To put the matter more concretely, when we see a dear friend we experience an emotional lift that is not quite like any other feeling. We do not at this moment ask whether we ought to feel this way about seeing the friend, nor do we ask whether he is worth our devotion. He seems intrinsically worthy of such devotion.

On the other hand, any value may have an instrumental phase; it may lead to other value experience. Few are the values that do not depend on other values for their own full development. Sunsets and the music of birds, to be sure, are free, but education costs money, so do art objects and admission tickets to plays and concerts. Even religious values, if they are to be realised in a congregation, require clergymen who need some material goods and a church building that is rarely constructed out of piety alone.

The reader can spell out these relations for himself by taking one value area at a time and noting what it contributes to every other value. The point to be stressed is that just as the intrinsic phase of value experience is certain, so is the instrumental phase problematic. For in the moment of valuing something, its ramifications and relations are not apparent. While we are enjoying the solution of a mathematical problem, the uses to which it may be put are not evident and may never become evident without investigation. The taste of wine does not foretell its effects, nor the good deed its blessings.

One type of value can be instrumental to others, but it can also be in conflict with them. The businessman may be too busy for the aesthetic or social values if he devotes himself too wholeheartedly to realising economic values; whereas, the artist may have to live in a garret if he ignores the conditions under which pictures are exchanged for money. We cannot cultivate all values with the same intensity at the same time; every choice is trailed by some sacrifice. Practical wisdom reduces this sacrifice, but the reduction is never complete.

Positive and Negative Values

It seems odd to speak of a negative value, but aversion, dissatisfaction and displeasure are as real as their opposites. Negative values are experiences we would prefer not to have and perhaps would give something to avoid.

By combining the intrinsic instrumental dimension with the positive-negative one we get the following combinations:

1. Intrinsically positive-instrumentally positive, *e.g.*, the eating of a flavourful nutritious food, the reading of a book that is both interesting and instructive.
2. Intrinsically positive-instrumentally negative, *e.g.*, the delights of the drug addict, the alcoholic, betting on horse races (at least for those who lose consistently), and overindulgence of the appetites.
3. Intrinsically negative-instrumentally positive, *e.g.*, a pain warning that medical attention is needed; the bitter pill or

painful surgery that improves health; the failure that inspires greater effort.

4. Intrinsically negative-instrumentally negative, *e.g.*, all instances of unnecessary and preventable suffering, painful incurable illnesses, cruelty, malice, envy.

In general, men yearn for the first class of values, often succumb to the second, endure the third, and hate the fourth.

Higher and Lower Values

In common usage the religious, intellectual, aesthetic, moral and some of the social values are often referred to as the "higher" values, whereas, the material and bodily ones are called the "lower" values. The quotation marks indicate that higher and lower are not self-evident in their meanings. Why are the intellectual values, for example, higher than the values of enjoying a beefsteak? If we examine the kinds of books men do buy, the kinds of pictures they seem to enjoy, and the number of times they prefer beefsteak to study, we can only conclude that often they prefer the lower to the higher, or that if they prefer the higher, they nevertheless choose the lower.

Underpinning the common judgement of lower and higher is a metaphysical belief that those activities which exercise the faculties peculiar to man or are most developed in man are more real than the activities which we share with the brutes. There also lurks the assumption that what is less common is more precious, so that excellence in the aesthetic, religious, and intellectual fields is more to be esteemed than bodily vigour and physical pleasures.

Such convictions may be sound, but it is difficult to see how one could prove them to a sceptic's satisfaction if that sceptic chooses to argue that what we share with the animals is, on the whole, more necessary and more pleasureful than what we enjoy as human beings. He might argue that the rare is the monstrous deviation from the type and endangers it, and is, therefore, less valuable than the common, the average, and the plentiful.

Another way of justifying the common use of higher and lower values is to argue as follows:

1. The aesthetic, religious, moral, and intellectual values are more self-sufficient than the others; they are, on that account, higher. Although truth, beauty, holiness, and good character do depend

on money, health, and friends, they can, if necessary, be cultivated and enjoyed with a minimum of such dependence. Granted one gets a more systematic education if he has the means to pay college tuition and book bills than if he cannot do so, an amazing amount can be learned with very little money. One may not be able to buy masterpieces of painting or season tickets to symphony concerts, yet are the opportunities for aesthetic satisfaction seriously limited by lack of money?

2. These values wear well over the long pull. Physical vigour and bodily delights wane with age; friends and family die; money is a mercurial commodity. Literature is replete with commentaries on the ephemeral nature of worldly goods and pleasures. By contrast the pleasures of intellectual, moral, aesthetic, and religious activity increase with age if for no other reason than that the older we get the less distracting the attractions of the bodily values become. Youth will never take the word of the aged in this matter and consequently will not undertake in the green years to establish resources for the serve ones. Educators who try to convince their charges that something ought to be learned for possible use in old age are wasting their time.
3. One can argue that the higher values—the values of the mind or of the spirit—pervade life more completely than do the lower ones. Every activity undergoes a change in quality when subjected to inquiry, when explored for its aesthetic possibilities, or for its character or religious value. Houses and food can be made beautiful as well as useful, and the spirit of godliness can pervade family life and conceivably even our economic life. The businessman of high character is a better businessman, and a beautiful dance is as hygienic as an awkward one.

In the long run both lines of justification have to be employed. That a life which is self-determined, realises potentialities, and is self-integrated, is good, rests on the belief that man's perfection lies in the direction of the higher values. This belief becomes empirically grounded to the extent that we actually find the cultivation of these higher values to be more satisfying than a life which does not cultivate them to the full.

Every man realises some sort of value in every value area. Every man has to have some material goods, some health and bodily pleasure, and some human associates. His knowledge is never zero; he enjoys some sort of beauty, has some code of conduct, and there are some objects he regards as worthy of his worship.[26]

Communist Value System

As per the communist viewpoint "Morals are the models and standards of conduct people adhere to. Morals as the actual being of good and evil in human behaviour are distinct from ideals as due to be. Morals taken as a whole bear on the morality of a social community. Morals differ in as much as there is difference between the being of different classes and social strata, their place in the system of social production and their cultural levels." Accordingly, the following principles of communist morality make up their moral code:

1. Devotion to the cause of communism.
2. Increase of social wealth by labour.
3. Collectivism.
4. Humanism.
5. Internationalism.

Prior to these proletarian moral principles, morals of the exploiters were prevalent in Russia, which cannot be called universal nor the above-mentioned morals can be called universal. Being a socialist pattern of society in Russia the main current trend in the development is the growing unity of its classes and social sections and consolidation of its social homogeneity. This is a stage on the way towards the supreme goal of the Soviet State, *i.e.*, building of classless society in which, as Lenin said, "all must work." Article 19 of the Soviet Constitution defines the main ways leading to that goal as follows:

> "The state helps to enhance the social homogeneity of society, namely, the elimination of class differences and of the essential distinctions between town and country and between mental and physical labour, and the all-round development and drawing together of all the nations and nationalities of the U.S.S.R."

Article 20 declares that "the free development of each is the condition of the free development of all." This serves to stress the humanistic orientation of the Soviet State's activities and the need to combine the vital interests of the individual organically with those of society. The article further adds: "The state is duty bound to ensure the realistic opportunities, and to develop the personalities in every way, this being an important prerequisite for the intellectual and moral development of the individual."

Politically USSR, with its collapse, is no more a power bloc. The very fallibility of Russian policies was predicted by various thinkers earlier. The advocates of recent Western theories of "Industrial Society" (Walt Rostow, Raymond Aron, John Galbraith), "Post-industrial Society" (Daniel Bell, Alain, Touraine, Peter Drucker), "Techetronic Society" (Zbigniew Brzesinski and others) attack the Marxist Leninist theory of socio-economic formations and its conclusion that capitalism is historically transient in nature; they attempt to show that the capitalist system may be perfected and, therefore, represents the future of the whole of mankind.

Referring to the enormous growth of the social significance of Science, bourgeois economists, philosophers and futurologists insist that, owing to this fact, modern capitalism has undergone radical changes, that such Marxist categories as class-struggle are now inapplicable to it, that state-regulated capitalism eliminates class-conflicts and easily overcomes them. Substituting technological for social determinism, they allege that the use of nuclear energy, electronics and other scientific and technological achievements may result in a radical restructuring of the social, political and intellectual life of capitalist society without the need for social revolution or class-struggle.[27]

Thus, we observe that the above futurology regarding communism and its ideology came to be true. With the collapse of Soviet Union and end of the cold war, indications are that the world is now moving towards a unipolar world led by the United States. Recently on 3rd January 1993, the then US President, Mr. George Bush and the Russian President, Mr. Boris Yeltsin, signed a landmark nuclear arms control treaty in Moscow, which calls for two-thirds reduction of the world's most terrifying weapons. Recently Sino-Russian summit was also held. Thus, the political equation, at the global level, is changing very rapidly. So is the case for changeability of values in the Marxist world-view. Before and even after the collapse of USSR, the most important gesture was stress on humanism. They regarded freedom as the central value and posed their faith in 'New Humanism', as M.N. Roy puts it: "Man is the archetype of society, co-operative social relationship contribute to develop individual potentialities. But the development of the individual is the measure of social progress collectively presupposes the existence of individuals . . . well being, it is actual, and enjoyed by individuals."[28]

Elaborating further the tenets and axiology of 'New Humanism' M.N. Roy says: "The axiology of New Humanism deduces all values from the supreme values of freedom. Freedom is the supreme value of life, because the urge for freedom is the essence of human existence. Indeed, it can be traced all the way down the entire process of biological evolution. Since, all ethical values are derived from the biological heritage of man, they require no sanction which transcends human existence. To be moral, one needs only to be human, it is not necessary to go in search for divine or mystic, metaphysical sensation. Humanist morality is evolutionary."[29]

Confucian Values

In spite of its limitations, the ethical quality of the work of Confucius is undoubtedly high. We find, of course, an excessive reverence for the past; filial piety is carried to a degree unknown to Western nations; and many of the rites enjoined on us appeared to be not merely superstitious, but obviously foolish. Yet the soul of his teaching is moral goodness, and this is so aided and broadened by the inculcation of right reason as to greatly increase its practical usefulness. From a passage in the Shu King it would appear that conceptions in which the claims of head and heart were happily united were known from a very early period, though as this work was compiled by Confucius, we cannot be sure that the words in question are not his own. A minister of the great king Shun (who reigned more than 2,000 years B.C.) being asked what were the nine virtues, replied:

> Affability combined with dignity; mildness combined with firmness; bluntness combined with respectfulness; aptness for government combined with reverence; docility combined with boldness; straightforwardness combined with gentleness; easiness combined with discrimination; vigour combined with sincerity; and valour combined with righteousness.[30]

This is far from being a simple classification of morals, and we may well feel the improbability that such a remote age could be in a position to represent each virtue as being a compound of other virtues; even if Confucius be the author of the passage, it must be admitted to indicate a comparatively advanced stage of both individual intelligence and social organization.

Confucius held office as Minister of Crime in one of the small Chinese States, but not for a sufficiently long time to admit of his theories being fairly put into practice. He believed that, if given a free hand, he would "effect something considerable in twelve months, and in three years the government would be perfected," and crime virtually abolished.

But jealousy, selfishness, and treachery undid his work. He held up too high a standard to suit the debauched tastes of the time. With a pride which did him credit, he gave up his post when a rival ruler sent eighty dancing girls as a present to his master in the hope of destroying his influence. The trick was successful: the philosopher was no match for the dancers.

His reverence for forms and ceremonial, his scrupulous observance of the details of Chinese etiquette, did not blind him to the perception of the real meaning, the essentially practical nature, of right conduct. Nor did the stress laid on filial piety cause him to overlook the obligations on parents to bring up their children worthily. On one occasion, when a father brought an accusation against his son, Confucius cast both into prison, and, in reply to remonstrances, is said to have uttered the following homily:

> "Am I to punish for a breach of filial piety one who has never been taught to be filially-minded? Is not he who neglects to teach his son his duties equally guilty with the son who fails in them? Crime is not inherent in human nature and, therefore, the father in the family and the Government in the State are responsible for the crimes committed against filial piety and the public laws. If a king is careless about publishing laws, and then peremptorily punishes in accordance with the strict letter of them, he acts the part of a swindler; if he collects the taxes arbitrarily, without giving warning, he is guilty of oppression; and if he puts the people to death without having instructed them, he commits a cruelty."[31]

Confucius placed an excessive faith in human nature and in the influence of example. "What do you say," he was asked by a chief, "to killing the unprincipled for the good of the principled?" "Sir," replied Confucius, "in carrying on your government why should you employ capital punishment at all? Let your evinced desires be for what is good, and the people will be good." Just as the nature of gold is hardness, and the nature of fire is heat, he held that the nature of man is benevolence, righteousness, propriety, wisdom, and faithfulness.[32] Everything around him gave the lie to this view, but he never relaxed his faith in human goodness.

Confucius was once asked if there was one word which might serve as a rule of practice for all in one's life. With remarkable penetration he replied: "Is not reciprocity such a word? What you do not want done to yourself do not do to others." He gave this aphorism a more positive form when he said:

> "In the way of the superior man there are four things, to none of which have I as yet attained. To serve my father as I would require my son to serve me; to serve my prince as I would require my minister to serve me; to serve my elder brother as I would require my younger brother to serve me; and to offer first to friends what one requires of them."[33]

It is worthy of notice that the virtues upon which Confucius lays most emphasis are not merely outward observances, but some of the primary and most natural dictates of the human heart. Faithfulness he ranks as the foundation of conduct, and as necessary to truly virtuous behaviour as a boat is to a man wishing to cross a river. "Hold faithfulness and sincerity as first principles," said he. "I do not know how a man is to get on without faithfulness." The earnestness with which he insisted over and over again on this requirement shows that his system was not so devoid of the spiritual element as is often supposed.

Tips from Confucianism

1. Do not wish for quick results, nor look for small advantages. If you seek quick results, you will not attain the ultimate goal. If you are led by small advantages, you will never accomplish great things.
2. The nobler man first practises what he preaches and afterwards preaches according to the practice.
3. If, when you look to your own heart, you find nothing wrong there, what is there to worry about, what is there to fear.
4. When you know a thing to recognise that you know it, and when you do not, to know that you do not know—that is knowledge.
5. To go too far is as bad as to fall short.
6. A man without virtue cannot long abide in adversity, nor can be long abide in happiness.

7. When you see a man of worth, think of how you may emulate him. When you see one who is unworthy, examine your own character.
8. Wealth and rank are what man desires, but unless they be obtained in the right way they may not be possessed.
9. Feel kindly toward everyone, but be intimate only with the virtuous.
10. Hold faithfulness and sincerity as first principles.
11. Benevolence is the tranquil habitation of man, and righteousness is his straight path.
12. Virtue is not left to stand alone. He who practises it will have neighbours.
13. The great end of learning is nothing else but to seek for the lost mind.
14. A man can enlarge the principles which he follows; those principles don't enlarge the man.
15. Virtue is the root, wealth is result.[34]

Exhorting the king once Confucius said: "To govern (Cheng) is to correct (Cheng). If you set an example by being correct, who would dare to remain incorrect."[35]

In Chinese language the word Cheng (to govern) and Cheng (to correct) are cognate. He further added, "Guide them by edicts, keep them in line by punishment and the common people will stay out of trouble but will have no sense of shame. The ultimate of government is the welfare of the common people. This is the most basic principle in Confucianism. Example is better than precept. This is what he impressed upon the ruler.

"Moral example is far more effective than edicts, and where edicts contradict the example, it is the example that the common people will need rather than the edicts. This point is most persuasively put by Confucius."

Taoist Values

Taoism negates all self-seeking and self-assertive processes and prefers inwardness of a man, and a man who is never forcing and never under strain. According to Tao the preliminaries to arriving at full self-knowledge are selflessness, cleanliness and emotional calm. By cleanliness of thought and body. He says: "Only where all is clean will it reveal itself, therefore, put self-aside. Perturbing emotions must likewise be quelled. Ruffling the surface of the mind they prevent introspection from seeing past time to the springs of consciousness beneath."[36]

The concept of inwardness or emotional calm is not to be taken as identified with inaction, as it has been said in *Bhagavadgita*:

> Only duty is thy concern
> And not the fruits.
> Don't stand for the fruit
> Nor indulge in inaction.[37]

Emotional calm means to be the pure embodiment of suppleness, simplicity and freedom. Thus a kind of pure effectiveness will emerge in which no motion is wasted on outward show:

> One may move so well that a foot-print never shows
> Speak so well that the tongue never slips
> Reckon so well that no counter is needed.[38]

Following the analogy of water, the Taoists rejected all forms of self-assertiveness and competition. The world is full of people who are determined to be 'somebody' or give trouble. They want to get ahead, to stand out. Taoism has little use for such ambition.

Behind the 'success story' of Japan one of the prominent factors is that they have discarded the ambition to be 'somebody', particularly in the industrial sector. Because there are no ethnic divisions in the Japanese society and regional divisions have disappeared as a result of rapid urbanisation and the powerful impact of the mass-media, people are no longer conscious of a division between 'upper' and 'lower' class. Everyone thinks himself or herself as middle-class. Therefore, following the ideology of Tao they prefer 'anybody' to 'somebody'.

There is always danger in being at the top. Chanakya (Kautilya) in his '*Neeti Shataka*' says that "in the forest tall and straight trees are cut first." Similarly Tao observes that "The axe falls on the tallest tree." Therefore, he alarms us:

> Standing tiptoe a man loses balance,
> Admiring himself he does so alone
> At no time in the world will a man
> Who is sane
> Over-reach himself
> Over-spend himself
> Over-rate himself.

Thus, we observe that there is a profound naturalism in Taoist value-system, but it is naturalism of Rousseau, Wordsworth, Thoreau rather than that of Galileo or Bacon.[39]

Gandhian Values and School Programmes

In order to create new social order Gandhiji introduced Nai Talim in the year 1937, which is popularly known as Basic Education. This system of education, which could not be continued for several socio-political reasons, is based on certain values cherished by him. He wanted that these values should be internalised by the younger generation also through new system of education evolved by him. The NCERT and Gandhi Peace Foundation had jointly sponsored studies on Gandhian Values at the school stage. These were the values which he practised himself in his personal and public life, experimented with them and suggested that our society should be instructed on the basis of these values if we want to remodel the social setup through education. These values are as follows:

1. Truth (Honesty);
2. Non-violence (Love for mankind, service of humanity, *satyagraha*, compassion, universal love);
3. Freedom (Fearlessness);
4. Democracy (Rights, duties, responsibilities, national integration);
5. Sarva Dharma Samabhava (Composite culture, reverence for others' beliefs, communal unity);
6. Equality (Removal of untouchability, social justice non-exploitation);
7. Self-realisation (Swadesh, dignity of labour);
8. Purity of ends and means (Integrity between thought and action);
9. Self-discipline (Self-control);
10. Cleanliness (Suddhi, simplicity of life, non-consumerism, aesthetic life).

For the realisation of these values in the system of education, a properly planned curriculum, organization of community life based on these values inside the educational institution and a programme of social service integrated to school life are very necessary.

Socially useful productive work (SUPW), which is now called 'Work Experience', should be integrated with the courses of study and participation in it should aim at developing dignity of labour, promotion of self-reliance, productive efficiency, co-operation, dutifulness, along with development of intellectual and aesthetic qualities such as sensitivity to beauty, spirit of inquiry, problem-solving capacity, productive skill, effective use of tools and implements.

Political Values

The political values in culture constitute an inseparable part of its total value-system. They are more important because of their pervasiveness, effectiveness, etc. These values affect the behaviour of all the citizens of the society during their life. Political values are visible in a country when citizens opt for one political party over another, when the President of India conveys his message on various occasions including those of national festivals, etc., when the ruling party annex a bill into law, etc.

The very existence of government policies reveals that there are rules of one kind or another which are to be enforced if people were to lead a harmonious and peaceful life in the society. According to James Madison, Government is "the political and administrative machinery of an organized state." When the word government is used as a noun it refers to the institutions and persons who exercise authority in a cultural group. If it is used as a verb, it relates to the exercise of the authority, to the processes of control, etc. It has been rightly said that if people were angels, no government would be necessary. But people are not angels, they are persons who may have conflicting interests and desires. Therefore, some kind of governmental arrangement is necessary for every civilised group. Government can never be a static arrangement. In the words of Woodrow Wilson, it is an ever-living thing.

As far as governments' policies are concerned, they are nothing but practical aspects as government in action as the values are political aspects of a religion. It encompasses such institutions or activities as political parties, the gaining and holding of political office, influencing public opinion and meeting any other demands imposed on individuals by the institutions of government.

Tips of Laotse

Laotse (6th century B.C.) is perhaps the best known of the ancient Chinese philosophers. His work, *The Book of Tao*, still fascinates the readers. The rhythm of life, unity of all world and human phenomena, the importance of keeping the original simplicity of human nature, the danger of over government and interference are some of the themes that often recur in the book. The following selections have been drawn from the *Wisdom of China and India* by Lin Yutang (Modern Library, New York, 1955).

Living for Others

The universe is everlasting
The reason the universe is everlasting
Is that it does not live for self.
Therefore, it can long endure.
Therefore, the Sage puts himself last,
And finds himself in the foremost place,
Regards his body as accidental,
And his body is thereby preserved.
It is not because he does not live for self
That his self-achieves perfection?[40]

Rulers

Of the best rulers
The people (only) know that they exist;
The next best they love and praise;
The next they fear;
And the next they revile.
When they do not command the people's faith,
Some will lose faith in them,
And then they resort to oaths;
But (of the best) when their task is accomplished, their work done,
The people all remark, 'We have done it ourselves'.[41]

Knowing the Eternal Law

He who knows the Eternal Law is Tolerant;
Being Tolerant, he is impartial;
Being impartial, he is kingly;
Being kingly, he is accord with Nature;
Being in accord with Nature, he is in accord with Tao;
Being in accord with Tao, he is eternal,
And his whole life is preserved from harm.

Degeneration

The man of superior virtue is not (conscious of his) virtue,
Hence, he is virtuous.
The man of inferior virtue (is intent on) not losing virtue,
Hence, he is devoid of virtue.
The man of superior virtue never acts,
Nor ever (does so) with an ulterior motive.
The man of inferior virtue acts,
And (does so) with an ulterior motive.
The man of superior kindness acts,
But (does so) without an ulterior motive.
The man of superior justice acts,
And (does so) with an ulterior motive.
(But when) the man of superior in acts and finds no response,
He rolls up his sleeves to force it on others.

The Individual and the State

Cultivated in the individual, Virtue will become genuine;
Cultivated in the family, Virtue will become abundant;
Cultivated in the village, Virtue will multiply;
Cultivated in the State, Virtue will prosper;
Cultivated in the World, Virtue will become universal.

Therefore:

According to (the virtue of) the individual, judge the individual;
According to (the virtue of) the family, judge the family;
According to (the virtue of) the village, judge the village;
According to (the virtue of) the state, judge the state;
According to (the virtue of) the world, judge the world.
How do I know the world is so.
By this.

The Three Treasures

I have three Treasures;
Guard them and keep them safe;
The first is *Love*.
The second is *Never too much*.
The third is, *Never be the first in the world*.

Through Love, one has no fear;
Through not doing too much, one has amplitude
(of reserve power);

Through not presuming to be first in the world, one can develop one's talent and let it mature.

If one forsakes love and fearlessness,
forsakes restraint and reserve power,
forsakes following behind and rushes in front,
He is dead!
For love is victorious in attack,
And invulnerable in defence.
Heaven arms with love
Those it would not see destroyed.

Negative or Demoniacal Values

Man is born with natural bliss of love and compassion, but everywhere he is found to be a victim of hatred, jealousy, anger, passion, etc. From the dawn of civilisation our social ethos have been disapproving these negative values. These vices weaken the human beings. That's what is prayed in *Rigveda:*

O Love-divine
You offer us a wide defence
Against hatred of aline
That wastes and weakens us.[43]

Negative values are so often spoken of as enemies of man that let him down in all activities of life. We are well aware of this fact. That is why we do not like others to be angry against us, we decry passion of all sorts when others succumb to this vice. We very often complain against them who are jealous of our rise and prosperity. We will never like that others hate us and despise our heinest shortcomings. All these are common to mankind of all ages and places.

Mahabharata[44] has rightly enjoined: "Do unto others as you would like to be done to you." This is such a common thread that it is found in almost all the religions of the world.

Divine values are regarded as conducive to liberation, whereas, negative or demoniacal values are supposed to be conducive to bondage.

In *Geeta* hypocrisy, arrogance, pride, anger, harshness and ignorance; these are mentioned as demoniacal values. men cherishing such type of values are not able to distinguish between good and bad. They do not know what is right activity and what is right cessation of activity. Therefore, they possess neither purity (internal or external) nor good conduct nor truth.

Possessed of hypocrisy, conceit and given to insatiable passion, and adopting false doctrines, they take to action with impure vows. Giving themselves over to endless cares terminating only with death, and given to the enjoyment of sensuous pleasures, they believe the highest limit of joy to consist only in this. Held in bondage by a hundred ties of expectations, given over to passion and anger, they strive to obtain by unlawful means hoards of money for the enjoyment of sensuous pleasures.

Towards the Age of Cultural Priorities[45]

The then Prime Minister of Japan, Mr. Masayoshi Ohira, in January, 1979, initiated several Study Groups in Japan with certain interesting terms of reference. They were: "The Garden City State Concept Study Group", "The Age of Culture Study Group", "The Study Group on Economic Performance in the Cultural Age", "The Historical Evolution of Science and Technology Study Group", etc. The reports of these groups are published by the "Foundation for Advanced Information and Research, Japan". The reports recognise that rapid industrialisation had produced what were referred to as the "advanced nation's disease", in the societal structure. One of such is the "growth of individualisation". They create neurotic individualistic possessive tendencies characteristic of an acquisitive society. These tendencies, the reports predicted, produce a conflict with the growing consensus for evolving a cultural society and fostering of inter-dependence. The Report on the Historical Evolution of Science and Technology says:

> "In the highly industrialised society isolated and alienated individuals have created the main cause of 'illness' of civilised countries which has reduced significantly the vitality of the society. It may be interpreted as an expansion of the living space of mankind being limited by the barrier of 'finiteness of the globe'."
>
> ". . . Life, for instance, cannot be understood simply as an aggregate of elements but the concept of self-organisation is the most important key to understand various life phenomena. It has been remarked in recent years that cells in a living body transform energy from one

form to another directly and very efficiently, by the co-operation of the whole and individual elements. This is a subject to be studied in the context of 'holistic path' concept."

Speaking on the "Economic Management in the Age of Cultural Priorities" the report says:

"In order to secure existence with honour and vitality in the coming 21st century, what harmony should be realised between people, culture and economic principle and how should economic management be undertaken? The following five basic philosophies may be sought after in economic management in the age of cultural priorities:

1. Respect for humanity
2. Respect for Independence
3. Respect for creativity
4. Respect for regionality
5. Respect of internationality."

Referring to what the values are, the Report says:

"In any age and in any society, if a question is made to the people living therein, 'Are you happy?', not a few of them would answer, 'Yes'. There exist some fundamental life values, including the feeling of happiness and worthiness of life, which will not change, even if time elapses and the environment changed. They are something relating to the essence of people's desires. However, the latter assumes various forms in the current of times, diversifies the contents of life values and thus, appears as the change. It is, therefore, important in the study of 'life values' to grasp the essence of people's desires which does not vary with the lapse of time and then study of the life values in the current of time."

Referring to Modernisation in the West, the Report says:

"The 'modern age' was ushered in with the industrial and civil revolutions in Europe. In science, this took the form of 'atomism'; in politics, economics, and society, it gave birth to 'individualism'. The Latin word 'individual' and the Greek word 'atom' are identical in meaning."

Referring to the 'Affluent Society at a Turning Point', the Report says:

"Faced with a deteriorating natural and living environment, scientific and technological stagnation, resource and energy restrictions, and the worsening trade-off between demand control and welfare policies, the economic vitality of the developed countries has fallen. In addition, they are plagued by the "developed nation's disease", symptoms of which are deep-rooted inflation, slowing economic growth, growing unemployment, loss of vitality in the private sector, the decline of business activity (loss of incentives to invest), government bankruptcy and huge fiscal deficits, balance of payments deficits, etc."

Second is a cultural and social viewpoint. The affluent society has altered the desires, behavioural patterns and social structures of its people.

These changes include the formation of a new middle-class, the fragmentation of values, and the appearance of a social pathological phenomenon, the so called 'advanced nations syndrome', in rich societies.

The influence of centuries of modernisation and industrialisation on society has been the appearance of the 'British disease', or more generally, the "developed nation's disease" or the 'Civilisation disease'. This malaise affects not only the economies of the countries involved, but its symptoms penetrate the political and social spheres as well. As a result, the advanced industrial societies are faced not only with declining economic vitality, but also with a variety of manifestations of anomie, such as decreasing political unity, terrorism, crime, juvenile delinquency, suicide, anxiety and depression, alcoholism, drug addiction, the loss of the will to work, and sexual confusion.

Does the ancient Indian tradition has any answers to these growing myths of modernity? "No other country in our planet earth", said a well-known artist, "has nourished and integrated human aspirations and spiritual wisdom in an amazing continuity for more than four thousand years, than this continent called India. From the beginning of time, perhaps even further back than imagination can take us, there is evidence of a sophisticated culture with both a social and political order".

The artist said: "The *guru-shishya parampara* emphasised the importance of learning and hermitages were their places of dwelling. Our civilisation was born from nature, the greatest thoughts were nurtured amongst sylvan surroundings. Students came from far and wide away and were integrated into a highly intellectual approach to living".

Gurudev Rabindranath Tagore said of India:

> "I love India, not because I cultivate the idolatry of geography, not because I have had the chance to be born in her soil, but because she has saved through tumultuous ages the living words that have issued from the illuminated consciousness of her greater sons: *Brahma* is Truth, and the unity of all beings is in *Brahma*."

Without the development of the inner culture of man all our worldly possessions become the means of his own destruction, science and technology, if recognised as ethic neutral, will surely destroy our great civilisation. Without a perception of the morality of the means and ends intellect becomes a self-stultifying instrument. The scòrnful impatience of the egoist wrecks his mission.

The ideals of the ancient Indian culture are not only '*Atmoddhara*' but also '*Jagath hithaya*'. Without respect for ethical principles, an acquisitive society cannot ensure happiness of its members. Indeed as Aldous Huxley points out:

> "The ethical doctrines taught in the Tao Te Ching, by Gautam Buddha and his followers on the Lesser and above all the Greater Vehicle, in the Sermon on the Mount and by the best of the Christian saints, are not dissimilar. Among human beings who have reached a certain level of civilisation and of personal freedom from passion and social prejudice there exists a real consensus gentium in regard to ethical first principles."

Indeed, happiness is the result of *Indriya Jaya*. If the leaders of the polity do not possess this attainment, the consequence will be that the political organisation will be corroded from within. Political power will then be perceived as an instrument of plunder and those exercising such power seek to perpetuate their own power irrespective of the morality of the means.

Concept of Progress and Cultural Values

The concepts of mass production, mass consumption and mass employment as enhanced by the social scientists like Karl Marx became the general creed of Marxism, which subsequently resulted into the value of social equality. The whole gamut of process necessitated the education for the masses. Therefore, in most parts of the world universalisation of education became the significant focal point of the educational process by the beginning of the twentieth century. Mass education was important not only to train employees for industrialism and the technology, but more importantly to teach the cultural values. Mass participation in education is much more important as the time rolls by.

If we turn over the pages of history we find that aims of education in different civilisations have been highlighted as per their cultural tenets including the concept of development. Referring to the story of Yajnyavalkya, a great seer and exponent of Brahmavidya and preceptor of the King Janak, we find that the base of Indian culture and thus of education was spiritualism. Material progress was secondary. Yajnyavalkya wanted to partition his mundane belongings between his two wives Katyayani and Maitreyi, before leaving his home. Katyayani meekly accepted the proposal, but the spiritual-minded Maitreyi's reaction was strange. She said that material wealth was of no avail to her and therefore, she would prefer to be taught the ways and means as to how to attain immortality, which mere riches could not bring. The sage agreed with her that all that wealth could do was to make its possessor happy in the sense of enjoyment of worldly pleasures and comforts but that it could not give one immortality. At this Maitreyi became more insistent on learning about the means to attain immortality. The husband was pleased at this attitude of his wife. But in modern time due to misconceptual notion of modernity and development the cultural values have deteriorated in India as in other parts of the world. It is a global crisis.

In fact, cultural values vary from time to time and place to place and so from country to country depending upon the cultural postulates of the groups. The rate of change in cultural values very much depends upon various socio-economic phenomena prevailing at particular phase of the development as well as basic inclination of the group towards philosophical speculation. As per Spellman, "The concept of development must be understood to be a projection, rather than a reality, based on identifiable Western images and stereotypes combined with a unique historical experience. The cultural values which arose from the dynamics of the nineteenth century industrial, technological, scientific, economic and social alterations are the basis for the criteria of today's development."[46]

In the Western context most significant of all cultural values is the concept of progress, which has been defined in many ways in various religious scriptures. In the Indian perspective there is no more significant value than *Dharma*. It has been the only yardstick by which each and every aspect of life was measured. It may be compared in many respects to Chinese concept of the *Tap* and to some degree the Western idea of Natural Law. *Dharma* is the source of law, the customs of the righteous, the order which unite the people and make the society harmonious provided it is understood and internalised in the right spirit, without much doctrinisation.

There are various interpretations of the term "progress". Nineteenth century sociology was interpreted under the guidelines of the concept of progress of Comte and Condorcet. Since the renaissance the idea of progress was interpreted in a different manner. A political, social and economic interpretation of progress was provided for the common man's benefit by Karl Marx. According to J.B. Bury, "This idea (Progress) means that civilisation has moved, is moving and will move in a desirable direction."[47]

This definition, like many others, does not cover the subtle aspects of the idea of progress. The criterion of desirability is based on one's value-system.

Something, person or place desirable for 'A', may not be so for 'B'. It depends upon the cultural values of the individual or the group concerned.

In life problems are faced by the individuals or groups in all parts of the world and they have also their own ways and means to solve various type of problems. They have different type of perceptions of the problems.

Spellman observes that:

> "As a society oriented towards mass production and mass consumption it will emphasise the new as opposed to the old—two other time concepts perceived very differently in the cultural values of other societies. Products will be advertised as new, improved, recent, youthful; all terms culturally understood as highly desirable. Indeed, development itself is sometimes called modernisation—suggesting that the most recent is the best. To be 'ahead of the times' is considered highly complimentary, while being 'behind the times' is close to an insult. To be 'old fashioned', 'archaic', or 'worse', 'obsolete', is highly undesirable."

Of course, cultural values are hardly ever so completely dominant as to annihilate all recessive cultural values. Such exclusive rigidity would be likely to result in the extinction of the culture through inability to adapt to changing environments. Some words such as 'senior', 'antique', 'venerated' still retain positive connotations.

But essentially the lineal time perceptions of technological societies is an anti-age focus.[48]

Attitudinal Change and Values: For any improvement in the institutions, economic, social or political, desired change in the attitude of the citizens and the concerned functionaries is very essential. It is the attitudinal change which leads to increase in labour efficiency, effective competition, mobility, enterprising attitude, etc., and ultimately make possible higher productivity and well-being of the nation. A sort of revolution can be brought out through the positive changes in the behaviour and attitude of the people.

Gunnar Myrdal has rightly observed:

> "The institutions envisioned in the modernisation ideals would imply a united and integrated national community within which there is solidarity and 'free competition' in a much wider sense than the term generally implies in economic analysis. In such a national community the social and cultural divisions would be swept away. There would be formed a nation with marked social and economic equality and mobility, where people were able to move from one area to another as well as from one economic level to another. The desire for such 'modernisation' of institutions is most clearly expressed in India, where, ironically, the barriers to free competition in the wider sense are strongest and most pervasive."[49]

There is no denying the fact that the Western countries have realised this ideal to a great extent. In the Communist countries in Europe, the standard of living is also growing day by day. Due to positive change in attitude, maintenance and upliftment of various institutions is a healthy sign. Through the attitudinal change, an ideal of social revolution can be materialised and the creation of the "new man" or the "modern man" is possible. For this, according to Gunnar Myrdal, the following values are very essential:

"(1) efficiency;
(2) diligence;
(3) orderliness;
(4) punctuality;
(5) frugality;
(6) scrupulous honesty (which pays in the long run and is a condition for raising efficiency in all social and economic relations);

(7) rationality in decisions on actions (liberation from reliance on static customs, from group allegiances and favouritism, superstitious beliefs and prejudices, approaching the rationally calculating 'economic man' of Western liberal ideology);

(8) preparedness for change (for experimentation along new lines, and for moving around spatially, economically, socially);

(9) alertness to opportunities as they arise in a changing world;

(10) energetic enterprise;

(11) integrity and self-reliance;

(12) co-operativeness (not limiting but redirecting egoistic striving in a socially beneficial channel; acceptance of responsibility for the welfare of the community and the nation);

(13) willingness to take the long view (and to forgo short-term profiteering; subordination of speculation to investment and of commerce and finance to production, etc.)."[50]

REFERENCES

1. G.E. Moore, *Principia Ethica*, p. 7.
2. J.N. Sinha, *Introduction to Philosophy*, p. 369.
3. The *Coming of the Kingdom*, p. 138.
4. Leo Tolstoy, *What is Art*?
5. शुग़ल अच्छा है इश्कबाजी का।
   क्या हकीकी का, क्या मज़ाजी का।।
6. Reynold A. Nicholson, *Rumi: Poet and Mystic*, (1950), p. 33.
7. Sathya Sai, *Education in Human Values*, Thailand (1988).
8. *Ibid.*, p. 128.
9. *Ibid.*, p. 130.
10. कल्पितश्रुतिमूलो वा मूले लौकैर्धृतः सदा।
    देशादिधर्मः संज्ञेयो देशे–देशे कुले–कुले।। —*Shukraniti* 4. 305.
11. Harry S. Brondy, *Building a Philosophy of Education*, pp. 131-32.
12. Will Durant, *Pleasures of Philosophy*, p. 74.
13. *Ibid.*, p. 75.
14. F.L.K. Hsu, *Clan, Caste and Club*, p. 142.
15. Will Durant, *op. cit.*, p. 74.
16. K.W. Kapp, *Hindu Culture, Economic Development and Economic Planning in India*, pp. 5-6.
17. *Ibid.*, p. 15.
18. For details please see Max Weber's *Religion of India*.
19. Max Weber, *The Protestant Ethic and Spirit of Capitalism*, p. 64.
20. त्यक्त्वा कर्मफलानि नित्यतृप्तो निराश्रयः।
    कर्मव्यभिप्रवृत्तोऽपि नैव किंचित्करोति सः।।
    न हि देहभृता शक्यं त्यक्तुं कर्माण्यशेषतः।।
    यस्तु कर्मफलत्यागी स त्यागीत्यभिधीयते।। —*Bhagavadgita*

21. *Elements of Philosophy*, pp. 300-14.
22. *Ethics*, Vol. 1.
23. For details the author's following books are worth referring—'Value Education: Theory and Practice' (1986), 'A Search for Human Values' (1992), *Education and Values in Mahabharata* (1995).
24. Rokeach, *Beliefs, Attitudes and Values*, p. 124.
25. *Ibid.*, p. 160.
26. On the basis of H.S Brondy's *Building a Philosophy of Education*, pp. 136-45.
27. *Philosophy in the USSR*, pp. 18-19.
28. M.N. Roy, *New Humanism*, p. 53
29. M.N. Roy, *Reason, Romanticism and Revolution*, p. 496.
30. R.K. Douglas, *Confucianism and Taoism*, p. 13.
31. *Ibid.*, p. 34.
32. Based on *The Living Thoughts of Confucius* by Alfred Doebin.
33. Confucius, The Analects (Penguin Classics), with an introduction by D.C. Lau, p. 34.
34. Huston Smith, *Religions of Man*, p. 187.
35. Quoted in *Religions of Man*, p. 190.
36. *Ibid.*, p. 192.
37. *Wisdom of China and India* by Lin Yutang, p. 586.
38. *Ibid.*, pp. 591-92.
39. *Ibid.*, p. 591.
40. *Ibid.*, p. 604.
41. *Ibid.*, p. 611.
42. *Ibid.*, p. 618.
43. त्वं सोम तनूकृदभ्यो
    द्वेषोभ्योऽन्यकृतेभ्यः।
    उरू यक्तासि वरूथम्।। —*Rigveda* 8/79/3
44. आत्मनः प्रतिकूलानि परेषां न समाचरेत्। —*Mahabharata*
45. Based on the Birla Memorial Lecture, delivered by the former Chief Justice of India at London Kendra of Bharatiya Vidya Bhavan on October 10, 1994.
46. J.W. Spellman, 'Development and Indian Cultural Values' in *India: History and Thought*, Edited by S.N. Mukherjee, p. 207.
47. J.B. Bury, *The Idea of Progress* (Oxford, 1920), p. 3.
48. J.W. Spellman, *op. cit.*, p. 209.
49. Gunnar Myrdal, *Asian Drama*, p. 31.
50. *Ibid.*, p. 33.

2

CONCEPT OF VALUES AND CULTURE

Better with the learned dwell,
Even though it be in hell
Than with the vulgar spirits roam
Palaces that gods call home.

—*Panchatantra*

Concept of Culture

The word 'culture' has been defined by many oriental and occidental scholars. In general it denotes "good manners and good taste". It is said that culture would not be culture if it were not an acquired taste. E.B. Taylor defined it as "that complex whole which includes knowledge, belief, art, morals, law, custom, and any other capabilities and habits acquired by man as a member of society". Mathew Arnold includes in it the ways of life, the habits, the manners, the very tones of voices, the literature, the things which give pleasure to the community, the words that come out of their mouths, the thoughts which make the furniture of their mind.

There is a difference between culture and civilization. Culture has certain components of permanent nature that are not changeable. Civilization represents material aspects of the age and place. Culture has non-material aspects, which can be enumerated as below:

(a) Group behaviour patterns such as folk-lores and, common folk-ways (clothing, manners of greeting, food habits and common superstition).
(b) Art, sculpture, music, dance, handicrafts, poetry, etc.
(c) Literary advancement which includes various forms of literature.
(d) Religious advancement which includes various faiths, sects, beliefs, etc.
(e) Scientific advancement through inventions and discoveries.

Culture: A Fountain-head of Values

One may ask what are values? What is the relationship between Culture and Values? There are multiple origins of values but our values owe a great deal to culture specially philosophy and religion. Our philosophical and religious tenets are significant originators of our values. This very idea has been elaborately discussed in the following chapter styled as "Value-tenets and Teachings", By the term 'teachings' we mean preachings of great religious and social leaders. Culture is one of the significant sources of values. Since culture differs from nation to nation, cultural tenets also differ. Consequently values and morals also differ from nation to nation, age to age and place to place.

American value-tenets are an admixture of religious and secular tenets and based on materialism. Indian value-tenets are based on spiritualism. Therefore, American and Indian values also differ to a great extent. This hypothesis will be clear if we compare the value-tenets of these two countries, which are as under:

Indian Value-Tenets	*American Value-Tenets*
1. Spiritualism is superior to materialism.	
2. Human body does not consist of physical body only.	Material progress is important.
3. The principle of universal soul.	
4. The principle of trans-migration of soul.	
5. *Moksha* is ultimate aim.	Individual is of supreme importance.
6. Law of *Karma*.	
7. Importance of knowledge.	Life has purpose.
8. Contact is vital factor for formation of character.	Man is rational.
9. Will of God is Supreme.	Certain basic social institutions are important.
10. The principle of other-worldliness.	Selected other miscellaneous beliefs and attitudes are important.

There is a very close link between values and culture. Values originate from cultural tenets and help to shape and maintain the cultural structure of the society. On the other hand culture conditions the various values developed by the individuals.

"In respect to individuals and cultures, values are circular. Existing in individuals, they flow into and help to shape the culture. Existing in cultures, they condition, without categorically dictating, the values developed by individuals in those cultures".[1]

Revival and Strengthening of Values

It is observed sometimes that values are originated from cultural tenets, but they are not adopted and developed by the individuals of the society for good many socio-economic factors. Consequently values remain dormant. But history reveals that in every society and nation at large there had been certain great personalities to counter several evils of the society and strengthen the various cultural values for the wider interest of the mankind.

Among such great personalities, who could revive and strengthen certain cultural values, the names of the following can be quoted, in the Indian context, who could change the course of ideas and thus, history itself by their revolutionary ideas:

Lord Krishna—Karma Yoga, spiritualism is superior to ritualism.
Krishna Dwaipayan Vyas—Subtlety of religion and ethics.
Mahavira—Non-violence and truth.
Buddha—Countering casteism, advocacy of compassion and reasoning.
Ashoka the Great—Benevolence and humanism.
Charak and Sushruta—Code of conduct for physicians.
Shankaracharya—Importance of knowledge and cultural unity.
Chandragupta II—Appreciation for good arts.
Rajendra Chola—Appreciation and propagation of one's culture.
Jnaneshwar—Spiritual knowledge.
Guru Nanak—Brotherhood.
Guru Govind Singh—Humanism and concern for other fellow beings.
Mahatma Gandhi—Freedom of Indians through non-violence.
Ishwar Chandra Vidyasagar—Upliftment of women.
Ramkrishna Paramhamsa—Realising presence of God and preaching the same.
Swami Vivekanand—Countering false notions of religion.
Raja Ram Mohun Roy—Abolition of *Satee*.
Bhimrao Ambedkar—Upliftment of Harijans.
Dr. Rajendra Prasad—Simplicity in life.
Pt. Jawaharlal Nehru—Hardwork and concern for other faiths and cultures.
Mother Teresa—Concern for orphans and handicapped.
Dada Murlidhar Amte—Upliftment of lepers and leftouts.

The Indian value-tenets mentioned above are mainly responsible for originating traditional cultural values. Traditional cultural values exist in many advanced countries also including United States. Such people, cherishing the traditional cultural values, are generally labelled as 'orthodox'. In every society we find 'orthodox' and 'progressive' both types of people. Right from the period of Epics we find these two groups in the society. That is why we find contradictory statements regarding flesh-eating, drinking, waging war, status of woman in society, etc. in our great epic, the *Mahabharata*. The same phenomena are applicable to the modern Indian society also. There is a group of people, who may not agree with the value-tenet styled as "Will of God is supreme" of "Principle of transmigration of soul".

Similarly in American society, there is a group of people who may not agree with the American value-tenet styled as "Material progress is important" or "Man is rational." Growing craze of the Americans for "Hare Rama Hare Krishna" cult and establishment of large number of temples over there are sufficient to prove that a class of American society is more prone to Indian value-tenets. Inspired by the Indian spiritualism and 'Yoga-Vidya', the American authorities established University for propagation of "Science of Creative Intelligence (SCI)," a refined and scientific term for *Dhyan Yoga*. Here it will not be out of place to quote Senator Robert C. Byrd on this point. He says, "Maharshi International University was established in 1971 under the laws of the State of California as non-profit educational institution with teaching programme leading to baccalaureate and doctoral degrees. The decision to establish Maharshi International University (MIU) arose directly from the enthusiasm of faculty, administration, students and parents at more than 600 college and university campuses in the United States who had witnessed the enlivening result of engaging in the practice of Science of Creative Intelligence (SCI) as taught by Maharshi Mahesh Yogi."[2]

Atheists do not believe in the existence of 'God', Atheists, though less in number, are found in every country, in every society. In Indian society also there are atheists, who may not believe in traditional cultural values originated from Indian philosophy. Similarly in United States "Individuals who subscribe to Orthodox Judaism or Christianity accept the reality of a personal God—the God of the Old and New Testaments, a God who is supreme, personal, noncontingent, and directly concerned with, and in daily lives and affairs of man. Individuals more liberal in orientation reject the simplicity of this orthodox view of God."[3]

Indian Culture

As far as Indian Culture is concerned, it would be incorrect and rather undesirable to use "Hindu" or "Hinduism" for Indian Culture even with reference to the distant past. In fact "Hinduism" is not a religion in terms of popular sense of the word. Pt. Jawaharlal Nehru has very rightly observed that Hinduism "as a faith is vague, amorphous, many-sided, all things to all men. It is hardly possible to define it, or needed to say definitely whether it is a religion or not, in the usual sense of the word." According to Dr. S. Radhakrishnan "Hindu religion can be described in one word, that is, do the right." If it is taken to be true, it is applicable to all the faiths and religions. But the concept of right and wrong may differ from place to place, age to age and tradition to tradition.

It is said that religion is a line of demarcation, which differentiates between the man-beast and the beast:

> For it there be no mind
> Debating good and evil,
> And if religion send
> No challenge to the will,
> If only greed be there
> For some material feast,
> How draw a line between
> the man-beast and the beast?
>
> —*Panchatantra*

Biologically speaking man's first inheritance is physical while the second inheritance is cultural. According to Swami Akhandananda "It is this second inheritance that makes for the uniqueness of man; through it, man becomes capable of rising above his physical limitations and achieving unlimited personality expansion through the expansion of his awareness and sympathy. This highlights the importance of this second inheritance for education, ethics, and religion." Thus, vertical growth in human personality has been the landmark in the history of mankind and has contributed a lot to the advancement of civilization and culture. Due to this change, a man has played wonders in the areas of art, literature, knowledge, etc. On this Julian Huxley's following observation is, noteworthy:

> "Man's evolution is not biological but psycho-social, it operates by the mechanism of cultural tradition, which involves the cumulative

self-reproduction and self-variation of mental activities and their products. Accordingly, major steps in the human phase of evolution are achieved by break-throughs to new dominant patterns of mental organisation of knowledge, idea, and beliefs—ideological instead of physiological or biological organisation."

Really speaking values in isolation are meaningless, may it be ethical, social or spiritual values. Ethics is inseparable from social context and social behaviour cannot be entirely devoid of ethics. Our ethical and moral values are vital integrating forces uniting man with man in society. Therefore, real synonym for '*dharma*' is 'integration', which has obviously two aspects—*abhyudaya* (social welfare) and *nihshreyasa* (spiritual liberation). The *Mahabharata*, therefore, puts *dharma* in its aspect as *abhyudaya* as that which holds together, that which sustains all human beings—'धारणात् धर्म इत्याहुः धर्मो धारयति प्रजाः' । It is also said that wherefrom a man derives social welfare and spiritual liberation as well, that is to be called '*dharma*'—यतो वाऽभ्युदयनिश्रेयः सिद्धिः स धर्मः" ।

The essence of "*dharma*" lies in the right conduct which includes love, truth, non-violence, concern for others, equanimity of mind, etc. Out of moral impulse and love for mankind, Jesus said "Love thy neighbour as thyself." Lord Krishna said "You should help the poor" (दरिद्रान् भर कौन्तेय"—गीता) ।

The Upanishads teach us about the futility of Karma (Karma Kand-rituals) and advocate the importance of ethical qualities. But the *Gita*[4] is emphatic in denouncing mere rituals. The *Bhagavadgita* strongly advocates the supreme necessity for developing *Atma Gunas*. Acharya Shankar has been more particular in exposing the hollowness of rituals. He has emphatically announced the significance of ethical qualities as the fundamental basis of spiritual life.

Karma Yoga

Individual's personality is based on three-fold activities, *i.e., icchha* (feeling), *jnana* (knowledge or thinking) and *kriya* (doing or action) respectively governed by heart, mind and sense-organs. In the process of learning they are reflected by affective domain (heart), cognative domain (mind) and motor skills (sense-organs) respectively. Similarly for spiritual pursuits *Shrimadbhagavadgita* has laid down three-fold *paths—Bhakti* (devotion). *Jnana* (knowledge) and *Karma* (action); but there is an emphasis on *Nishkam Karma Yoga* (action without attachment). One should not bother for fruits of actions, howsoever troublesome it is. With the sense of 'mine' comes the sense of 'fear'. The moment we throw out all idea of 'mine' we lose all fear, which destroys our ego and make our life tension-free. Therefore, *Gita* exhorts, "If you regard pleasure and pain, profit and loss, victory and defeat—all alike, and then fight, no harm will befall you. Regard all sense-pleasures only as misery. If with a heart full of renunciation, you go on working, then you will not fall into misery. If you wish to work in the world, this is the only method, which when followed is able to cut the fetters of your Karma. Be equanimous to both pain and pleasure. This equanimity of mind toward all dual expression of life is known as *Yoga*."

In this way in '*Gita*', the whole human beings are exhorted through Arjuna to fight, to give battle to the unrighteous, to the unholy, to the enemy of our progress in life, without fear or remorse, being steadfast in *Yoga*. With a unwavering faith in God if one works with all his zeal and sincerity, success is sure. Thus, succeeded by practising Yoga he will be able to sing with Longfellow:

> "Trust no future, however, pleasant
> Let the dead past bury its dead
> Act, act in the living present
> Heart within and God on head."

Secularism

Ours is a secular state, secularism is one of the significant values enshrined in our Constitution. But our secularism is of quite unique nature and different from that of Western countries specially United States of America. According to them it means a tendency or attitude towards belief which discards all forms of religious faith or worship. Indian secularism is, on the contrary, very accommodative, comprehensive and sympathetic towards all religions. The following salient features can be attributed to Indian secularism:

1. It means equal protection, treatment and respect for other religions and faiths.
2. It incorporates concern for every sect and culture.
3. It inspires people to have sense of purity in spiritual and material things as well.
4. It enjoins freedom for adoption of religion or faith of one's own liking and choice.

5. One can exercise synthesis of more than one faith or religion to shape one's life-style.
6. It is conditioned by very wider concept of 'universal brotherhood'.
7. It lays emphasis on the formulation or moral, social and spiritual values based on common elements found in all religions.

Salient Features

Unity, continuity and power of assimilation are three most prominent characteristics that can be attributed to the composite culture of India. In a country like that of ours, where different religions, faiths, languages, sects and customs have been flourishing, unity bears a very vital importance. This is also necessary for national solidarity, because conflicts caused by religions, faiths or sects are very fatal to the national unity and also to the socio-cultural development of the countrymen. In this connection, India has a very sound and splendid tradition. She has been enjoying unity in religions throughout the ages. It has been sustained by the sincere and constant efforts of saints and many socio-religious reformers and has been very helpful in maintaining peace and harmony in the society and country at large.

India's spiritual greatness is and has been famous in the world. Because of its supreme leadership in the field once it attained the rank of spiritual preceptor ('गुरुपदमधिष्ठत्') ।[5]

Vedas, full of very vibrant vision of life, are the oldest literary works of the world. They represent most organised efforts made by man in his search for internal, moral and spiritual values. *Vedas* visualize human personalities in all its complexity and totality. Accordingly to *Mahabharata*, man is the supreme being in the world and there is no better creation than man in the world ("न हि मानुषात् श्रेष्ठतरं हि किंचित्"—महाभारत) ।

From the pages of history, we see that the supremacy of Indian culture has been acknowledged by various occidentals. In this connection, the following observations of Maxmuller, a noted Indologist are noteworthy:

> "If I were asked under what sky the human mind . . . has most deeply pondered over the greatest problems of life, and has found solutions of some of them which well deserve the attention even of those who have studied Plato and Kant—I should point to India.

> And if I were to ask myself from what literature we . . . who have been nurtured almost exclusively on the thoughts of Greeks and Romans, and of one Semitic race, the Jewish, may draw the corrective which is most wanted in order to make our inner life more perfect, more comprehensive, more universal, in fact more truſy humane a life, not for this life only, but a transfigured and eternal life—again I should point to India."

The early Hindus of the Vedic culture, no doubt, worshipped many gods and goddesses and thus, they seem to be polytheistic. The following lines from the *Vedas* expressly indicate that the concept of multiplicity of God was in vogue during the Vedic period. But gradually they began to perceive the oneness of Godhood.

एकं सद्विप्रा बहुधा वदन्त्यग्निं यमं मातरिश्वानमाहः।
सुवर्ण विप्राः कवयो वचोभिरेक सन्त बहुधा कल्पयन्ति।।

The above verse of the *Rig Veda* declares that what is one in reality is called by many names by the wise. Our six systems of philosophy (*Nyaya, Vaisheshik, Sankhya, Yoga, Mimansa* and *Vedant*) indicate the gradual development of this concept. Acharya Shankar had examined critically the merits and demerits of the five earlier systems and ultimately propounded 'Monism', according to which only Brahman (Cosmic Soul) is true and the rest is '*Maya*' (illusion). Shankar asks us to believe in the authority of the *Vedas* and identify the self with *Brahman*. That *Atman* is one for the whole universe.

A great task of fostering National Unity was achieved by Shankaracharya through numerous measures. The four Vedantic shrines and monasteries in far-flung four corners of India played a historical role in inculcating the feeling of oneness among its people. For further reinforcement of the value of unity—spiritual, cultural and political—he reestablished the value of pilgrimage.

Four *dhamas* (Kedarnath and Badrinath in the Himalayas, Puri in Eastern India, Dwarika in Western India and Rameswaram in South India); the seven *puris* or sacred cities (Ayodhya, Mathura, Maya or Haridwara, Kasi or Banaras, Kanchi or Conjeevaram, Avantika or Ujjain and Dvaravati or Dwarika); the seven rivers (Ganga, Yamuna, Godavari, Saraswati, Narmada, Sindhu or the Indus, and Kaveri); besides other shrines like the five Saiva shrines of South India embodying the five elements (Kanchipuram, Jambukeswara, Tiruvannamalai, Kalahasti and

Madurai); and the eleven Jyotirlinga shrines in other parts of India—all these, together with the great pan-Indian fasts, feasts and festivals, like Janmashtami (or Birthday of Krishna), Ramanavami (or the Birthday of Rama), Siva-Chaturdasi, Durgashtami, Dipavali, etc., made the people of India conscious more than ever of the fundamental unity of their country in its history, its religion and its culture.

Threefold Paths

According to Hindu scriptures, the way of salvation (realisation) from the bondage of life and death is three-fold. It can be attained by *Jnana* (knowledge), *Karma* (action or *Bhakti* devotion). During Sultanate period a number of Hindu saints and reformers started a movement to do away with undesirable religious practices and inculcate a greater faith in the Almighty. For this purpose, they adopted *Bhakti Marga* (path of devotion). It was called Bhakti Movement. According to A.L. Shrivastava, "The movement was not altogether new, and it did not owe its origin to Islam, as has been erroneously supposed by some modern writers. What really happened was that this movement received impetus from the presence of iconoclastic Muslim preachers, who stressed the unity of God, vehemently criticized the Hindu religion and thought and attempted to convert Hindus to their religion by resorting to all kinds of means. Hinduism, therefore, tried to defend itself purging of some of its evil practices, particularly those relating to rigours of caste and image worship."[6]

The system of Shankaracharya of attaining salvation through *jnana marga* (path of knowledge) was highly intellectual and philosophical and as such it could not worked upon. In fact it miserably lacked in appeal for the masses. Therefore, *bhakti marga* became very popular. The preaching of the saints and reformers of this movement were in vernaculars and local dialects like Awadhi, Bundelkhandi, etc., that appealed most to the masses. The most prominent features of this movement was 'escapism'. The leaders of this movement were—Ramanuj, Nimbark, Madhavacharya, Ramanand, Kabir (1440-1500), Nanak (1469-1538), Mirabai (1498-1546), Vallabhacharya (1479-1531), Chaitanya (1486-1533), Namdev, Tukaram, Surdas, Tulsidas, etc.

Alike the common masses these saint-poets and religious leaders also sought solace in other-worldliness. In their preaching they preached right conduct and clean-play in a very lucid way. As the other-worldliness is related to the law of *Karma,* law of *Karma* is related to the transmigration of the soul, at times their teachings also bear the philosophic touches here and there. Even then in their teachings there was a great appeal for the people.

Unity in Diversity

This has been one of the most prominent features of Indian culture. In spite of divergent streams of caste, creed and colour, different languages, sects, food-habits, faiths, etc. there has been undercurrent of unity in our country, which has been quite obvious from time to time. This has been feasible because of uniquely wider canvas of our values.

We have common traditions in as much as we reveal in chanting the same *Vedic mantras* and reading the epics because they narrate the history of our common forefathers who lived and died for the cause of our country and gods. Rama, Krishna, Yudhishthira and others are our common heroes. Our social and cultural traditions have been the same during the last several thousand years. It will thus be clearly seen that if at all real Indian nationalism is to thrive, it will become possible only under the roof of the Sanskrit language.

Our social framework has been the same for several millenniums, although it is getting loosened now as a result of the domination of western ideologies. There is a complete and thorough unity of religion and culture all over the country. The difference between the Dravidian culture and the Hindu culture which is often referred to is a myth. Indian culture means tradition of religion and philosophy, general mode of life, the repertory of convictions and beliefs and outlook upon life as a whole. There is no provincial or cultural variation. Difference in language, literature or local customs is no cultural difference. The one common thought, ideal and focus has been the mythology of India from Brahmaputra to Comorin. The difference is superficial and not fundamental.

Fostering of Values: A Challenge

Ours is a land highly rich in cultural heritage. India's pluralistic composite culture has been enjoying all high tributes and appreciations from the dawn of world civilization. Its assimilation power has been so strong and effective that whatsoever race entered into its fold became Indian, only Indian shedding off their own colours. In ancient India all the activities of the society had the profound base of '*Dharma*'. Our social institutions, customs, duties, etc. used to be within the radius of '*Dharma*'.

Educational theories and practices were not the exceptions to this. Thus, it was beyond imagination, even to think, whether any educational thought or practice could be without the tint of 'Dharma'. Teachers ('*Acharya*' or '*Guru*') commanded so high repute, respect and prestige that teacher-taught interaction used to play very significant and effective role in the formation of character, building up of personality and cultivation of high spiritual values in the minds of the pupils. Teachers used to take it as their moral obligation. They were morally bold enough to own the responsibility if they failed in this very pious task.

In our present set-up of the society the above-mentioned teacher-taught interaction is not found to be effective and as such the outcome is not the desired one. It is very much due to a few lapses and constraints on the part of the teachers, a part of the present social set-up. Teacher alone is not responsible for this apathetic phenomena. Good many socio-economic factors also have been responsible for this.

Realistically it is said that "Values are not taught but caught". In fact, spiritual values are not to be taught but to be lived. This is why in the present set-up teacher finds himself, in most of the cases, unable to teach morality to the students or inculcate spiritual values in them. The apparent reason for this is that he has not himself imbibed these values in him. The thing which one does not possess how can it be imparted. Our values have become more and more materialistic, because the society as a whole is materialistic. Teacher or administrator alone is not to be blamed.

The question arises what should be done under the above circumstances. Should we be disappointed and pull on with the vicious circle and allow the society to be deteriorated even further. No, we have to do something. Here it will be worth to recall the wisdom of *Shwetashwetar Upanishad*—

श्रुण्वन्तु सर्वे अमृतस्य पुत्राः
आ ये धामानि दिव्यानि तस्थुः।

वेदाहमेतं पुरुषं महान्तम्
आदित्यवर्णं तमसः परस्तात्।
तमेव विदित्वाऽतिमृत्युमेति
नान्यः पन्था विद्यतेऽयनाय।।

(श्वेताश्वेतर उपनिषद् 2-5, 3-8)

Consoling over the helplessness and despair of human beings the sage exclaims: "O, the sons of nectar! O gods residing in the heavenly abodes! I have known that eternal embodiment of soul, who is beyond ignorance and illusion. After having known him only you can be free from the bondage of life and death. There is no other way out for self-protection".

By quoting these lines from *Shwetashwetar Upanishad* what is to be impressed upon is that we should not be disgusted and disappointed. After all, the present set-up of the society is our creation and we, only we can improve upon this by cumulative and collective efforts with firm faith and determination. We should bear in mind that the present situation is not a creation of overnight and as such it will be absolutely unwise to think that it may be improved overnight. The worsening process has taken decades together. The pages of our history will be able to reveal this fact to us expressly. Similarly the improvement can be brought about through continuous process only. 'Value-oriented Education' is one of the many tools to be reinforced by us.

Thus, 'Value Education' is like a movement, which started comparatively earlier in Western countries. Let us start now, better late than never. On this score Franklin D. Roosevelt has aptly remarked:

> "Men are not prisoners of fate, but only prisoners of their own minds."

Let us not be prisoners of our own minds thinking that we are not capable to do this. Let us take it as a challenge and strive with firm faith and self-confidence to meet it.

Enriched Heritage: An Asset

India's cultural heritage is so varied, and so enriched that it is capable of meeting any challenge. The present value-crisis has been brought about mainly by wrong conceptualization of modernity and cut-throat competition for acquisition of more and more material wealth, which is uniquely intensified due to rapid growth of Science and Technology.

Once Pt. Jawaharlal Nehru, describing a culture, has mentioned that a culture that cannot understand modern times is an incomplete culture. Our composite culture has been standing the test of completeness, from time to time, by assimilating all those elements generated by the needs and aspirations of the country for its smooth advancement and self-strengthening. This has been one of the most eminent factors for its seniority and nobility among the cultures of the world. In the context of value-orientation also it would stand the test of modernity, it is believed.

> "India, ever since the formation of her culture and the establishment of her distinctive Weltanschauung, her view of the World with her Way of Thought and her Way of Life, has acquired her place in the forefront of Civilised Peoples and her "seniority among the nations of World." Her place of Seniority has been given to her because of her services to the nations not so much in their mundane affairs, but rather in the direction of the things of the mind and the spirit—in bringing to Man the sense as well as the need for certain intellectual and moral approaches in the problems of existence and in the way of living."
>
> —Suniti Kumar Chatterji

REFERENCES

1. *Values in Transition*, p. 3.
2. *Congressional Record: Proceeding and Debate of the 93rd Congress*, Second Session, Washington, January 28, 1974.
3. *Values in Transition*, p. 21.
4. *The Bhagavadgita* II, 42.46, IX 20-21.
5. तुलनीय–

   यूनानियों को जिसने हैरान कर दिया था।
   सारे जहाँ को जिसने इल्मोहुनर दिया था।।

   –इकबाल
6. A.L. Shrivastava, *Medieval Indian Culture*, 1975, p. 43.

3

VALUE-TENETS AND TEACHINGS

From the time immemorial to the present time, there had been many philosophers and socio-religious leaders, who contributed to different facets of Indian philosophy. They differed from each other on many points, but still there are certain common tenets available in their works. These tenets are the bases of moral, social and spiritual values. On this score all of them (except Charvak,[1] who propounded the philosophy of eat, drink and be merry) agree. As such there is no controversy with regard to moral, ethical and spiritual tenets, which form the bases of values. They are as follows:

1. Human being does not Consist of Physical Body Only

The principle of soul or spirit is one of the subtle ideas the Indian philosophy has given. The self (soul) is not only revealed by *Vedas* or *Shastras* but it is self-evident. The self of man is 'knower' of all, may it be spiritual knowledge or ignorance. When we say 'I know this' or 'I do not know this' we mean the same 'knower' (self). Here knowledge or ignorance are the objects to this knower, which is immortal, imperishable and eternal. The body of flesh and bones may ruin but not the self. Self is different from mind. It understands the states of mind whether it is sad or glad, etc. An object of knowledge is apprehended through cognition, so cognition is automatically known as pleasure and the like—wherefore cognition is self-revealed, and therefore, also is the cogniser self-revealed.

Describing the characteristics of this self (soul), it is said:

> "Weapons cannot cut it nor can burn it, water cannot drench it nor can wind make it dry. For this soul is incapable of being cut, it is proof against fire, impervious to water and undriable as well. This soul is eternal, omni-present, immovable, constant and everlasting. This soul is unmanifest; it is unthinkable; and it is spoken as immutable. Therefore, knowing this as such, you should not grieve."[2]

It is not attained; but it is the attainer. *Upanishads* tell us that *Atman* (soul) is the fountain of bliss and that he has to know his real state. It is possible only when the cobwebs over the *Atman* are removed by *Shastras*.

2. The Principle of Universal Soul (Cosmic Soul)

According to *Vedas* and *Shastras*, there exists supreme consciousness as the source of all that constitutes the universe. It is denoted by the Sanskrit word *Brahman*, or *Ishwar* or *Parameshwar*. Acharya Shankar contended that only '*Brahman*' is true, rest else is '*Maya*' (illusion). *Brahman* is realised through the discipline of meditation and not by rituals.

It has no form, no smell, no sound, no body, etc. It is beyond senses. Senses cannot grasp it. It is said that all other souls are just offshoots of this Cosmic Soul (*Brahman*).

3. The Principle of Transmigration of Soul

The individual soul is embodied in physical body. It is in bondage, till it is liberated. After the decay of the body (death) the soul parts with the body. "As a man discarding worn-out clothes takes other new ones, likewise the embodied soul, casting off worn-out bodies, enters into others which are new."[3] In Sufism soul is compared with the bird and body with the cage in which the bird lives in.

4. The Law of *Karma*

> A calf can find its mother cow
> Among a thousand kine;
> So good and evil done, returns
> and whispers, "I am thine".
>
> —*Panchatantra*

In philosophical terminology, *Karma* means *Karma Kand* (rituals), which does not pretend to deal with *Atman*, nor it can be an instrument for attaining *Brahman*. But hereby *Karma*, we mean 'action' only. 'As you sow, so you reap' is the common dictum applicable to the performance of *Karma*. According to the nature of *Karma*, *i.e.*, good or bad, man has to reap its fruit.

Regarding *Karma*, it is advised—

1. Your right is to work only.
2. You should never think of fruits thereof.

3. Fruit of action should not be your aim.
4. You should not have any attachment to inaction.[4]

In *Suttpitaka* it is said that a man enjoys joy and happiness even by performing vicious acts, till they are ripened. Similarly a man suffers even by performing good acts, till his good acts are ripened. Once '*paripak*' (ripening) is complete people are destined to get the good or bad fruits as per the nature of *Karma* performed by them.

In this spiritual sense, *Karma Marga* (the path of action = rituals) as taught in the *Shastras* is the cause of bondages.[5] Simply because a *Karma* is prescribed by such a great authority as the *Vedas*, it does not mean that it has not the evil effect of bondage. Even good *Karmas*, done mechanically as prescribed by the *Vedas* (and without detachment as to the fruits), cause bondage.

Therefore, the positive attitude of detachment is essential for purity. If that is not present, bondage is the result.

The pleasure and pain, joys and miseries, which are the fruits of these *Karmas* respectively, as produced by contact of the senses with the sense objects and no more. These pleasures and pains are not supersensuous at all, as in the case of bliss of realization. According to our scriptures the fruit of *Jnana* is far different from the fruit of *Karma*. The fruit of *Jnana* is described as superior to the fruit of *Karma* as the former leads to *Moksha* (realization) while the latter leads to attainment of Heaven.

5. Importance of 'Knowledge'

There are two paths of worship—*Jnana Marga* and *Karma Marga*. Here knowledge (*jnana*) means '*Atma Jnana*' (knowledge of self). The purpose of *Atma Jnana* is the removal of the non-self created by *Avidya* (ignorance of self). *Jnana* is like the flashlight inherent in onself. Acharya Shankar maintains that "This flashlight, latent till now, becomes patent by proper meditation (stillness of the mind). The attainment of self by *Brahma Vidya* which has been taught, is but the removal of the non-self created by the superimposition of the physical body, etc. as the self".

Knowledge of the self (self-realization) leads to instantaneous realization—"सद्यो मुक्तिकारणं आत्मज्ञानम्" । The proposition established by all *Upanishads* is that final release results from knowledge ("ज्ञानात् मोक्ष इति च सर्वोपनिषदां सिद्धान्त")।

The realization that there is but one self (in all) is the supreme aim of discipline of *Jnana* (knowledge). Result of *Jnana* is certain as it can be experienced in this life. It is different from the reward of *Karma* to be attained in heaven after death.

6. Moksha is the Ultimate Aim

In Indian culture, four legitimate goals of life are prescribed—*Dharma* (righteousness), *Artha* (material wealth), *Kama* (pleasure), *Moksha* (realization or salvation). Of these, *Moksha* is said to be the supreme aim of knowledge. *Moksha* or realization is attained by knowledge only and not by rituals (*Karma Kand*). Even *Dharma* (righteous act) is injurious or harmful to a seeker of liberation (*Moksha*) from the cycle of life and death as it causes bondage.[6]

Commenting on *Gita*[7] Acharya Shankar has mentioned that the mind refined by the control of body, the senses and the lower mind, and equipped with the teaching to the scripture and the teacher, constitutes means to realise self (in its true nature). *Sama* and *Dama* (the internal and external control of the mind), are the greatest purifiers of mind, not *Nitya Karma*, charity, etc. A purified mind is the instrument for realization, not the sense-bound mind. Therefore, it has been very aptly concluded that mind is the only instrument for bondage and liberation of a man.

7. Will of God is Supreme

The *Hindu Shastras* state that relation between cause and effect is rigid and of permanent nature, but can be altered at God's will. For those, who believe in the existence of God, His will is supreme. It is said that there is no effect without its appropriate cause—"कारणेन विना कार्यं नोदेति" I The permanency of the relation of cause and effect gives rise to natural laws. At His will natural laws also cease to function.

When Indumati, wife of the great Raghuvanshi King Aja, succumbs to death with a mere stroke of a wreath Kalidasa has rightly said—

विषायतेऽमृतं कुत्र विषं चाप्यमृतयते ।
विषत्वं अमृतत्वं च जायते हीश्वरेच्छया ।।
ईश्वरस्य वशे सर्वं चराचरमिदं जगत् ।
कटाक्षेण विभोस्तस्य स्वरूपेणाधिगच्छति ।।

(Nectar sometimes acts like a poison and a poison like nectar depending on the will of God. Everything in this Universe is under His control and its nature at any particular time depends on His Will.)

Great *saint*-poetess and staunch devotee of Lord Krishna Meera was compelled to take a bowl of poison. She did so with firm faith in God. At His will the bowl of poison was turned into the bowl of nectar. In fact poison has been created as poison and nectar as nectar and therefore, ordinarily they behave as such. It is only when God wills it, that poison acts like nectar though even then it remains a poison.

8. The Principle of Other-Worldliness

The principle of other-worldliness is linked with the theory of transmigration of soul. Transmigration of soul is indicative of rebirth. It is believed that as per one's good or bad acts in this birth man gets its return in this world as well as in the next world. It is not necessary that a man will take rebirth in this very world. The concept of hell and heaven is also indicative of other-worldliness. It is believed that those, who perform righteous acts and lead a spiritual life in this world, enjoy the happiness of heaven. On the contrary those, who commit sins, practise hatred and cruelty, go to hell. Those, who get themselves liberated from the cycle of life and death and the fruits of their action by attaining *Moksha* (liberation or salvation), are free from heaven or hell.

Jataka stories, more than 500 in number, are said to be the stories of several births of Lord Buddha. Each story relates to one birth wherein Buddha was born in one form or the other and led a very righteous life. In each birth, may it be of deer or cow or novice, he excelled in his conduct and character. He was called 'Bodhisattva'. Buddhists, believe that through the gradual refinement through these births Gautam Buddha, propounder of Buddhism, could become so enlightened and accomplished.

It has been said that man does not undergo in this life all the effects of his action. Therefore, man takes birth again to experience the effects which he has not realised in this life. The indestructibility of *Karma* and its partial realization in one life lead inevitably to rebirth. The birth of a living being is due to its own *Karma* and so is its death. Its joy and sorrow, its fear and protection all spring from the same inexorable cause.[8] Living being is born from *Karma*, which he cannot see and becoming patent in this life, again becomes latent in death, under the influence of its own *Karma*. Impelled by *Karma* which is the most powerful of all, it is born of parents in a family where it can experience its own *Karma*.[9]

For future life, one should be righteous and straightforward. Fate is nothing but a sum total of actions performed by a man in his previous life. Therefore, one should make an effort manfully without being slothful. "Just as a potter makes whatever he likes out of a lump of clay, so does a man reap the fruit of the action done by himself."[10]

9. Contact is Potent Factor of Character Formation

Our scriptures say that contact is omnipotent. By contact (संग or संसर्ग) all living beings acquire good and bad qualities and, therefore, persons who wish to become saints themselves constantly seek the company of real saints.[11]

With the king condemned a parrot for crying all day "Catch him and cut him to pieces", he was addressed thus by another parrot, with which the king was immensely pleased for reciting the *Vedas* all day long— "Oh king! I listen to the talk of saints and he hears constantly the talk of a butcher. It is not his fault, nor my virtues that we talk so differently. Vices and virtues always arise from contact."[12]

Our scriptures declare that contact (संग) is supreme and almighty. It works miracles and shapes, moulds and alters character in a way nothing else can do. In Panchatantra we find a number of verses to prove what has been said above.

It is said that "a piece of glass, by being in contact with gold, possesses the lustire of emerald; similarly a fool attains proficiency by being in the company of the good."[13] It is also said—"The intellect is impaired, O friend, by the society of inferiors; it remains what it is with one's equals and is improved by association with one's superiors."[14]

As objects on the rising mountain appear bright by the near presence of the sun, so a person of humble rank too shines by being in the company of the good.[15]

Thus, contact makes a saint of hateful sinner and leads even saints astray. To proclaim with a clarion call the absolute irresistibility of almighty contact, King Bharat, the devout *Avatar* (incarnation) that he was, choose of his own free will to become a deer and by doing so administered the most solemn warning to all men alike— "Beware of almighty contact. None can withstand its bewitching charms end enthralling fascinations, not even as *Avatar* or God incarnated. Yearn and pine for *Satsang* (good contact) or association with saints and shun all evil contact as a deadly poison, that will not destroy the body in this birth, but will spell ruin in births to come."

10. Spiritualism is Superior to Worldliness

Spiritualism has been the identity of ours. India has been the leader, still she continues to be, in the field of spiritualism. "The mist of worldly desires obstructs one's vision and he does not know good from bad, both in this world and in the next, and does not perceive that time is fleeing and his valuable life is running rapidly to a close." That is why our sages have been advocating spiritualism. Our literature in Sanskrit, Pali and Prakrit languages is replete with such episodes and illustrations wherein spiritualism has been shown as victor over materialism or worldliness. There cannot be two opinions that discovery of 'Indianness' lies in spiritualism and not in materialism.

On this score observation of Swami Vivekananda is noteworthy. He boldly declares, "The question has yet to be decided whether peace will survive or war, whether patience will survive or non-forbearance; whether goodness will survive or wickedness; whether muscle will survive or brain; whether worldliness will survive or spirituality. We have solved our problem ages ago. Our solution is unworldliness renunciation."

To lead a spiritual life four *purushartha* have been mentioned:

1. *Dharma* (the discharge of religious duties).
2. *Artha* (the acquisition of money by fair means).
3. *Kama* (the gratification of desires so as not to trespass on *Dharma*).
4. *Moksha* (liberation, final emancipation).

Moksha has been described as the ultimate goal of life by our ancient sages and saints.

Religious Leaders

It is a universally acknowledged fact that union with the divine spirit is the ultimate aim of all faiths and religions. Means and paths to achieve this aim may differ from religion to religion and faith to faith.[16] For the cultivation of right type of character, one's conduct must be consistent with his feeling and thinking. It has been rightly said that "you must live as you think."

In the Christian and Jewish scriptures it has been obviously observed that man has been created in the image of God. In other words we can say that man was recognized as a symbol of God. Thus, all types of rituals and prayers are symbolic in nature. In real sense man's most important ritual is performed through his righteous dealing with his fellow-men.

It is rightly said that "service to the humanity is service to the God."

If this maxim is followed, man's life will become sacred. If one has to practise the presence of God, there is no need of Sundays or special religious holidays for its observance. One can practise the presence of God in every day, every hour, every minute.

Jesus rejected the extreme, meticulous ritual of the Jewish theologians of his day. He laid great emphasis himself on right action, right dealing with fellow-men, etc. Similarly Lord Buddha and Mahavira condemned many outdated and deleterious rituals of the Hindus and laid stress on the right conduct of character of the man.

In our *Upanishads*, rituals have been criticised. Therein more and more stress is laid on the righteous conduct of a man and purity of heart. Buddha suggested Eightfold Path consisting of Right View, Right Aim, Right Speech, Right Action, Right Means of Livelihood, Right Effort, Right Thought, Right Contemplation. In this Eightfold Path, there are many substantial elements to be followed for right conduct.

In *Bhagavad Gita* it is said, "No man shall escape from act by shunning action; nay, and none shall come by mere renouncements up to perfectness. Nay, and no jot of time, at any time, rests any actionless; his nature's law compels him, even unwilling, into act (for thought is act in fancy). . . . Find full reward of doing right in right. Let right deeds be thy motive, not the fruit which comes from them. And live in action! Labour! Make thine acts thy piety, casting all self aside." The *Gita* goes on to explain that selfless service for others, work without ambition, action "without desire for fruit of works," is one of the three great ways to attain union with God. This is called *Karma Yoga, Karma* here meaning action and *Yoga* meaning union (with God).

Confucius put great stress on ethical action.
There is a strong ethical emphasis in Judaism.
The Mohammedan Quran is full of calls to right action.

If we sincerely compare the main teachings of various religions we can easily conclude that the central idea or ultimate aim of all the religions is one and the same. We may call it *Moksha* (liberation or salvation), union with God, attaining heaven, or gaining of Paradise. To achieve this very ultimate aim, our religious leaders have been spreading the message of the presence of God in various ways.

In India, we have a very grand galaxy of such leaders. Right from Lord Krishna to Mahatma Gandhi, there had been a number of preachers who taught the people to have right conduct and brotherly behaviour with other fellowmen. It may be gospel from *Bible* or Sermon from *Quran* or conversation between Lord Krishna and Arjuna, everywhere we find the emphasis on right action and dutiful attitude towards life. In *Bhagavad Gita*, law of *Karma* has been explained in detail. Our spiritual leaders have tried to convey the message of spiritualism. They have repeatedly mentioned that spiritualism is far superior to worldliness. This is the nucleus of our religious philosophy and culture. It may not seem to be consistent with value-tenets of Western countries. Value-tenets of Western countries are different than that of ours and as such their social and ethical values are also different to some extent.

We may mention Krishna, Vyasa, Arishtanemi, the sages of the *Upanishads*, Mahavira, Buddha, Panini, Valmiki, Pradyota, Udayana, Chandragupta Maurya, Chanakya, Susruta, Patanjali, Salivahana, Kumarajiva, Chandragupta Vikramaditya, Harshavardhana, Vasubandhu, Dharmakirtti, Sankaracharya, Ramanuja, Rajendra Chola, Prithviraj Chauhan, Jnaneswara, Bukkaraya, Sayanacharya, Krishnadeva Raya, Chaitanya, Sankaradeva, Nanak, Guru Arjun, Akbar, Dara Shikoh, Samartha Ramadas, Sivaji, Tukaram, Zain-ul-Abidin, Guru Govind Singh, Raja Ram Mohun Roy, Iswar Chandra Vidyasagar, Ramakrishna Paramahamsa, Bankim Chandra Chatterji, Mahadev Govind Ranade, Swami Vivekananda, Rabindranath Tagore, Mohandas Gandhi, Subhas Chandra Bose, and a number of others.

Teachings of Buddha and Mahavira

Buddha appeared on the stage when the religion was "bleak, corrupt, defeatist, and irrelevant, matted with superstition and burdened with worn-out rituals." As a firm reformer Buddha determined to clear the ground so that truth may spring again in freshness, strength and vitality. He tried successfully to dissociate the religion entirely from six corollaries and preached the religion devoid of authority, devoid of ritual, devoid of theology, devoid of tradition, devoid of grace and devoid of supernatural. Buddha challenged each individual to do his own religious seeking. "Be self-enlightened" ('आत्मदीपो भव') was his most cherished preaching based on individual reasoning.

In *Kalama Sutt* he called upon his followers with the following preachings, which can be said as 'Magna Carta' of the individual freedom, ever advised by any religious leader:

"Do not accept what you hear by report, do not accept tradition, do not accept a statement because it is found in our books, nor because it is in accord with your belief, nor because it is the saying of your teacher. . . . Be ye lamps unto yourselves. . . . Those who, either now or after I am dead, shall rely upon themselves only and not look for assistance to anyone besides themselves, it is they who shall reach the very topmost height."[17]

In Buddhism as well as Jainism *Nirvana* state of spiritual illumination is given the greatest significance. The *Dharma-Chakra* (wheel of *Dharma*) of the Buddhists with its eight spokes signifies the 'Eightfold Path' of purity of sight, thought, speech, action, means of livelihood, day-to-day living, purpose or goal of life and finally keeping one's inner being turned to the Divine. Buddha preached one more important thing, *i.e.*, *Madhyam Marga* (Middle path of life), which conveys the message that a man neither should get engrossed in lustre nor practise severe penances but follow the middle path in all walks of life to make his life harmonious and peaceful.

Mahavira was fore-runner of Buddha. Both of them laid stress on the values like truth and non-violence. Both were born of the Kshatriya clan and were great reformers of their times. With the popularity and acceptability point of view Buddhism enjoyed far wider recognition specially outside the country. Jainism more or less remained confined to the country only for several reasons. The teachings of Mahavira are almost based on the same lines as those of Buddha. To facilitate living on this sublime plane, both the religions insist upon a life of self-discipline and self-restraint through the practice of truth (*satya*), non-violence (*Ahmisa*), non-covetousness (*Astheya*), Celibacy (*Brahmacharya*) and non-hoarding.

REFERENCES

1. यावज्जीवेत् सुखं जीवेत् ऋणं कृत्वा घृतं पिबेत्।
   भस्मीभूतस्य देहस्य पुनरागमनं कुतः?
   [*Live happy till you die, consume ghee even by borrowing. If the body is perished, it would not be back again.*]
2. *The Bhagavadgita*, II. 23-25.
3. *Ibid.*, II. 22.
4. *Ibid.*, II. 47.
5. शास्त्रविहितविषयः कर्ममार्गः बंधहेतुः।

   —श्रीमद्भगवद्गीता 18.30

6. *The Bhagavadgita*, VI. 21.
7. शास्त्राचार्योदेशशपमदमादिसंस्कृतं मनः आत्मदर्शने कारणम्।

   Commentary on Gita 2.21
8. कर्मणा जायते जन्तुः कर्मणैव विलीयते।
   सुखं दुःख भयं क्षेमं कर्मणैवाभिपद्यते।।
9. लन्ध्वा निमित्तमव्यक्तं व्यक्ताव्यक्तं भवत्युत।
   यथायोनि यथाबीजं स्वभावेन बलीयसा।।

   —पंचतन्त्र, प्रस्ताविका, 34
10. यथा मृत्पिण्डतः कर्ता कुरुते यद्यदिच्छति।

    —पंचतन्त्र, प्रस्ताविका, 34
11. संसर्गजा गुणा दोषा भवन्त्येव हि जीविनाम्।
    तस्मात् सतां हि संसर्गं सन्तो वाञ्छन्ति सन्तम्।।
12. अहं मुनीनां वचनं श्रुणोमि श्रुणोति राजन् स गवासवाक्यम्।
    न तस्य दोषो न मद्गुणो वा संसर्गजा दोषगुणा भवन्ति।।
13. काचः कांचनसंसर्गाद्धत्ते मारकतीं द्युतिम्।
    तथा सत्संनिधानेन मूर्खो याति प्रवीणताम्।।

    —पंचतन्त्र
14. हीयते हि मतिस्तात् हीनैः सह समागमात्।
    समैश्च समतामेति विशिष्टैश्च विशिष्टताम्।।

    —पंचतन्त्र
15. यथोदयगिरेर्द्रव्यं संन्निकर्षेण दीप्यते।
    तथा सत्संनिधानेन हीनवर्णोऽपि दीप्यते।।

    —पंचतन्त्र
16. रुचीनां वैचित्र्यान्नानाऋजुकुटिलपथजुषाम्।
    नृणां गन्तव्यस्त्वमसि पयसामिवार्णव।।

    —शिवमहिम्नस्तोत्र
17. E.A. Burtt, ed., *The Teachings of Compassionate Buddha*, New York, 1955, pp. 49-50.

4

CORRELATION BETWEEN VALUES AND CREATIVITY

Relationship between creativity and values is an integral and important part of creativity-personality relationship. It is so for the obvious reason that values stand as intrinsic part of one's personality. A personality of an individual is a psycho-physical organism consisting of one's attitudes, belief, faith and various personality traits. Similarly personality is reflected through one's moral, social, cultural, aesthetic, spiritual and environmental values one cherishes. This is why creativity-personality relationship has been centring around value-orientation of creative individuals.

Role of Values in Creative Process

Eiduson (1957, 1958, 1962) has adduced evidence to show that creative individuals have more theoretical and abstract interests. He has also found creative to have a deep-seated concern for intellectual activities. Myden (1959) has also found creative to be intellectually oriented towards the outward world. Similarly, Reid *et al.* (1959) have found creative individuals to tend to value intellectual attainment. MacKinnon (1961) has found them to possess a high degree of theoretical and aesthetic value. This has been attested by Yamamoto (1963) and Drevdahl (1964) who found scientists to have greater interest in scientific investigation as compared to a more socially-oriented activity. Barron (1965) has found the creatives to have concern for philosophical problems in Windholz's (1968) view the creatives as characterized by a higher level of literary interest. Most of these studies have consistently found the creative individuals to possess a significantly higher degree of aesthetic value. The hypothesis advanced by Dr. C.R. Parmesh in his research work is also noteworthy:

> There is a significant difference between the high and the low creative individuals in their value orientation, and the high creatives are higher on theoretical and aesthetic values as compared to the low creative individuals.[1]

The above hypothesis has received a widest confirmation from the researchers in the field of creativity and values. MacKinnon (1962), using Allport-Vemon-Lindzey study of values with American architects, found that his creative subjects scored very high on these two values (aesthetic and theoretical values). Walberg and Welch (1967) in their study of personality characteristics of 36 innovative male physics teachers found that on the Allport-Vemon-Lindzey study of values these teachers scored significantly higher on aesthetic and theoretical values than teachers in other fields. Cooke (1975) in his study of behaviour value and personality measures of academically superior adolescent in creativity art curriculum, the design of which provided for test-retest control and experimental groups over a six months period (the experimental group was given a specialized art curriculum), found that on the Allport-Vemon-Lindzey study of values the high creatives showed improvement in theoretical and aesthetic values.

All the creative persons cherish some moral values and are found to be in possession of certain virtues, may it be poet or scientist or a painter. Certain researchers have supported the viewpoint that creative people are low in religious value. It may be so partly because of their more rational attitude towards life, argumentative nature and scientific temper.

With the rapid advance of science and technology the necessity for exploring the correlates of values and creativity has become a must in order to maintain peace and harmony in the society. If creative innovations are not guarded by various moral and social values they may lead to utter destruction and land our culture in peril. Therefore, it is very essential to explore the correlates of values and creativity and make the creative innovations more meaningful and beneficial to society and nation at large. It can further be added that creative innovations especially in the field of science and technology can be better used to the benefit of the society provided they are guarded by our various value-tenets. It may also be asked why to hanker after creativity while conformity guarantees a relatively comfortable position in a culture bound community.

To this question Carl Rogers (1959) has provided the most sensible and fascinating answer in the following words:

> In a time when knowledge, constructive and destructive, is advancing by the most incredible leaps and bounds into a fantastic atomic age, genuinely creative adaptation seems to represent the only possibility that man can keep abreast of the kaleidoscopic change in his world. . . . Unless man can make new and original adaptations to his environment as rapidly as his science can change the environment, our culture will perish. Not only individual maladjustment and group tensions but international annihilation will be the price we pay for a lack of creativity.[2]

Three Phases

There is a close link between human values and creativity. All creative persons may be virtuous; but all the virtuous persons may not be having creative ability—as all the intellectuals may be intelligent but all intelligent persons are not intellectuals. Some human values work as motivators, some help the individuals to decide as how to use their creative thinking or an object in the wider interest of the mankind whereas by the virtue of certain ethical, moral and social values, teachers, parents and administrators are motivated to inspire the creative talents to nurture and enhance their creativity.

In fact an encouragement is just like oxygen and nobody could live without it. For the purpose of creativity proper motivation is also a must. It has been rightly remarked by Robert Thomson—"Creative thinking is only possible for an individual who not only has the ability but the motivation to submit both to disciplined preparation and the self-discipline needed in all original work."[3] Motivation is an important determinant of all the creative activities. But in the books of Psychology, very little has been said on this point. The role of Value is very vital at the motivational phase of the creative thought or activity. According to Patrick creative thinking proceeds through a series of stages. *viz.*:

Preparation—Here the subject makes himself familiar with his situation and its material.

Incubation—The problem begins to be defined. Suggestions occur and fragments of the final product appear.

Illumination—A specific goal is envisaged and the subject begins to work towards it.

Verification—The results are worked out fully, revised, altered, completed (Testing in case of hypothesis).

The above stages may be applicable for various creative activities like writing of a poem, the painting of a picture or the solving of a scientific problem. In this process the time-gap between one stage and another is not distinct or definable. In many cases it may be quite negligible. But even before the start of the first stage (preparation) formation of certain belief, attitude or temperament is essential. It is here that our ethical, moral, social and spiritual values play a very significant role.

At the applicational level also values play a determinant role. After achievement of some creative idea or novel thought (knowledge) the subject may think as how to use it. Whether he should keep it confined to himself or publicise it in the interest of many people or all. Gautam Buddha, the propounder of Buddhism, was caught in such dilemma after attaining enlightenment under 'Bodhi' tree at Gaya. The spiritual values cherished by him were the decisive factor for formulating his course of action. Ultimately he decided to use the knowledge attained by him for welfare of suffering mankind. In the life of creative persons many such moments are confronted and the values cherished by them work as guiding stars and enlighten their path of life.

In this way we have observed that the *values function at three phases of creativity—motivational phase, encouragement phase and application phase.* What are those values which influence creativity at these three phases. Here we are enumerating phase-wise functional values, which should be taken as suggestive only and not exhaustive.

Motivational phase—Appreciation of cultural values of others, common good, curiosity, courage, devotion, discipline, self-control, leadership, quest for knowledge, sincerity, self-discipline, self-confidence spirit of enquiry, truthfulness.

Encouragement phase—Consideration for others, courtesy, dignity of the individual, duty, gentlemanliness, helpfulness, humanism, loyalty to duty, proper utilization of time, and sympathy.

Application phase—Concern for others, compassion, fellow-feeling, patriotism, sense of social responsibility, sympathy, universal brotherhood.

Creative Aspect of Values

To create is an urge with a human being. At the same time an individual cherishes some values to fashion his life-pattern. It is different thing that the values and its nature and extent may not be fully clear to a man and because of this at times his value-judgment is not well framed. But in the process of creation individual's value-judgment should be quite proximate to perfectness, if not perfect at all, then only the creation will be meaningful and purposeful. Then only human values can influence the creation in the right perspective. Then only human values can work as a source of creation.

It is an established truth that there is a vital relationship between moral values and human behaviour, between one's critical thinking and his acts. Hence, there is a very significant relationship between one's values and creative acts. This relationship has not so far been fully recognized and understood. We should not forget that our moral and ethical values always influence the development of individual creativeness. They also influence our relations with people from various strata of society.

In Hindu scriptures specially in *Upanishads* the truth has been described as beautiful, as perfect, as just and also compared with all pervading *Brahman* (the cosmic soul). Our modern psychologists also mention that truth is beautiful, truth is good, truth is perfect, truth is just, truth is unitary. But this view cannot be universalized. Our experiences go contrary to this view. The truth may not be good always and the good may not be true and just always. Clark Moustakas has rightly pointed out that "truth sometimes exists without ethic, without moral, without value. *For example*, the existence of leukemia is a matter of truth but it is not beautiful or just or good. That which is true—that is, real, genuine, correct, and lawful—may also be damaging, harmful, or impoverishing. The unique is not necessarily just or good. The real is not necessarily simple or perfect or whole. The correct or lawful is not necessarily just or beautiful or complete. The true may be without ethic or moral, and consequently corrosive and ugly. Value is required to create a truth which is good, just, and beautiful, a truth with meaning and substance."[4]

One cannot forget that the great values of justice, liberty and equality defined in Plato's Republic' or 'Justice' apply to the Spartan tribal aristocracy and not to the vast majority of slaves, who grew to the proportion of 1 : 13 of citizens and slaves, by the time the revolt of Spartans undermined the foundations of the slave society and ushered in the medieval age. Here in the value—judgment creativeness is found to be a very forceful guiding factor.

Personality Traits of Creative and Intelligent

Getzels and Jackson (1961) interviewed intensively the parents of the high IQ students and highly creative students separately.

The following differences were found with respect to their personalities:

Parents of High IQ Students	*Parents of Highly Creative Students*
1. Tended to recall greater financial difficulties during their childhood.	1. Not as much as those of high IQ students.
2. Expressed greater real or imagined personal security.	2. do.
3. Seemed to be more "vigilant" with respect to their children's behaviour and academic success.	3. Not so vigilant.
4. More critical of both their children and the school.	4. No so critical.
5. Focus their concern on immediately visible virtues such as cleanliness, good manners and studiousness.	5. Focus their concern on less visible qualities such as child's openness to experience, his value, and his interests and enthusiasm.

From the differences indicated above, it is obvious that the parents of highly creative adolescents are found to be more concerned with the values cherished by the child. Creative children do cherish certain moral, ethical and cultural values. On the basis of elaborate psychological studies, Hammer (1961) found that the "truly creatives" differed from the "merely faciles" in that "they exhibited deeper feelings, greater original responsiveness, preference for the observer role over the participant role, stronger determination and ambition, integration of feminine and masculine components, greater independence, rebelliousness, and self-awareness, stronger need for self-expression, greater tolerance for discomfort, and fuller range for emotional expression."

Creative persons are found to be more firm and determined towards their cherished aim of life and they claim to have specific view of life calling for more honesty, sincerity and firm convictions. Their qualities at times may not be so visible but interact with the creative process and lead to form unique personality. According to Clark Moustakas.[5] "There are two basic requirements for creative experience (a) that the person be direct, honest, consistent in his own feelings and his own conviction; and (b) that he feels a genuine devotion to life, a feeling of belonging and knowing." To him "creativity is an abstraction that attains a meaningful, concrete form in a particular and unique relation." This relationship closely involves various moral, ethical, social, cultural, spiritual and aesthetic values. It has already been said that all the virtuous persons cherishing certain values strongly may not be creative, but all creative persons do cherish certain positive human values, which guide and motivate the individuals to proceed with more zeal and vigour to attain their aim.

Values: Canalisers of Motivation

Earlier we have elaborated correlationship between values and creativity at three levels, *i.e.*, self-motivational, encouragement and applicational. Out of these two, *i.e.*, self-motivation and encouragement are very vital as far as teaching-learning process is concerned. In other words they can be termed as motivational (self-motivation) and exomotivational (motivation to others). Firstly, teacher is required to be self-motivated for creativeness, then only he can motivate his students for various creative activities in order to develop their creative talents. Najder Z. (Values and Evaluation, 1975) in an excellent discussion, speaks of values as being *the strongest or ultimate motivational factor* in a person's behaviour. It is also explained by the analogy of ingredients and cake. Values are like ingredients and behaviour is like a cake. As the ingredients govern the quality of a cake, so one's cherished values decide one's behavioural pattern. It is rightly said that "a person's values, then, may be seen as the basic motivational constituents of his intentional behaviour and in view of which it may be explained. It is as a consequence of this fact that people try to use values as touch-stones for setting disputes about the relative worth of things. Where people share the same values, it is supposed that such disputes will always be capable of resolution, in principle, by reference back to the basic values."[6]

In the context of creativity values canalise motivation for nurturing creative talents of the students. This is a sort of exomotivation. Motivation is forerunner of exomotivation. Only kindled lamp can enlighten others. To make others to learn self-study is essential. It is a different matter that all may not agree to this maxim. But some scholarship is essential on the part of teacher to become a successful teacher.

To become a successful secondary school teacher whether scholarship is essential or not—is a matter of dispute. Similar controversy exists in respect of professional training and personality, which are, by a group of educationists said to be essential. Much dispute is recorded over the relative importance of these three, *i.e.*, scholarship, training and personality of a teacher. Some have emphasized sound knowledge of the subject, others have stressed proficiency in methods, whereas, many observe personality as the most important for a successful teacher. Out of these three components which is valued most depends upon the ethical and moral values cherished by a teacher or those beliefs and attitudes internalized by a teacher. There is no gainsaying the fact that there are some subjects, particularly humanity subjects, which expressly demand thorough knowledge, at least more than the subject matter, from a subject-teacher, who claims to be a good and successful one. If the teacher is sincere to his duty and loyal to his profession, if he has taken teaching as a mission he/she will try his/her best to acquire broader knowledge and wider vision in the discipline concerned. Otherwise a teacher not having values like sincerity, loyalty, devotion, dedication, etc., will harbour totally on skill and his/her personality for so called success without realizing the responsibility. Here we are recalled of a Chinese saying that "dominating personality and clever mannerism has nothing to do with man-at-his-best." This is very true particularly of a valueless teacher.

In recent years there has been a definite trend towards minimizing scholarship. Administrators have become mentally entangled with the slogan. "We are teaching pupils, not subject-matter." The tendency has been to disparage the scholarship of the teacher. All will agree that we are teaching pupils, but the question still remains. How are we teaching them or with what are we teaching them? In order to obtain the desirable changes in pupils, we must be well grounded in the materials that will aid to produce those changes."[7] May it be teaching in school, college or university the ingredient of good teaching cannot be devoid of scholarship. However, there may be a difference of quality. This difference of degree is partly because of academic and moral values cherished by the individual.

Sharing of Creative Products

World-wide concern is being expressed for sharing of creative ideas and objects accrued to the scientific and technological world due to relentless and untiring efforts of the scientists of the world. This is indicative of the truth that the application of creative products for the benefit of mankind is a must if science and technology have to survive. The application or sharing of creative products should be for the welfare of mankind or its destruction much depends upon the values cherished by the creators and nation at large. There is consensus of opinion that these products should be used only for welfare of mankind if we want to vanquish the possibility of nuclear war.

Recently (Jan. 1987) a five-day conference was organised on "Towards New Beginnings" by the Indira Gandhi Memorial Trust wherein deep concern was shown by the eminent scientists and thinkers against the "tight veil of secrecy" in the field of science and technology. They emphatically said that the knowledge pertaining to scientific development and technology made particularly by advanced nations should be shared and used for the benefit of mankind. During this conference, Prof. Yash Pal, Chairman of UGC and distinguished space scientist chairing the discussion, expressed his concern to the unfortunate phenomena that a dominant fraction of the people were engaged in generating new knowledge in science and technology for military activities or private co-operate entities. Consequent upon this phenomena much of the new knowledge did not exist for the rest of the world because of secrecy or confidentiality of such new information. Dr. Raja Ramanna, Chairman of Atomic Energy Commission, said that mankind should be able to distinguish between knowledge and information as between "signals and noise" in a radio.

On this occasion Gerald Piel, editor of the U.S. Science Magazine—Scientific American, observed that humankind was living today in a "non-living moment in History." Passing remark on the progress of the developed world at the expense of the developing world he said that it is no longer necessary to increase one's well-being at all at the expense of others. Development in Science and Technology should be to abolish "poverty and misery" from the world. Renowned British poet Dr. William Radice said that the difference between genuine knowledge and useless information, good and bad and between what was true and false in the world should be underlined.

Thus, we see that there are innumerable dimensions wherein the correlation between human values and creativity stands well established. Some of the areas of correlation between scientific knowledge and human values include; judging the validity of creative product, selection of parts of scientific field to be cultivated, exploring the ways to share scientific knowledge, deciding the modes of application of scientific discoveries, etc. In this regard observation of A.N. Whitehead is noteworthy:

> Mankind have raised the edifice of science, because they have judged it worthwhile. In other words, the motives involve innumerable judgment of values. Again, there has been conscious selection of the parts of the scientific field to be cultivated, and this

conscious selection involves judgment of value. These values may be aesthetic, or moral, or utilitarian, namely, judgments as to the beauty of the structure, or as to the duty of exploring the truth, or as to utility in the satisfaction of physical wants. But whatever the motive, without judgment of value there would have been no science."[8]

Role of Science Teachers

Today, the world has advanced so far that at the press of a button one can avail of all the luxuries that we have at our disposal through the benevolence of the goddess of knowledge. With the advance in the fields of science and technology, gigantic changes have taken place that have transformed the world into a mini utopia (materially). However, there is a yawning gap between materialism and spiritualism and this gap may be lessened or even bridged by the combined efforts of dedicated people who are genuinely interested in the welfare of the human race.

Teachers take the place of the parents in the School by helping to mould young minds and souls that are yearning for someone to guide them and lead them on the correct path towards perfection. Among the various subject teachers, the teacher of science can and should play a very prominent role by trying to instill some value or the other in the course of his/her lecture. In the sphere of Science, there are no limits or restrictions. The wells of knowledge are deep and hold untold treasures. These treasures have to be dug out by delving deeper and deeper and by piercing the sometimes hostile walls of ignorance or sheer lethargy.

If Einstein were alive today, he would have been absolutely horrified and dismayed to see the hostility and venom that exists in the world and especially more so because of the threat of a possible nuclear war. Scientists should try to emulate Einstein by providing knowledge strictly for constructive purposes. The Science Teachers should inculcate in their students an undying love and interest in the preservation of life and all living creatures. They can influence young minds by stressing on the beauty of life and the ugliness of death and destruction. Through the means of nature clubs, by instructing them to preserve wild life and instilling a love for flora and fauna, the Science Teachers can help to arouse the interest of the students and generate undying love for beauty and life.

Though the world has advanced greatly today, there are still some spheres of areas in the world where people, even some educated people still cling to age-old customs and rites that are absolutely barbaric and ruthless. For example many people still believe in offering human sacrifices in order to appease some God or the other or to beg for rain or good crops. Many people even believe in superstitions. Here the Science Teachers can help by trying to convince the students of the utter futility of such beliefs and rites.

While imparting knowledge of Science, the teacher can suggest the possibility of other supernatural forces that cannot be seen but are definitely felt by millions of people some time or the other in their lives. *For example*; when many doctors have despaired over a critical patient whose case has baffled them, they are astonished to see him hale and hearty due to God's grace. Can anyone explain such an incident? Can anyone shrug it off as sheer luck? Such questions can set the students thinking. Through various devices and techniques students should be made to understand that without scientific base some traditional values, at time, may prove to be sheer superstitions and valueless application of scientific products may prove to be destructive and disruptive for the mankind. Statements given in various religious books regarding creation of world need scientific enquiry. Leucretus says: "Nothing is ever produced out of nothing by divine powers." This statement stands in contrast with various statements of the religious books. This contradiction requires careful examination with due application of scientific temper. In this direction a tip given for students of science by Har Dayal is very thought-provoking:

> Thus you must reject all the legends of Creation that are related in the *Vedas*, the *Koran*, the *Purana*, the *Bible*, the *Zend-Avesta*, and other ancient religious scriptures. The authors of those valuable books were great and good men, but they were ignorant of modern Mathematics, Physics and Chemistry. In Cosmogony, our teachers are the living scientists, and not old prophets. You need not also pay much attention to the queer and absurd notion of Plato, Augustine, and J. Jeans, that Time had a beginning. The idea of eternity , both in the past and the future, is implicit in the very definition of Time. "Time with a beginning" is a meaningless phrase, like 'cold fire' or 'hot ice'. Alfarabi has well defined Time as "the movement that holds things together."[9].

Teacher should endeavour to make the students understand powers as well as limitation of science. There are certain areas where one's self-conscious can only work. As far as sublimation and refinement of individual's emotions are concerned externalization and internalization of positive values can play a significant role. Externalization and internalization of values must go together, then only positive results may come out. Before internalization of certain desired or positive values an individual should evaluate himself. For this self-evaluation externalization of values is a must. By externalizing certain moral, social or spiritual values he gets an opportunity to interact with others, *i.e.*, peer group, colleagues, visitors, seniors/juniors, etc. This role can be performed by values only and not by science. Judging this very limitation of Science Einstein had rightly remarked, "Science can denature plutonium but it cannot denature the evil in the heart of man."

REFERENCES

1. *Creativity and Personality*, p. 98.
2. Carl C. Rogers, "Toward a Theory of Creativity," reprinted in Harold H. Anderson (ed.), *Creativity and Its Cultivation*, New York, Harper & Row, Publishers, 1969, p. 70.
3. *Psychology of Thinking*, p. 195.
4. Clark E. Moustakas, *Creativity and Conformity*, p. 93.
5. *Creativity and Conformity*, p. 28.
6. *Values and Evaluation in Education*, p. 76.
7. Bining and Bining, *Teaching the Social Studies in Secondary Schools*, Tata Macgraw Hill, p. 194.
8. A.N. Whitehead, *The Aims of Education*, 1929, pp. 153-54.
9. Har Dayal, *Hints for Self-culture*, 1961, p. 12.

5

VALUES AND VALUE EDUCATION

The Contents of education still belong to the past. Education suffers basically from what the report describes as the gap between its contents and living experience of its pupils between the system of values that it preaches and the goals set up by society, between its ancient curricula and the modernity of Science.

—Learning To Be (the Report of the International Commission)

Concept

Moral Education has been most popularly used term for the topic. Value Education is the term propounded by Eastern and Western Educationists. Here it should be borne in mind that the term 'Value education' is rather misleading and confusive, being the term having two annotations—'Value-Oriented Education' and 'Education of Values'. In the first annotation, the world 'value' is used as an adjective, whereas in the latter it denotes an area, which is not our concern at least in the present context, at all. There is consensus of opinion among the educationists that in order to respond to the needs and aspirations of the changing society, spiritual values should be inculcated in the minds of the students of schools and colleges through various subjects of the curriculum and not as a part of curriculum itself. The students are already overburdened with the heavy load of curriculum and as such it would not be just and right on our part to add one more subject on regular basis in the curriculum.

Therefore, 'Education for Human Values' seems to be a more justified term, which involves inculcation of several spiritual values, mostly common in all faiths and religions, through various subjects including Physical Education, Social Sciences, Languages, S.U.P.W. etc. According to John F. Emling "Values are those aspects of anything which, when reorganised and understood, encourage, induce or incline to use them for the purpose." A functional application of the Piagetian Principles of continuity to learning and teaching indicates a growing conviction that process and response are essential to relevant involvement with values in their tridimensional aspect: truth, beauty and goodness. Indian thinkers have been applying the principles of the truth, the beauty and the goodness to the words and deeds of human beings to testify their validity with reference to human behavioural patterns.

The Western scholars have propounded several ethical theories. Main theories to judge the act of a man are as below:

1. *Hedonistic Theory:* In this theory pleasure is the main base. Human words and deeds are termed as good or bad on this very basis.
2. *Intuitional Theory:* In this theory intuition is taken as standard instead of pleasure. Man's act is judged by intuition only.
3. *Rigourist Theory:* In this theory neither pleasure nor intuition but duty is the sole standard. In this theory there is more and more objectivity and rationalism, no place for emotion. According to this theory duty is the supreme concern and no other worldly matters.
4. *Legalistic Theory:* According to this theory the authority of law of the land is the supreme. Morality is equated with leading of life according to law only.
5. *Idealistic Theory:* According to this theory perfection is the only standard. Any personality or idea is termed as good, if it is perfect. There may be several measures for rating the perfection.
6. *Religious Theory:* According to this theory Religion is the standard, which binds a group, a community, etc. It (religion) may be revealed or natural. Revealed religion is the one, which is governed by various supreme personalities (saviours) like Lord Rama, Krishna, Christ, Buddha, Mahavira, etc. Natural Religion is based on several compassions governing the human behaviour through very broad spectrum. In the context of 'Value Education' Natural Religion is to be preferred as it has a secular outlook, a vital requirement of our educational system.

Value Education intended for desired modifications in the individuals' (students) behavioural patterns apparently involves four factors—society, environment, individual and school. Individual's personality is projected as good or bad as a result of his/her interaction with society, environment and school synchronically. An individual's personality in terms of two such different 'models' can be analysed in the following manner:

Individual		
Good Model 'A'		*Bad Model 'B'*
Society	civilizes	demoralizes
Environment	uplifts	degrades
School	educates	diseducates

From the above two models it is obvious that both environment and school together play a very significant role in building the personality of the individuals; because values grow from our purposes, aspirations, beliefs, attitudes, feelings, interests, convictions, etc., that have close link with the society and environment around us. The term 'value' is a complex term. There is no consensus among the scholars like Macmillan, Kneller, Superka, Ahrens and so on for its definition. This is such a pivotal term that each school of thought invests the word with its own definition. In the Indian perspective it can be roughly said that the term 'virtue' is the nearest, if not identical, to the term 'value'. In our scriptures the terms like non-violence (*Ahimsa*), truthfulness, purity, spiritual wisdom, self-discipline, piety, friendliness, charity, devotion to duty, etc. are called virtues. These and other similar terms are termed 'values' by the Western psychologists and philosophers. There are traditional values inherited from the past. In order to match the emerging aspirations and needs of the changing society many fresh values are also envolved, which will be explained through the lines to follow.

Need

The need for Value Education cannot be over-emphasised particularly in the present set-up of the society. According to Dr. J.E. Adamson ('The Individual and the Environment') we have the educated treated in relation to three worlds that make up his complete environment—the natural world, the social world, and the moral world. Obviously all the natural and physical sciences belong to the first, all the humanist studies to the second and all the ethical and religious to the third. Our educationists have spent lot of ink in formalizing the curriculum regarding the natural and social world; but very little has been brought about for the third, the most subtle world—moral world. There has been lot of controversies about the separation of religion from the state. In order to make our system of education more and more secular in nature, the moral uplift of the child has been neglected. Since last few decades, the Western World has taken it up as a challenge and devised several ways and methods for cultivating moral and spiritual values in the minds of the students. We also come across a sort of syllabus for Moral Education.

But in our society the awakening in this direction has been too late. Till recently there was no substantial move. In May, 1981, a High Level Seminar on Moral Education was held at Shimla. On the recommendations of this seminar there is a move to form syllabus for value-oriented education for different classes; but it has not yet been finalised so far because of several socio-cultural constraints. The Education Commission, 1964-66, headed by Prof. D.S. Kothari has very rightly observed:

> "A serious defect in the school curriculum is the absence of provision for education in social, moral and spiritual values. In the life of the majority of Indians, religion is a great motivating force and is intimately bound up with the formation of character and inculcation of ethical values. A national system of education that is related to the life, needs and aspirations of the people cannot afford to ignore this purposeful force. We recommend, therefore, that conscious and organized attempts be made for imparting education in social, moral and spiritual values with the help, wherever possible, of the ethical teachings of great religions."

From the reports of several committees and commissions appointed from time to time it is obvious that there has been consensus of opinion regarding inclusion of values in educational system. This is the high time to do so, if we intend to safeguard the present set-up of society from further deterioration and degeneration.

The resolutions adopted at Wardha Conference (1937) do not contain any reference to moral and religious education. When Mahatma Gandhi was asked about this he remarked very aptly—"We have left out the teaching from Wardha Scheme of Education because we are afraid that religions as they are taught and practised today lead to conflict rather than unity. But on the other hand, I hold that the truths that are common to all religions can and should be taught to all children, these truths cannot be taught through words or through books—the children can learn these truths only through daily life of the teacher. If the teacher lives up to the tenets of truth and justice, then alone can the children learn that Truth and Justice are basis of all religions."

Thus, we may firmly conclude that there has been consensus of opinion regarding the teaching of moral and spiritual values but the main setback is the present social set-up itself, in which positive teacher-taught interaction does not seem to be to the mark. This is why in spite of nice resolutions and recommendations of so many commissions and committees we have not been able to introduce 'Value Education' in our schools and colleges. As far as necessity part of 'values' is concerned, it is the need of the hour for which we have to strive in spite of all odds and obstacles.

Objectives

The main aim of value-oriented education is to make the students good citizens who may share their responsibilities in the changing set-up of the society in order to give the desired shape and image to the society and the country at large. The following can be enumerated as the general objectives of moral education for the school stage:

1. To promote in children such basic and fundamental qualities as truthfulness, co-operation, love and compassion, peace and non-violence, courage, equality, justice, dignity of labour, common brotherhood of man and scientific temper;
2. To train children to become responsible citizens in their personal and social lives;
3. To enable them to understand and appreciate the national goals of socialism and democracy and to contribute to their realization;
4. To create in them an awareness of the socio-economic conditions and to motivate them to improve the same;
5. To enable them to become open and considerate in their thought and behaviour and rise above prejudices based on religion, language, caste or sex;
6. To help them understand and appreciate themselves and continually strive for their inner development and becoming, thus moving towards the goal of self-actualization; and
7. To develop in them proper attitudes:
   (a) towards oneself and fellow beings.
   (b) towards one's own country,
   (c) towards people of other countries, leading to international understanding,

(d) towards life and environment, and
(e) towards all religions.

Value: Dynamic Side of Philosophy

It is an acknowledged fact that philosophy is the origin of our values. As the philosophy differs from nation to nation, so the values also differ. There are three branches of philosophy:

1. Epistemology, which deals with nature, origin, validity and extent of knowledge.
2. Metaphysics (Ontology), which deals with nature of reality, life, soul, God, etc.
3. Axiology or theory of value, which deals with the following:
   (a) Logic or reasoned thought,
   (b) Ethics or moral values, and
   (c) Theology or religion.

There is a difference in eastern and western philosophy and as such the occidental and oriental values also differ.

The tenets of philosophy form the various bases for values. Ecology of a particular place or age also plays a very significant role in formulating the theory of values. It has been said that education is the dynamic side of philosophy. Any education devoid of moral and ethical values may not be acceptable to the society. Vivekananda has rightly said, "The education which does not help the common mass of people to equip themselves for the struggle for life, which does not bring strength of character, a spirit of philanthropy, and the courage of a lion—is it worth the name? Real education is that which enables one to stand on his own legs."

Traditional and Functional Values

There are two types of values—traditional and functional. Some of the traditional values, which might have been very significant in the past, may not be useful and relevant to the present time because some morals are subject to change from time to time and place to place. These values, which are subject to change, are called as '*Yuga Dharma*' in our scriptures. Contrary to this, there is '*Sanatan Dharma*' consisting of eternal and fundamental principles, which does not change in any time or place.

The central ingredient of India's wisdom is enshrined in her concept of *Sruti* (श्रुति) and *Smriti* (स्मृति). The former is supposed to be of eternal nature while the latter is subject to the change caused by various socio-cultural factors. Thus, we come across the following two sets of elements:

1. A set of universal, eternal and fundamental principles.
2. A group of values derived from the first and finding expression in individual and collective attitudes and behaviour.

These latter are limited, temporary and relative in their scope and authority. The first should be upheld, while allowing the second to respond to the urge for change. *Dharma* or spiritual tradition has two aspects—the '*Sanatan Dharma*' and the '*Yuga Dharma*', the tradition eternal and tradition valid for only an epoch or an age. The first connotes the *Sruti* and the second the *Smriti*. In *Manu Smriti* itself the very distinction between the two sets of values has very rightly been pointed out. It mentions that "there is one set of *Dharmas* for man in the *Krita Yuga*, a different set for each of *Treta, Dvapara*, and *Kali Yugas*; the *Dharmas* change according to the change of the *Yugas*."[1]

Dr. S. Radhakrishnan has also rightly endorsed this very view. According to him, "The Hindu view makes room for essential changes. There must be no violent break with social heredity, and yet the new stresses, conflicts and confusions will have to be faced and overcome. While the truth of spirit are permanent, the rules change from age to age."[2]

The difference in these two sets of values should be understood clearly, without which the process of clarifying the values may not attain fruitful completion. Any misconception in this regard may lead to further confusions. Laying down very distinctive demarcation between these two sets of values Swamy Vivekananda has very aptly mentioned:

> "The one set is that which abides for ever, being built upon the nature of man, the nature of soul, the soul's relation to God, the nature of God, perfection and so on; there are also the principles of cosmology, of the infinitude of creation, or more correctly speaking, projection, the wonderful law of cyclical procession, and so on; there are eternal principles founded upon the universal laws in nature. The other set comprises the minor laws, which guide the working of our everyday life. They belong more properly to the *Puranas*, to the *Smritis*, and not to the *Sruti*. These have nothing to

do with the other principles. Even in our own nation these minor laws have been changing all the time. Customs of one age, of one *Yuga*, have not been the customs of another, and as *Yuga* comes after *Yuga*, they will still have to change."[3]

Besides customs, philosophy, teachings of great social reformers, etc. ecology also play very prominent role in formulating the values. "Morals are changing today like clouds before the wind. Customs and institutions older than human memory melt under our eyes as if they were superficial habits, recently acquired and easily forgotten. . . . The family, once nurse of social order, yields to the individualism of urban industry, and is broken to pieces in a generation, homes built with sacrificial toil to shelter sons and daughters are silent and desolate, the children scattered in loyalty to wandering tasks, the father and mother left alone in their bleak houses, every other chair vacant, and every room echoing with the absence of familiar sounds."[4]

The picture of a family visualized above by Will Durant may not reflect Indian 'homes' in general, but due to rapid growth of industrialization and consequential Western impact instances of such families are not rare where 'familiar sounds' are absent. In a family where father does not act as father and son does not act as son, we cannot imagine of cultural and spiritual values. Moreover, this situation signalizes a very dangerous symptom of degeneration of the institution. In an institution like family the responsibility of preserving social values rests more upon the elderly members, specially the heads of the families, than the younger ones. It has been rightly said that it is the parents, rather than the younger generation, at whose door we must lay the change. The following piece of advice for parents by Will Durant is quite interesting and useful:

> "We stand between the two worlds—one dead, the other hardly born; and our fate is chaos for a generation. We are like Socrates and Confucius, conscious that the morality of restraint and fear has lost its hold upon men; and we too must look for a natural moral code that shall rest upon intelligence rather than fear, and be able to convince even educated men. Those of us who have children are faced by a thousand questions in morals and psychology for which our old answers will not serve. We are compelled, despite ourselves, to be philosophers, to scrutinize our assumptions and our habits, to build for ourselves a system of life and thought that shall be consistent with the experience and demands of our time. We stand before the

stars almost naked of supernatural creed and transmitted moral code; everything must be rebuilt, even as if we had been cast into the wilderness and forced to begin civilization anew."[5]

According to Dr. S.C. Dube there are two fundamental views about values. One is to regard some of the values as internal and perennial for the whole of society while the other view is that values emerge from definite socio-economic, historical and cultural contexts and are related very much to the class to which certain groups of people belong. In the world of social sciences, by and large, the absolutists' view of values has been given up and has been relegated to the realm of metaphysics. But in connection with human behaviour, the values have been found to be relative.

One cannot forget that the great values of justice, liberty and equality defined in Plato's 'Republic' or 'Justice' apply to the Spartan tribal aristocracy and not to the vast majority of slaves, who grew to the proportion of 1 : 13 of citizens and slaves, by the time the revolt of Spartacus undermined the foundations of the slave society and ushered in the medieval age.

Even in Indian history the hoary tribal values of collective ownership of land and other property, of equality, of the 'Rajan' being a servant of the people and of the equality of man and woman in public affairs, in due course of time, were transformed into values of the four-tier social system known as '*Varnashram Dharma*'. But "*Manu Smriti*" had relegated women to the level of the home and hearth alone and had forbidden any induction into intellectual realms or ascent to the higher reaches of the mind.

The very story of the emergence of the State in India, on the ruins of the primitive communal and collective tribal society, is the story of how values in society change and how a homogeneous society may have values which all may adhere to. It is also observed that a society divided into classes has different values for different classes, and so different norms of behaviour for them.

Here one is recalled of Einstein's "Special theory of Relativity" for which he was awarded Nobel Prize for Physics in 1921. Since then the concepts of space and time took a new form. The "Theory of Relativity" can be translated as "*Sapekshwad*", which very much resembles with Jain theory of '*Syadwad*', a very subtle aspect of Indian philosophy. That is why Dr. Radhakrishnan has translated '*Syadwad*' in his "History of Indian Philosophy" as 'Theory of Relativity'.

In understanding and clarifying several values and minimising the tension, the Jain theory '*Syadwad*' can be of great help. Jain Acharyas observe that various contradictory qualities do exist in the same things in various relative conditions. Prof. Albert Einstein explained what relativity is to his life in these terms—"I will give you one example, when a man talks with a beautiful girl he feels that an hour is just like a minute but if the same person is asked to sit on a hot oven, he will feel every minute like an hour."

Such contradictory qualities may be observed with many other ideas and objects. Once Gautam asked Lord Mahavira: "Respected Sir, how many colours, odours, tastes and touch-sensations are possessed by the molasses?" Mahavira replied, "I can answer your question from two viewpoints. From the point of view of *Vyavhara Naya*, it is said to be sweet, but from the point of view of *Nischaya Naya*, it contains all the 5 colours, 2 tastes, 5 odours and 8 feels."

In sum we can say that the nature of things as comprehended by sense-organs is quite different from the absolute nature. According to Einstein, "We can only know the relative truth, the Absolute truth is known only to the Universal observer." If this attitude is adopted in clarifying the values, we can avoid lot of confusion and misunderstanding and restore peace and harmony in the society.

Values and Environmental Conditioning

Behavioural patterns of a child are set as he reacts to his environment. In a broad sense we can say that a child is exposed to a triangular environment—home, school and society. His behavioural patterns in this triangular environment tend to persist for a long time and shape his attitude towards himself and others. Therefore, it should be the responsibility of home, school and society as well that they set up desirable situation in which children learn to behave according to set norms and such , behaviour is aptly awarded. From various investigations it is proved that children who are punished severely build up an undesirable amount of aggressive behaviour. His feelings of fear and anxiety lead to the feelings of insecurity in a repressive adult atmosphere.

Children learn by imitation. In this sense they are like little apes. They do not easily sense the difference between good and bad behaviour, but they can be made to behave in more socially acceptable ways if their elders set good examples through their conduct. Children will definitely emulate them. In a child we should create the sense of confidence, reassurance, support, being reasonable with him. We should help him to achieve the desire conduct without recourse to forms of discipline that build up conflict and resistance.

It is an established assumption that a child's speech and action reflect the environment of which he is a part. The kind of home in which a child is brought up determines the behaviour he brings to school to a great extent. If we want children to be unselfish, dependable, self-reliant, co-operative, altruistic, honest and sincere, then we must provide environment capable to inculcate these values in him. Home and community can play a very significant role in this matter. If the home and community influences fail in these respects, the school has an added responsibility. In this way we see that home, school and community—these three are main components mainly responsible for environmental conditioning of a child.

To establish peace and harmony in the society and global peace at large, it is very essential that the value-orientation is started at home itself. Family is said to be the eternal school of life. It means that family starts its work of educating the individual from early childhood. In a family where parents do not act as parents, son does not act as son and daughter does not act as daughter, such family is really in danger. For the right conduct of the kids of the family, exemplary behaviour of the parents is very essential. Club-goer parents cannot stop their children from going to the places of recreation. It is difficult for idle parents to advise their children for hardwork.

Exemplary behaviour of the parents and congenial and conducive atmosphere of the family go a long way in fostering right values in children at the right time. It is observed that in the family where the parents present exemplary behavioural patterns children do emulate them. In the family where prayer is offered in the morning as well as in the evening children do get some sort of inspiration and encouragement for devotion and concern for others.

Authoritarian attitudes in child's training at home and school do not generally teach a child better self-discipline, because they deprive the child of opportunities for practising self-selection, appraisal, judgement and self-management. If children are trained in autocratic style they respond only in a mechanical way to external control. Thus, they will be conditioned in external discipline only. The results of over-protection are equally devastating. Punishment proves to be something of a deterrent, essential in some instances, but intrinsic rewards for positive effort are more useful and fruitful in improving child's conduct. The proverb "spare the rod and spoil the child" has now become outdated. At least for inculcation of desired values mentioned above, it is not found to be sound psychologically.

According to Educational Policies Commission good community is one in which—

(a) The status of teacher is enhanced.
(b) The economic security of the teacher is insured at the professional level.
(c) The people help to plan the programme of education.
(d) The special resources are used in every way possible. With value-inculcation point of view *the good school* is one which:
   (i) can create an atmosphere where children feel accepted and wanted,
   (ii) acquires the teacher who loves and accepts and wants to work with the children,
   (iii) creates conducive atmosphere for good and desirable rapport between parents and teachers, between student community and teachers,
   (iv) directs all its efforts towards developing a child's confidence in his abilities to use skills as tools for learning and to be creative,
   (v) cultivates in the students the feeling of true happiness, which lies in giving, not in taking, in manifesting one's best and not in preserving the same for oneself,
   (vi) considers that children differ in physical and emotional health and in social maturity, as well as in mental ability and caters to their individual needs and aspirations for their balanced growth.

Teacher is one of the most important factors responsible for environmental conditioning. In an affluent country like USA teacher enjoys better economic and social security. Therefore, teachers devote more time and energy for planning the things. They share the success also. Enhancement of teacher's social status is very essential. All the commissions and committees set up on education have realised and recommended this very matter to the authorities. No doubt, the things have improved, but still there is a scope to do more. This is necessary for several socio-economic reasons.

According to S. Harman: "The strongest point in favour of a teacher's position or respect in society would seem to be his being a law-abiding citizen. He is not at all aggressive or violent outside school, is not interested in economic exploitation, and, as a rule, has a good control over his desires, greed and sex-urges. Teachers form the smallest proportion of persons involved in crimes against property or person. Crimes like stealing, robbing, swindling, hurting, injuring, raping, etc., are rarely committed by teachers. As a class teachers are non-criminal. Teachers live in close proximity to young boys and girls, some of whom are in age group in which they are prone to be sexually more excitable and yet are not sensible or experienced enough to be invulnerable."[6] Because of all these traits teacher can play a very significant role in cultivating desired values in the students, provided he possesses a few qualities mentioned in the lines to follow.

The following qualities have been ascribed to a good teacher—

The Good Teacher

1. Is trained, skilled and sympathetic instructor.
2. Has economic security.
3. Has a feeling of adequacy and of belonging.
4. Shares in planning the life at the school.
5. Stands by group decisions.
6. Recognizes the vital role of the school, but also the part of home and community in education of children.

Lastly our administrator has a very vital role to play to give an impetus to value-oriented education. All our measures devised for value-oriented education may go stray if the resources available are not utilised and energy of teachers and co-operation from parents are not channelized properly. Therefore, our administrator should possess certain traits of leadership.

The Good Administrator

1. Should be a skilled teacher, trained teacher, and an experienced worker with people.
2. Should have vision, insight, and understanding.
3. Should encourage parents, teachers, children to share in planning and carrying out the educational programme.
4. Should accept the responsibilities of leadership and share the rewards of success.

For the administrator, to my mind, two things are of utmost importance—exemplary conduct and ability to create congenial and conducive environment in the school. In fact all other qualities of the administrator centre round these two qualities, which are very essential to make a programme of 'value-orientation education' a success.

Indiscipline among the students is a universal phenomena. This is because of crisis of ethical, moral and social values in our present social system. Educational system is a sub-system of our social system. Who is at fault for this growing unrest and indiscipline among the students? Neither teachers nor parents are prepared to own the responsibility for this indiscipline. The responsibility is shifted from one quarter to another. Teachers blame the parents. Parents, concealing their own inability to provide right type of lead and guidance, blame teachers, political leaders, and executive machinery of the Government. Our political leaders, at times, do not hesitate to exploit the phenomena to meet their ends.

In order to identify the causes of indiscipline among students in school situation a very interesting and useful study was undertaken.[7] An opinionnaire was given to 30 students of the school. On the analysis of the opinionnaire it was found that 60 per cent of 30 students held the home responsible for indiscipline among them. Similar percentage of students held school responsible for indiscipline among them. Community and peer group were found less effective in creating indiscipline. An opinionnaire was given to 30 teachers. The opinionnaire was divided into four parts, *viz.*, causes due to home, community, school and teachers. The Tables 5.1 and 5.2 indicate the percentage of students and teachers respectively who hold several agencies responsible for indiscipline.

TABLE 5.1

Causes at	*Percentage*
Home	60
Community	50
School	60
Peer group	40

TABLE 5.2

Causes at	*Percentage*
Home	60
Community	60
School	30
Teacher	20

Further it was found that "lack of healthy atmosphere at home, improper training at home, parental over-indulgence, unhindered freedom and not teaching the rudiments of discipline at home were considered to be the causes for indiscipline among students. 50 per cent of them blamed school and teachers for indiscipline. Lack of adequate opportunities to satisfy student's desire for scholastic achievements, non-recognition by his teacher, not feeling emotionally secure, unrelaxed and unfriendly classroom atmosphere, pathetic attitude of the authorities, despotic head, purposelessness of life, biased attitude of teachers and their views about punishment and reward and faculty examination system were considered other reasons for indiscipline. . . . Teachers, parents and students agreed that the responsibility of disciplining the young is that of the home and the school but particularly that of the home. To this, we may add conditions in the school which play an important part in creating indiscipline among the students. The impact of the peer group and the community particularly of political parties and unions is of course very much. But it can be minimised under the healthy and sound conditions at home and school.

One of the causes reported for indiscipline in school was lack of moral teaching also. In sum we can say that right conditioning in the triangular environment, *i.e.*, home, community and school is very essential for inculcation of ethical, moral, and social values.

Conservation of Environment and Values

Preservation of environment is the demand of the day. World authorities including UNESCO have been expressing great concern to this burning problem. After formation of the National Association on Environmental Education in the U.K. in 1972 and the law on environmental protection and conservation in 1972 in the U.S.A., there has been worldwide awakening to find out ways and means to protect the nature by stopping deforestation, etc. With the help of UNESCO, the Stockholm Conference was organised in 1971. Since then, more and more stress has been laid on the conservation and scientific use of our natural resources.

Nature is to be befriended. Our cultural tradition is that our sages, at times, did not see the difference between animates and inanimates and behaved alike with them. An orientalist, who first reached the Everest, stated that their adventure is generally termed as "the conquest of Everest." But he put the matter differently by saying the befriending of Everest. We find profound naturalism in the thought of Tao also, as ancient religious thinker and preacher of China.

Tao maintained that "Man should avoid being strident and aggressive not only toward other men but also toward nature. How should man relate himself to nature? On the whole the modern Western attitude has been to regard nature as an antagonist, something to be squared off against, dominated, controlled, conquered. Taoism's attitude toward nature tends to be the precise opposite of this. There is profound naturalism in Taoist thought, but it is the naturalism of Rousseau, Wordsworth, Thoreau rather than that of Galileo or Bacon."[8]

The attitude towards nature found in Indian scriptures is of much higher values. In *Kenopanishad*[9] '*Wan*' (forest) is regarded as *Brahman*. Therefore, it is advised that *Brahman* nomenclatured as '*Wan*' should be worshipped. Sankaracharya commenting on this very verse has explained the meaning of '*Wan*' like this—वन=वननीय=भजनीय (worthy to be worshipped). There cannot be more higher sense of reverence to the nature than this.

On the conservation of environment, the following observation of Tao is noteworthy:

> Those who would take over the earth
> And shape it to their will
> Never, I notice, succeed
> The earth is like a vessel so sacred
> That at the mere approach of the profane
> It is married
> And when they reach out their fingers it is gone.
>
> (ch. 29)

Religious Instruction *vs.* Value Education

In Wardha Scheme (Basic Education) moral and religious education were not included under the fear that it may lead to conflicts rather than unity. The very fear was not baseless. Though the constitutional guarantee of religious freedom is there, but the operation of instructions from a particular religion is likely to lead to controversy and conflicts.

It will not be out of place to quote the classical ventures of Mrs. Martha Howard (U.S.A.).[10] At the behest of Mrs. Martha Howard of Owensbora, Kentuchy, who spent about a decade to the task of bringing religion more fully into school, Kentuchy Assembly in 1878 passed a law requiring that copies of 'Ten Commandments' be pasted in every one of State's 31,000 public school classrooms. What was the result? Conflict between two ideologies was the result. On the one hand the fundamentalists and parents being motivated by religious freedom guaranteed by the constitution sued the state claiming that denial of accreditation violated their rights. On the other hand a group of parents and state brought suit against the same education officials over 'Ten Commandments'.

Any sort of restriction against religious freedom may lead to undesired scenes and at times to legalities also. Recently in U.K. wearing of a turban by a Punjabi lad was objected. Consequently the decision of the Principal was challenged in the court of law. Ultimately the verdict of the court of law went in favour of the student and subsequently he was allowed to wear a turban in the school. The writer of these lines also had come across with a partly similar situation as a Principal. There was one Tamil gentleman, who used to come to the school with *lungi*, which was a very uncommon phenomenon in a co-educational institution run by the Central Government. As a Principal I objected to it many a time, but of no avail. Lastly I had to give up the idea for fear of complications.

From the above discussion, it will be clear that religious instruction in the institutions cannot work particularly in a secular state like that of ours. Here we can well imagine the insignificance of 'Value Education', which is a more deeper and broader concept than 'moral education'.

Ours is a vast country where there are so many different religions. Each religion has something to give to us. Tolerant attitude in religious matters has been one of the most prominent features of our composite culture. Many races have found very pleasant refuge on our land. The scriptures of different creeds—the *Bible*, the *Quran*, the *Upanishads*, the *Zend-Avesta*—appear different but their goal is one and the same, *i.e.*, to establish the brotherhood of man and to bring about peace and harmony in the society.

Therefore, some basic facts and common teachings of all religions may be made known to the students. Some of them can be enumerated below:

1. What does the *Yoga* mean for the Hindus?
2. What was the Confucius' ideal of the Gentleman?
3. Who was Lao Tzu?
4. What are Islam's five pillars?
5. What did the Exodus mean to the Jews?
6. What is *Quran*?
7. Who was Guru Nanak?
8. What did Confucius teach the Chinese people?
9. What is the most important thing that Jews believe in?

10. What are the three religions you find in Palestine today, why?
11. What did Christ teach his disciples?
12. Who are the Parsees? What religion do they follow?
13. What is the difference between Buddhism and Jainism?

To illicit the proper responses from the students, the class may be divided into certain groups. To make the enquiry more purposive and fruitful, the finding of the students should be discussed in the class as and when it is convenient.

National Solidarity and Values

Inculcation of values in the students of schools and colleges has considerable learning on our national solidarity. Restlessness starts first in the minds of the students and then, if not reconciled or channelized out properly, it comes on streets in the form of ugly and undesired scenes. In the present set-up and circumstances 'National Solidarity' should be given paramount place in the hierarchy of our traditional as well as functional values. Aurobindo Ghose has rightly observed on this score. According to him Nationalism is a religion that has come from God. To maintain and transmit the sanctity and sublimity of this very religion after his escape to Pondicherry he started an Ashram over there. He devoted his life for propagation of nationalism as a religion. This is the need of the hour for the progress and prosperity of the nation. The nation can advance in the right spirit of advancement when it is protected and safeguarded well from the divisive and disruptive social forces. It has been very rightly said that the progress and advancement in knowledge and learning can be perceived when the nation is protected well through arms:

"शस्त्रेण रक्षिते राष्ट्रे शास्त्रचिन्ता प्रवर्तते"

Therefore, the values like nationalism, national integration, patriotism, respect for other religions, etc. should attract our attention with an emphasis on suitable practical line of action.

According to Vivekananda three things are necessary to make every man great, every nation great:

1. Conviction of the powers of goodness
2. Absence of jealousy and suspicion
3. Helping all who are trying to be and do good

—Swami Vivekananda (VIII. 299)

These days parents also come across conflicting ideologies. At times there is utter lack of clarification of values. From time to time they have orientation in values through good reading, listening to discourses of socio-religious leaders, discussions with their friends, etc. The students get their first lesson in values like truthfulness, charity, concern for others, kindness to birds and animals, honesty, obedience, etc. at home only. Therefore, values must be clear to the parents. Then only we may hope their right and apt inculcation or internalization.

Clarification of Values

Clarification of different values at different levels for the persons from different strata of the society is very essential. In the traditional terminology of virtue (*dharma*) and sin and through different situations these values can be clarified well. Our spiritual leaders and social reformers have been doing this fine job through their speeches, writings, etc. *For example*, we may go through the following words of Swami Vivekananda—

> "Doing good to others is virtue (*dharma*); injuring others is sin. Strength and manliness are virtue; weakness and cowardice are sin. Independence is virtue; dependence is sin. Loving others is virtue; hating others is sin. Faith in God and one's own self is virtue; doubt is sin. Knowledge of oneness is virtue; seeing diversity is sin."
>
> —Swami Vivekananda (V. 419)

Clarity in values alone can satisfy the individuals and stand the test of utility in their social life. If it is not materialized students' restlessness will be growing constantly to the deleterious extent. For national integration, clarification of values should be taken as continuous programme. It should be through various mural and intramural activities. The best of our traditional (ancient) values should be brought about and students should be exposed to them through several situations.

On different occasions Swami Budhananda has emphasized the need of well-defined values for national unity—

> "In today's India, the scene that presents itself before any impartial observer is a welter of conflicting ideologies amidst drift and restlessness. The ancient values, which had once given to the nation strength and hope, have been pushed into the background, and many new ideas are contending to fill the gap. Thus, there is a quest

for well-defined values, satisfying the aspirations of all. In such a situation, the youth of the country are restive."

Value-orientation aims at modification of behaviour, which may be treated as different from psychological behaviourism because it would not work in the context of value-education. In this context, two approaches are important: (1) value clarification and (2) moral development stage theory or, as Lawrence Kohlberg its propounder would put it, the cognitive developmental approach. These two approaches have attracted the attention of educators as these approaches offer solutions to meta-ethical relativism and pluralism. Generally educators are confronted with these twin problems. According to Kohlberg, "A more differentiated and integrated moral structure handles more moral problems, conflicts of view in a more stable or self-consistent way. Because conventional morality is not fully universal and prescriptive. It leads to continual self-contradiction, to definitions of right which are different for Republicans and Democrats, for Americans and Vietnamese, for fathers and sons."

Therefore, right or wrong action should be defined in terms of their conditioning by the environment (students, teachers, peer-groups, community, etc.) and their consistence with one's cultural value-tenets. As far as possible indocrtination should be avoided.

Some thinkers have criticised the seven points put forth by Raths, L.M. Harmin and S. Simon for clarification of values. The critics maintain that seven criteria (1. choosing freely, 2. choosing from alternatives, 3. choosing after thoughtful consideration of the consequences of each alternative, 4. being happy with the choice, 5. willing to affirm the choice publicly, 6. doing something with the choice, and 7. acting repeatedly in same pattern of life) are dubious if only because, as Lockwood (1975) points out, the criteria rule out much of our axiological experience. Do we really have to consider the consequences of each alternative before we can be said to have a value? And do we have to be happy with and cherish the choices we are sometimes forced to make? The definition of value here is "programmetic" (Scheffler, 1960) rather than descriptive; it is a concealed recommendation to adopt the speaker's own programme that is otherwise subject to evaluation.

Self-Discipline: Basis of Values

The body of modern society seems to be lacking in self-discipline. Self-discipline is, in fact, the basis of all values which not only moulds the individual's character, but also determines his reactions and responses to other values and society at large. Self-discipline is the maintenance of orderliness and obedience with regard to the self and one's conscience. It takes into account various spheres of one's conduct and style of life, like respect for values such as truth, punctuality, responsibility, adjustment, devotion for duty, faith or trust in others, care and concern for others and their feelings and devotion to one's aims and objectives or fulfilment of one's duty. Thus, indiscipline of the self and of one's individuality can be called the main crisis of values that has hit our society. The crying need of modern society is to inculcate the spirit of self-discipline and the values that follow from it in every individual from his childhood through proper education and training.

It is widely believed that the modernization process is responsible for the crisis in values to a large extent. The reasons are not far to seek. Modernization involves industrialization, use of modern and advanced techniques in agriculture and all other spheres of life and work. With modernization comes better communication that bridges the gap not only between places but also between people. The result is that the traditional values of a small closely knit society which demands co-operation, loyalty, dependence on relations, neighbours get eroded and people tend to ignore these values. They become more self-reliant and more impersonal in their conduct. Had the modern society consciously tried to retain or imbibe the values of self-discipline in individuals, the crisis of values that is so widespread could have been contained. Self-discipline teaches one not only to value one's rights but to respect those of others equally.

The process of disintegration of values would soon prove to be disastrous, unless a conscious effort is made to reverse this trend and to inculcate in one and all, a spirit of self-discipline.

Teaching and Values[11]

The values that the teachers are supposed to uphold, cannot be delinked within the values that education, in general, is supposed to cherish. In the long history of mankind, education has always accomplished two major tasks:

(a) To enable the younger generation to wrest from nature and shape according to requirement that which is needed by humanity for its survival and comfort; and

(b) To mould the consciousness of the younger generation in such a manner that they would become useful and by and large satisfied members of the society to which they belong.

In terms of the first task, education, whether formal or informal, has taught the younger generation to become useful, productive members of the society, whether it be as an agriculturist, a potter, an astronomer, a modern scientist, technocrat or a management expert. In the modern period, there has been great expansion in the educational system at all levels, particularly at the tertiary and the higher tertiary level to enable the young to become useful productive members of a highly scientific and technological society.

Coming to the second task, education again, both formal and informal whether it was through the magic dances, stories, mythology or through the teaching of literature, social sciences, mass media, etc., is an attempt to so mould the consciousness of the young that they will remain parts of the society and not revolt against it. It would be good to remember here that the educational system is a sub-system of the socio-cultural system and both affects the values of the system and is also affected by them.

In both the processes, whether of turning out young people as useful productive units of society or in the process of building up their consciousness, certain values are perceptibly or imperceptibly inculcated in them and the education system of any country, in any age, becomes a vehicle for the transmission of values. These values can be values both for the preservation of an existing system or its transformation.

Role of the Authorities

To facilitate this transformation in a constructive and revolutionary manner, the International Commission exhorts governments to undertake three major tasks:

(a) Governments should initiate a fundamental reshaping of national educational systems and participate in a global diagnosis of the education and training systems. The Commission expresses the hope that national authorities will "recognise the primordial necessity of placing educational problems in an overall context, and seek answers to this all important question—does the educational apparatus, as now conceived, really satisfy the needs and aspirations of man and societies in our time?"

(b) National authorities should undertake a deeper scrutiny and understanding of the educational life of their societies and probe far beyond the previous trends of being mainly concerned with quantitative and qualitative aspect of education.

In the past our main concern has been to do more than before and later on, better than before. We must now ask ourselves how to do different than before, because what was before is no longer either suitable or relevant. "Education is such a huge undertaking, it has so radical an influence on man's destiny, that it will be damaging if it is only considered in terms of structures, logistical means and processes. The very substance of education, its essential relationship to man and his development, its interaction with the environment as both product and factor of society must all be deeply scrutinized and extensively reconsidered."

(c) National authorities should reshape their educational system on two parallel lines: (1) internal reforms and continued improvements of existing educational systems, and (2) search for innovative forms, for alternatives and fresh resources.

Indeed, the most significant change in the world of education should be the advent of democracy which will be living, creative and evolving. For this to be achieved, social structures must be changed and the privileges built into our cultural heritage must be reduced. "Educational structures must be remodelled, to extend widely the field of choice and enable people to follow lifelong education patterns. Subject-matter must be individualized; pupils and students must be aware of their status, their rights and their own wishes; authoritarian forms of teaching must give way to relationship marked by independence, mutual responsibility and dialogue; pedagogical training must be geared to knowing and respecting the multiple aspect of human personality; guidance must replace selections, those making use of educational institutions must participate in their management and policy-making, the bureaucratic aspect of education must be broken down and its administration decentralized."

(Intro. XV-XVI)

Such a programme of action obviously calls for a revolutionary transformation of the contemporary educational scene everywhere.

Guidelines

Dr. Anil Vidhyalankar presented a paper in High Level Conference on Moral Education held at Shimla in May, 1981 in which he has enumerated some Basic Principles for Moral Education. According to him these principles had been evolved as a result of the Status study of Moral Education in Indian States and Union Territories conducted by NCERT, the joint study on Moral Education in Asian countries conducted by the National Institute of Educational Research, Tokyo, and a dialogue with a number of teachers and educational administrators and planners:

1. Moral education should not be regarded just another school subject.
2. Moral education is not education in religion.
3. There should be an integral approach in the moral education.
4. Teaching of social responsibility should be the main aim of moral education.
5. Moral education cannot be separated from the socio-economic conditions prevailing in the society.
6. Atmosphere in the school influences moral development.
7. Instruction in moral education should be appropriate to the age-group of children.
8. Instruction in moral education should be problem-based.
9. All moral problems should be discussed frankly and sincerely.
10. No views should be imposed on children.
11. Moral education should have an integral practical part.
12. Moral education should be imparted in the context of the peculiar problems faced by the young people.
13. Moral education programme should be independent of ideologies and personalities.
14. All teachers are teachers of moral education.
15. Nothing should be done in connection with moral education that would directly or indirectly induce immoral behaviour.
16. Moral education should have both compulsory and voluntary components.

Constitution of India and Values

The question of what kind of values the Indian education system should propound, promote and cherish, to a very great extent, has been decided in the Constitution of India. The Preamble would have India as a Democratic, Secular and Socialistic Republic. The Directive Principles of State Policy express a very acute concern for the deprived masses, for the universalisation of education of the age-group of 6 to 11, for the equality of those who get left behind in the race for a productive set-up of society, *i.e.*, the tribal people and the scheduled castes and nearly 50 per cent of Indian humanity, *i.e.*, the women. The 42nd amendment to the constitution devolves certain duties, particularly the promotion of a scientific temper, preservation of the environment and India's long cultural heritage, etc. on the citizens of India.

One of the main recommendations of the Kothari Commission was to transform education into an instrument of social change, this can only be conceived in the dimension already delineated by the Constitution of India, which the great leaders of this country and the founding fathers have bequeathed to the people, basing it on the values which had been so dearly promoted in the struggle for freedom against British imperialism and colonialism. Therefore, when one starts thinking about the values for the vast community of teachers at all levels—whether elementary, secondary or higher—one cannot but think in terms of the constitutional imperatives.

Conclusion

From the above elaborate discussion it will be expressly clear that 'Value Education' is much more broader concept than 'Moral Education'. 'Moral Education' is a traditional term whereas, 'Value Education' is a new concept, which has not even been well founded in our educational terminology, especially in the Indian perspective. In order to make the 'Value Education' more effective we should adopt new approach to value education through different subjects. For this it is very essential to understand properly the relationship of 'Moral Education' to the broader concept of 'Value Education'. After this we should plan our strategies as per availability of time, environment and other desired resources.

Inculcation or teaching of values is a great task for teachers and other informal agencies including homes involved therein. For them the following recommendations put forth by the International Commission will be quite useful:

> "The teacher's duty is less to inclucate and more and more to encourage thinking; his formal functions apart, he will have to become more and more an adviser, a partner to talk to; someone who helps seek out conflicting arguments rather than handling out readymade truths. He will have to devote more time and energy to productive and creative activities: interaction, discussion, stimulation, understanding, encouragement."[12] The Commission further points out that "one of the essential tasks of educators at present is to

change the mentalities and qualifications inherent in all professions; thus, they should be the first to be ready to rethink and change the criteria and basic situation of the teaching profession, in which the job of educating and stimulating students is steadily superseding that of simply giving instruction."[13]

REFERENCES

1. अन्ये कृतयुगे धर्माः त्रेतायां द्वापरे अपरे।
   अन्ये कलियुगे नृणां युगह्यासानुरूपतः।।
   —मनुस्मृति 1.85
2. *Religion and Society*, p. 113.
3. *Complete Works*, Vol. III, Eighth Edition, p. 112.
4. Will Durant, *The Mansions of Philosophy*, p. 112.
5. *The Mansions of Philosophy: Our Changing Morals*, p. 131.
6. S. Harman, *Plight of Pupils in Schools*, D.L. Publications, London, p. 158.
7. *Research in the Classroom*, NCERT, 1979, Project Report No. 6.
8. *The Religions of Man*, p. 193.
9. तद्धि तद्वनं नाम तद्वनमित्युपांसितब्यं स य एतदेव।
   वेदाभि हैनं सर्वाणि भूतानि संवांच्छन्ति।
10. Robert M. O'Neil, *Classrooms in the Crossfire*, Indiana University Press, Bloomington, 1934.
11. Based on 'Professional Values', National Commission on Teachers, NIEPA, New Delhi, pp. 16-17.
12. *Learning To Be* (the Report of the International Commission on the Development of Education), pp. 77-78.
13. *Ibid.*, p. 216.

6

LISTING AND CLASSIFICATION OF VALUES

We have already explained how 'values' are evolved from the experiences of the individual with the interaction of the society and environment around him. Every individual, may he be an economist, poet, saint, social worker, teacher or doctor has certain cherished values. Almost all professions, except a few undesirable ones, prescribe certain rules of conduct, popularly known as 'code'. In '*Charak Samhita*', a famous treatise on ancient Indian system of medicine, Charaka has described in details the ethical mandate to be followed by all the physicians. In several scriptures there are distinct codes of ethics for saints, teachers as well as students.

Keeping in view the nature of professional requirements values can be classified into several categories, such as economic values, social values, political values, spiritual values, modern values, aesthetic values, religious values, material values, etc. It is a matter of great regret that in our society the values in fields like politics, trade, etc. are not encouraging and inspiring to the young generation.

We note the wide discrepancy between what people do and what they say. Many political leaders, business executives, military leaders, workers of all sorts, and even professional people are known to do things that are inconsistent with what they say are their values; charges of corruption are not unusual. So many people can be 'bought'. All this clearly suggests that approaches to values that have been so widely used in the past have been quite ineffective.

In the "Documents of Social, Moral and Spiritual Values in Education," a booklet published by NCERT, a list of 83 values is appended. In this list there are values like abstinence, citizenship, cleanliness, compassion, courtesy, devotion, duty, endurance, fellow-feeling, honesty, gratitude, kindness, purity, regularity, self-help, self-control, team-work, etc. As stated earlier these terms are very akin to the terms described as virtues in our scriptures.

Forty Virtues

There are certain virtues common to all religions like Hindu, Sikh, Jain, Buddha, etc. Such forty values (virtues) are enumerated below with brief explanation:

1. *Harmlessness (Ahimsa):* It means refraining from injury to anyone through mind, speech or action.
2. *Truth:* It means representing a thing precisely as one has perceived it through the mind or the senses, and in agreeable language.
3. *Non-Stealing:* It means refraining from all forms of theft or illegal possession of others' property.
4. *Brahmacharya* (abstinence): It consists in abstaining from all the eight forms of sexual gratification.
5. *Non-accumulation of Things:* It means refraining from accumulation, from a sense of possession.
6. *Purity:* It connotes freedom from bodily and mental impurities.
7. *Contentment:* It means complete absence of thirst for material objects.
8. *Austerity:* It means enduring hardships for discharging one's religious obligations.
9. *Scriptural Study:* It includes study of sacred books, repetition of Divine Names and recounting the virtues of the Lord.
10. *Devotion to God:* This is expressed through faith in and attachment to God.
11. *Spiritual Wisdom:* It means discrimination between what is real and what is unreal.
12. *Dispassion:* It denotes complete absence of attachment to anything pertaining to this world or the next.
13. *Self-discipline:* It is exercising control over the mind.
14. *Control of the Senses:* There are five senses of perception and five organs of action. Their control means bringing them all under subjugation and using them according to one's discretion.
15. *Endurance:* It means the capacity to bear heat and cold and to remain unaffected by pleasure and pain, etc., that is not to be influenced by diverse experiences.

16. *Piety:* It means absolute faith in the *Vedas*, the scriptures and the teaching of *Mahatmas*, one's preceptor truths. It may also be termed as 'Purity'.
17. *Forgiveness:* It means entertaining no thought of inflicting punishment on one who has wronged you.
18. *Courage:* It means boldness, *i.e.*, absence of cowardice.
19. *Compassion (Karuna):* It means melting of the heart at the sight of suffering of a creature. It is termed as 'consideration for others' or 'fellow-feeling' by the psychologists.
20. *Sublimity:* 'Sublimation' is a wellknown term in 'Psycho-analysis. In our scriptures it is equated with '*tej*'. It is the power of superior souls under whose influence, even those who are attached to worldly enjoyments and are of a base nature, are deterred from sinful acts and take to noble pursuits including the excellence in Fine Arts, etc.
21. *Arjava:* In the modern terminology it can be termed as 'simple living', which involves straightness of body, the senses and the mind.
22. *Unselfishness:* It means not seeking satisfaction of any selfish desire connected with this world or the next. In the NCERT list of values it is termed as 'common cause' and 'common good'.
23. *Amanitva:* It consists in not seeking honour, respect or homage for oneself and observes 'gentlemanliness, or shows 'respect for others'. These two values are included in the list given in NCERT booklet.
24. *Freedom from Hypocrisy:* Hypocrisy consists in putting up a false show of 'piety' or 'purity'. This should be avoided scrupulously by all because one cannot befool all the persons at all the times.
25. *Absence of the Back-biting Spirit:* Back-biting or slandering proceeds generally from jealousy and this should be completely eschewed.
26. *Straightforwardness:* It means not attempting any thing from a selfish motive.
27. *Humility:* This is antonym of 'boasting' meaning to have very high estimate of oneself.
28. *Fortitude:* It means not to be perturbed in the face of the greatest difficulty and danger.
29. *Spirit of Service:* It means constantly striving to the best of one's ability through mind, speech and body and in a

disinterested spirit to contribute to the happiness of all creatures according to their respective need. It indicates many values like concern for others, co-operation, compassion, fellow-feeling, helpfulness, humanism, etc.

30. *Satsang (Good Company):* In its religious sense it means association with saints and holy men.
31. *Japa:* It is muttering or mental repetition of a name of God or of a *Mantra* (sacred formula). It is different from meditation in some respects.
32. *Meditation:* It means concentration of the mind on a form of God to which one is specially attached.
33. *Freedom from Malice:* It means entertaining no enmity even towards an enemy.
34. *Fearlessness (Courage):* It means complete absence of fear.
35. *Evenmindedness (Equality) or Equanimity:* It means looking on all as equal from the point of view of the soul even though differences may be observed in dealing with them according to the *Varna* (caste) and *Ashrama* (order) to which they belong, just as one uses the limbs of his own body differently.
36. *Absence of Egoism:* It means absence of the feeling of 'I' in respect of the body, mind and intellect, and of the sense of doership in respect of actions performed by them.
37. *Friendliness (Universal Love):* It consists in extending the feeling of love towards all creatures, whether high or low.
38. *Charity:* It consists in gratuitously supplying that which is needed in a particular place, at a particular time and by a particular person, gladly and respectfully, without expecting any return or reward.
39. *Devotion to Duty:* It includes the values like 'sincerity', 'integrity', 'honesty', 'loyalty to duty' etc. contained in the list of 83 values given in NCERT booklet.
40. *Tranquillity:* This state is attained when the mind is completely free from desires and is peaceful, contented and perspicuous.

These are traditional values inherited from the past. Some of these values like 'non-accumulation of things', 'contentment', and 'dispassion' are practicable for saintly persons only. We may say that they are too righteous to cultivate in the individuals of this space-age for want of sufficient exemplary situations in the present set-up of the society.

Eighty-three Values

The following is the list of 83 values given in NCERT publication styled as "Documents on Social, Moral and Spiritual Values." Shri B.R. Goel, the compiler, claims that the list has been compiled on the basis of documents included in the publication as well as a study of the Gandhian literature.

1. Abstinence
2. Appreciation of cultural values of others
3. Anti-touchability
4. Citizenship
5. Consideration for others
6. Concern for others
7. Co-operation
8. Cleanliness
9. Compassion
10. Common cause
11. Common good
12. Courage
13. Courtesy
14. Curiosity
15. Democratic decision-making
16. Devotion
17. Dignity of the individual
18. Dignity of manual work
19. Duty
20. Discipline
21. Endurance
22. Equality
23. Friendship
24. Faithfulness
25. Fellow-feeling
26. Freedom
27. Forward look
28. Good manner
29. Gentlemanliness
30. Gratitude
31. Honesty
32. Helpfulness
33. Humanism

34. Hygienic living
35. Initiative
36. Integrity
37. Justice
38. Kindness
39. Kindness to animals
40. Loyalty to duty
41. Leadership
42. National unity
43. National consciousness
44. Non-violence
45. National integration
46. Obedience
47. Peace
48. Proper utilization of time
49. Punctuality
50. Patriotism
51. Purity
52. Quest for knowledge
53. Resourcefulness
54. Regularity
55. Respect for others
56. Reverence for old age
57. Sincerity
58. Simple living
59. Social justice
60. Self-discipline
61. Self-help
62. Self-respect
63. Self-confidence
64. Self-support
65. Self-study
66. Self-reliance
67. Self-control
68. Self-restraint
69. Social service
70. Solidarity of mankind
71. Sense of discrimination between good and bad
72. Sense of social responsibility
73. Socialism

74. Sympathy
75. Secularism and respect for all religions
76. Spirit of enquiry
77. Team-work
78. Team spirit
79. Truthfulness
80. Tolerance
81. Universal truth
82. Universal love
83. Value for national and civic property.

In the list of above values there is repetition as well as overlapping of purport conveyed by certain values. *For example,* we can take a few values from the above list—self-confidence and self-reliance, self-control and self-restraint, tolerance and endurance, concern for others and consideration for others, kindness and kindness to animals, national unity and national integration, common cause and common good. In fact, owing to complex nature of human feeling, psycho-cultural bent of mind, divergent individual and social differences there cannot be regimentation of words sounding different values. Therefore, there cannot be any fixed and exact number of values nor there can be any exhaustive list of values. In the above list even the number being as high as 83 a few important values like coexistence, preservation of cultural and natural environment, etc. are missing. One may argue that this value (coexistence) is connoted by other values like 'universal love' already included in the list. This argument may stand the test of brevity. With the brevity point of view the list may be incorporated under the following six sub-heads:

1. *Righteousness*—abstinence, cleanliness, compassion, common cause, common good, co-operation, courage, courtesy, discipline, endurance, friendship, faithfulness, good manners, hygienic living, justice, obedience, proper utilization of time, purity, quest for knowledge, simple living, self-help, self-study, self-reliance, self-support, self-confidence, self-respect, sympathy, sense of discrimination between good and bad, truthfulness, tolerance.
2. *Self-Discipline*—forward look, self-control, self-restraint, punctuality, regularity, honesty, sincerity, loyalty to duty, integrity, initiative, resourcefulness.
3. *Fellow feeling*—helpfulness, concern for others, respect for others, reverence for old age.

4. *Humanism*—consideration for others concern for others curiosity, dignity of the individual, dignity of manual work, gentlemanliness, gratitude, social service, solidarity of mankind, sense of social responsibility, spirit of enquiry, team-work, team spirit.
5. *Democratic sense*—citizenship, democratic decision-making, equality, freedom, leadership, national unity, national consciousness, patriotism, social justice, socialism, value for national and civic property.
6. *Non-violence*—appreciation of cultural values, anti-untouchability, kindness, kindness to animals, secularism and respect for all religions, universal truth, universal love.

In one of the circulars of Kendriya Vidyalaya Sangathan on Moral Education, the following seventeen values have been enumerated:

1. Freedom
2. Truth
3. Honesty
4. Hard-work
5. Self-discipline (punctuality, responsibility, devotion to duty, etc.)
6. Love for one's country
7. Justice
8. Non-violence
9. Secularism
10. Care for public property
11. Consideration for others
12. Scientific temper
13. Team spirit
14. Cleanliness
15. Humility
16. Co-operativeness
17. Service to the people.

Hutchin's Code lists ten qualities of character which we all might strive to attain:

1. Health
2. Self-control
3. Loyalty

4. Kindness
5. Self-reliance
6. Reliability
7. Duty
8. Team-work
9. Good workmanship
10. Clean play.

According to a section of educationists search for new human values, which would be more consonant with the global consciousness of our times and responsive to the changes brought about by science and technology and to the urgency of wide-scale problems being faced by mankind, is suggested.

Dr. Prem Kirpal, former Secretary of Education, Government of India has rightly pointed out that "the charter of the United Nations, the Constitution of UNESCO and the Declaration of Human Rights embodied statements, principles and norms for the observance by the member-states are very conducive to the evolution of proper human values that can be practised and shared by all in the making of a new humanism for the emerging global community." In this context he has mentioned the following value-concepts:

1. Man and his own self: The human person, The Inner Man.
2. Man and his fellowmen: Society, Human Relations.
3. Man and his habitat: Natural, Space
4. Man and his Work.
5. Man and his Art.
6. Man and Technology.
7. Man and his Technology.
8. Man and time: The stream of past, present and future.
9. Man and his cosmos (Man and his universe; the meaning and purpose of existence).

Besides these traditional and modern value-concepts mostly applicable to the individual there are a few values to be observed by societies and nations for the harmonious growth of human beings and global peace. Some of such value-concepts have been enumerated in the declaration of Congress for Human Unity held at Philadelphia in May, 1976. They are as follows:

(a) Compassionate love.
(b) Intrinsic worth of each human being.

(c) Right for all people to develop their creativity.
(d) The inter-dependence of all nations.
(e) Solidarity.
(f) Freedom and justice for all people.
(g) Complete disarmament.
(h) Decentralization of power.
(i) Freedom of expression of thought.
(j) The right to work for just rewards.
(k) Preservation of natural and cultural environments.
(l) The adjustment of economic structures for greater equality and justice for people.
(m) Abolition of all forms of slavery, torture and capital punishment.

To inculcate these values among the people some high level decisions are to be taken, authority is exercised and bills are passed by the competent bodies, if necessary, that is why they are called global values, national values and so on whereas to cultivate the value-concepts stated earlier personal influence, experience and several other strategies are used. As per the new approach of value education no pressures are to be used, rather more situations for clarification of values and free choice are to be provided. Under the sub-head 'Methodology' we will discuss here itself a few modes and methods of internalization of these value-concepts.

Classification of Values

1. *Academic Values*—Like regularity and devotion in teaching, impartiality in assessment, honesty and integrity in research and publication, healthy competition and objectivity, search for excellence and originality.
2. *Moral Values*—Like honesty, integrity, sense of responsibility and compassion. The realm of moral values is rather a debatable one.
3. *Socio-political Values*—Like national integration and international understanding, society *vs.* individual, social responsibility and citizenship, democracy and humanism. These are the values required for the survival of a socio-political system. The difference between moral values and socio-political values is very subtle. Among all socio-political values national integration is of utmost importance particularly for teachers.

4. *Scientific Temper*—Objectivity, rationalism, fact-base and investigative approach, looking into the hows and whys of problems.
5. *Global Values*—Global values consist of all those values pertinent and significant for global peace and order, solidarity, freedom and justice for all, complete disarmament, abolition of all forms of slavery, torture and capital punishment, etc., can be enumerated under this sub-heading.
6. *Environmental Values*—Preservation of natural environment, forestation, awareness and concern towards pollution, etc., can be called environmental values.
7. *Cultural Values*—Cultural unity, respect for others' culture, preservation of culture, etc. "Although we speak of the culture of a group, or of a country the essence of cultural elements is individual help to make for cultural unity, for functional group interaction and for organized, purposeful living together. Differences in cultural elements among individuals and conflict in values and purposes within individuals, often lead to tensions and to changc in cultural characteristics and values."[1]

Traditional and Functional Values

Values are also classified as traditional and functional values. Here we are concerned mostly with functional values. But at times traditional values also influence human behaviour. Therefore, while clarifying the value or values our approach should be pragmatic.

Idealized and Behavioural Values

Idealized values are of more theoretical character whereas behavioural values are usually less ideal, less perfect and less theoretical. Behavioural values reflect actual behaviour of the individual directly. According to Griffin and Pareek "Idealized values may be those found in ancient scriptures or philosophical treatises. They may be representative of the actual way of life that existed, or they may represent only the way of life of a particular class or group in the past. Nevertheless, people have to idealize those values, to worship them, and so long for resurrection of the way of living they represent. Behavioural values are those reflected in the day-to-day life of individuals and groups."[2]

Education is a sub-system of the wider sub-system. Other sub-systems of the society are economic, religious, political, etc. Problems of education are not to be seen in isolation of these other sub-systems as these are interlinked with each other. Moreover the systems like economic, political, etc. exert powerful influence on the goals and instrumentalities of education.

"In point of fact the educational sub-system is not the only agency offering education; to begin with the domestic group, the neighbourhood, and peer group have important educational roles and the educational process continues beyond the formal school stage through books, mass media, cultural, political and religious intercourse, and inter-personal contacts of a wide variety. The formal educational system has to take account of early socialization and has to anticipate future end processes."

Moral Values

The realm of moral values is rather a debatable one. Can anyone dispute that values like honesty, integrity, sense of responsibility and compassion be not part of teachers' personality make-up and still can it also be disputed that teachers are also part and parcel of socio-economic system that regards making the fast buck, of investing the minimum amount of money, labour, effort, attention and reaping the largest profit and results out of it as independent value in the present-day society—a value that seems to transcend all others? Educational institutions are supposed to be places where moral values have to be inculcated in the younger generation. But, as one analyses the present situation, one is struck by the paradox that the very agency which is to inculcate the desirable values in its own self-perception and in the perception of the community and the students, has few adherents to these values.

From one of the surveys made by the National Commission on Teachers in Higher Education reveals that the pessimists and optimists are equally balanced.

Professional Values

In fact teachers are finding it hard to uphold the banners of moral values. If the entire educational process beginning with admissions, instruction, examination, selection, retention, promotion and upward growth of teachers is getting distorted, would it be wise or practical to preach morality to the teachers alone?

It is only in this context that one finds that 14.69 and 18.46 per cent of the university and 19.82 and 24.45 per cent of the college teachers found nothing wrong with earning money by publishing *bazar* notes or undertaking too many tuitions to earn lots of money.

If one was to analyse world religions as they originated, one would find that all religions have a core of moral values common to them. These values are basically humanistic values necessary for sustenance of society, without adherence to which society would disintegrate; "धारणात् धर्म इत्याहु:" says the Indian sage. These are values like those prescribed through the Ten Commandmends or enshrined in great thoughts of '*Upanishads*' like '*Satyam Shivam Sundaram*' or in *Quran*, etc.

Values in the Good Elementary School

Independence and Initiative

— must be developed in each child by means of thorough mastery of many kinds of learnings;
— knowledge and practised skill in health—to protect himself and others;
— skill in reading—so that he can understand others;
— skill in writing and speaking—so that others can understand him;
— accuracy and understanding in the use of numbers and measurements—so that he can deal with things in quantity;
— practice in understanding and weighing the opinions of others—so that he may make good judgements;
— practice in critical thinking—so that he will be in the habit of examining his own motives and the purposes of others.

Skills of Communication and Understanding Ought to be Stressed in the Elementary School

The Humane and Constructive Talents

— of each child should be stimulated to full development. Each child ought to learn to feel;
— concern for the general welfare;
— kinship with others;
— respect for each person as an individual;
— respect for laws and social institutions.
— self-respect and Respect for Others Must Be Taught and Practised in the Good Elementary School

Social Responsibility and Co-operative Skills

Must be learned and practised by every child through:

— sharing in the gathering of data—so that the best evidence may be obtained;
— sharing in the forming of group decisions—so that the decisions may reflect the opinions of all;
— planning changes and improvements of institutions—so that progress may be made;
— practising the use of reason rather than force—so that the rights of minorities may be respected.

Habits of Responsible Citizenship should Begin in the Elementary School

When the Educational Policies Commission made its survey of the imaginary schools of the state of "Columbia"—Farmville, Oak Hill, American City, Woodland Park, and Patsburg—these principles were found to be the basis for good practices of teaching and learning: (1) Development and growth are continuous, (2) Behaviour is learned, (3) Each individual is unique, (4) We learn what we live, (5) We always learn several different things at once, (6) We learn a great deal by imitation, and (7) Learning and growth are stimulated by security and adventure.

American Values

In 1951, the Educational Policies Commission defined for public schools certain values which could be considered a common denomination of American democracy. These values included:

— Respect for human personality
— Moral responsibility of the individual
— Institutions are servants of men
— Common consent (peaceful adjustment rather than violence)
— Devotion to truth (freedom of expression)
— Respect for excellence
— Moral equality for all
— Brotherhood (the golden rule)

— The pursuit of happiness (happiness considered as the fullest expression of one's potentialities—not mere "fun")

— Spiritual enrichment.[3]

In 1959 the California Teachers Association choose seven of these values for inculcation in the students of the schools. American scholars[4] have listed many other values, which we may also like to endorse. One of these is "respect for the contribution of all peoples to our civilization," which is of great importance for the students and teachers of Social Sciences.

REFERENCES

1. Willis H. Griffin and Udai Pareek, *The Process of Planned Change in Education*, p. 31.
2. *The Process of Planned Change in Education*, p. 28.
3. *Educational Policies Commission: Moral and Spiritual Values in the Public School*, National Education Association (Washington, D.C. 1951).
4. R.H. Gabriel, *Traditional Values in American Life*, U.S. National Commission for UNESCO (New York: Harcourt, Brace and World, 1963).

7

MODERNITY *Vs.* VALUE-CRISIS: A CHALLENGE

Misconceptual notion of modernity and rapid growth of science and technology and subsequent industrialization have caused a great threat and danger to our old morals and values. In the changed social set-up, our definitions of good morals stand questioned. Old values seem to be lost but new are yet to be evolved and brought into practice and as such we can term the present era as 'transitional' one. Will Durant has very aptly put forth this phenomena. According to him, "These, then, are the varied causes of our moral change. It is in terms of their transit from farms and houses to factories and city streets, that we must understand the generation which so boisterously replace us. Their lives and problems are new and different. The Industrial Revolution has them in its grip and transforms their customs; their garb, their work, their religion, and their conduct; to judge them in terms of the old code is as unfair and unhistorical as to force upon them the corsets and bustles, the beards and boots of our ancient days."[1]

Several scientific inventions have also their role in challenging our old and traditional, but very useful values to a great extent. It is difficult to compile a list of changes brought about by these scientific inventions in our daily life. Similarly it is not easy to compile a comprehensive list of 'good' or bad actions of mankind—as moment after moment a man is confronted with new situations and problems. It is said that the actions, speech or thoughts which are motivated by or admixed with perverted emotions, called sex-lust, anger, greed, attachment, arrogance and sloth or lethargy (*Kama, Krodha, Lobha, Moha, Mada* and *Matsar*), called six sins, are enemies of a man (*shadripu*).

Of these, sex-lust is the arch-enemy of man; it is the chief sin or vice because due to this very weakness a man falls prey to other vices easily. But here also our scientific invention has come to 'rescue'. Contraceptives have intruded to adulterate the sanctity of individual's private life also. "The invention and spread of contraceptives is the proximate cause of our changing morals. The old moral code restricted sexual experience to marriage, because copulation could not be effectively separated from parentage, but today the dissociation of sex from reproduction has created a situation unforeseen by our fathers. All the relations of man and woman are being changed by this one factor; and the moral code of the future will have to take account of these new facilities which invention has placed at the service of ancient desires."[2]

Nowadays newspapers, magazines and other news media are flooded with reports of crime, murder, agitation and eve-teasing. We read in newspapers of several such occurrences where the landlord and tenants have exchange of hot words leading to stabbing. Disputes between father and son, between wife and husband, between son-in-law and father-in-law are not rare. For want of endurance in one's dealings all family ties are broken, people leave homes for ever out of disgust and anger. All these occurrences indicate deterioration in our ethical standards, loss of our moral and social values resulting in great loss to families, society and the nation at large.

It is widely believed that modernization is responsible for the crisis in values to a large extent. The reasons are not far to seek. Modernization involves industrialization, use of modern and advanced techniques in agriculture and all other spheres of life and work. With modernization comes better communication that bridges the gap not only between places but also between people. The result is that the traditional values of a small closely knit society which demands co-operation, loyalty, dependence on relations, neighbours get eroded and people tend to ignore these values. They become more self-reliant and self-centred which makes men more impersonal in their conduct. Had the modern society consciously tried to retain or imbibe the values of self-discipline in individuals, the crisis of values that is so widespread could have been contained. Self-discipline teaches one not only to value one's rights but to respect those of others equally.

Incidents of violence and destruction are increasingly reported. People take a certain irrational pleasure in discriminating between their faith and that of others and resort to communal riots. Strikes and lock-outs are becoming more and more common-place. Rarely does a man read a newspaper without coming across an item reporting strikes, lock-outs and crimes. What few people realise is that strikes and lock-outs hamper economic development and advancement of society. The total loss which the people suffer due to such anti-social and anti-national movements runs into millions of rupees each year. The major cause of such incidents is the loss of self-discipline in the average human-being, who is taken in by anti-nationalistic elements and ignores his duty and harms the economy and thus society in general.

Lack of self-discipline has led to an ignorance of one's values and duty which has adversely affected the structure of the society in the modern day. Indian society has also been affected by this trend and the process of disintegration of our basic social infrastructure and system is discernible all-around. The hazards we now face are far more dimensional than we had ever imagined earlier. Nietzsche says "When a tree grows up to heaven, its roots reach down to hell." We must not therefore, be overwhelmed by the failure of many individuals to maintain self-discipline. Instead, we must try to make them understand, as Dr. Radhakrishnan wrote that "Error is not crime, it is only youth, immaturity", which can be controlled and corrected with the right effort.

This process of disintegration of values would soon prove to be disastrous, unless a conscious effort is made to reverse this trend and to inculcate in one and all a spirit of discipline of the self. This cannot be done by simple physical processes. The initiation of the spirit and the awakening of the mind are the two modes of efficiently implanting values such as discipline of the self in people in all walks of life. Whittier has written:

"When faith is lost, when honour dies, the man is dead."

Thus, any man can be called a man as long as he guards his values, as soon as they are gone, the very reason for his being called 'Human' vanishes and he is lowered to the level of animals. Let every man realise that his values are guarded by his conscience and that these are not derived by nature or from reason, but by custom.

The crying need of the modern society is to inculcate the spirit of self-discipline and the values that follow from it, in every individual, from his childhood, through proper education and training.

Without any values, the world could not be a place worth living in and, unfortunately, it is heading towards this state due to the present crisis. If no person is interested in life, in the true sense of the word, then we can carry on without bothering at present. But it is obviously not so.

The trend towards modernity is being grossly misinterpreted to mean removal of values. We witness very often a total lack of regard for the values of others amongst people. Today, very few people care for or have respect for the age-old values—like freedom, belief, sincerity and self-respect, the right to work and freely express one's views. While we cherish individually these values for ourselves, we show a total disregard for similar values of others. Very rarely are people found making true sacrifices for the benefit of others, selfishness fills the atmosphere and corruption and other immoral acts reflect totally corrupted values. Individuals take pleasure in misleading the stranger. Most people today refrain from or at least avoid taking so called 'unnecessary' responsibilities making themselves morally accountable for some particular things, whether done by one or the other. Very few people are disciplined enough to fulfil and do justice to such responsibilities and duties, though they heartfully partake of all benefits they can derive from taking that responsibility.

Man is gradually losing the sense of duty which played a prominent role in human behaviour until recently. Today, all of us know that men not only ignore their duty, but also do just the opposite of what they are supposed to be doing. The glaring and repugnant example of the assassination of our ex-P.M. Smt. Indira Gandhi, by two of her own bodyguards, brings forth a reflection on the state of affairs. To be sure, no one could imagine earlier that two men could kill the Prime Minister, that too a lady, 66 years of age, whom they were paid to guard. Again, the spy-ring unearthed in the Prime Minister's Secretariat had been leaking out vital secrets to other nations. Such are the traitors who have been completely taken in by this crisis, the crisis of values. Hundreds of examples reflect this. A single day of observation of the pattern of life in any city would reflect this too. The prevalence of a crisis is confirmed. That it has spread to all spheres is indicated by incidents all around us. In the recent Bhopal gas tragedy the fault lay in the lack of sense of duty in the factory's administration. The recent incident at St. Stephen's College in Delhi was another example of vanishing and corrupted morals. All of us have thus to channelise our efforts to ease this crisis, so that we may leave, behind us, a world more worth living in.

India used to take pride in its rich traditions, art, culture, ideals and teachings of great personalities. But all these seem to be dormant and polluted to a large extent. Our media like cinema, TV, video, etc. could not provide desired nourishment to our culture, on the contrary, due to commercial type of competition in gaining cheap popularity and material benefits, they have polluted our culture. Except a very few they could not provide healthy and nourishing environment to our culture. Because of this cultural pollution, our work-culture has also been polluted. It is polluted work-culture that has affected the sincerity and devotion to duty in various walks of life. That is why we have to come across the incidents referred to above. Self-discipline and self-restraint lack very much in the society. Discipline is regarded as a check on one's liberty or ceiling on one's right. In these circumstances, it is crying need of the day that inner discipline is generated among the new generation. It should not be a sort of imposition. Moreover, it should be more and more practical. In education, therefore, we need a genuine faith in the existence of moral principles which are capable of effective application. This application requires to be in the social-settings. John Dewey, noted educationist, has rightly remarked on this point. According to him, "To isolate the formal relationship of citizenship from the whole system of relations with which it is actually interwoven; to suppose that there is some one particular study or mode of treatment which can make the child a good citizen; to suppose, in other words, that a good citizen is anything more than a thoroughly efficient and serviceable member of society, one with all his powers of body and mind under control, is a hampering superstition which it is hoped may soon disappear from educational discussion."[3]

Therefore, in moral education indoctrination should be avoided and defects of value clarification and cognitive developmentalism should be removed by the educators, before they plan any strategy of value-oriented education. It will be possible when the teacher avoids imposing his own judgements or ideals and approving or disapproving the moral judgement of the individuals under his or her charge.

In America (U.S.A.) "In the past decade the topic of moral education in the schools has received a great deal of discussion. In part this is a response to a variety of events that have, to say the least, shaken public life: Vietnam, Watergate, Koreagate as well as tales of perfidy and corruption in industry, unions, and the professions. As usual, the schools have received their bit of the blame for allowing us to come to this sorry state through the indictment that they are failing to morally educate individuals. And since the schools, contrary to many observations, are one of the least rigid institutions in our society, educators have scrambled to include some component on moral education in the curriculum. Similarly in our country also many schools specially convent schools have some sort of moral education in their curriculum. Certain periods are allotted to moral education.

But our experiences have revealed that moralizing has not served the purpose in the past nor it is going to serve the purpose in the present.

It becomes a mechanical process, neither it touches heart nor provides any scope for intellectual exercise, on the contrary, it becomes problematic specially when the question of indoctrination is raised. As values are governed by meta-ethical relativism, moralizing appears to be a form of indoctrination. Therefore, the strategy of Value-oriented Education is a challenge for teachers, parents and the society at large.

REFERENCES

1. *The Mansions of Philosophy: Our Changing Morals*, p. 130.
2. *Ibid.*, p. 119.
3. *Moral Principles in Education*, p. 9.

8

HOW TO INCULCATE VALUES?

"The problem of fostering ethical and spiritual values in a society raises the question of the source of these values. It is precisely in this field that sharp differences of opinion have developed in the modern age leading to utter confusion and bewilderment. Broadly speaking, these differences reduce themselves to *two viewpoints*, one of which holds that matter or outer nature is the focus of all values and the other which affirms man as that focus. The first leads to undue emphasis on the creation, possession, and enjoyment of material wealth and the search for organic satisfactions, whereas, the second, while putting due emphasis on the above, leads to the pursuit of values and satisfaction lying beyond the sensate level of life, and to the experience by man of spiritual freedom and integrity."

—Swami Akhandanand (p. 540)

The value-orientation is not confined to those only who are in schools, but also for those who are outside. It is a time-bound process; but it is a very long and continuous process. If education is a life-long process, as some educationists have put it, value-orientation is also to be observed as a life-long process. It is more so because it is more informal than education. Moreover, the faculties of mind of an individual take different shapes at different phases of life. Therefore, the principle of 'individual difference' is to be followed more carefully in the context of value-orientation. In this regard the following remarks are noteworthy:

"The development of values is a personal and life-long process. It is not something that is completed by early adulthood. As the world changes, so we change, and as we strive to change the world again, we have many decisions to make and we should be learning how to make these decisions. We should be learning how to value. It is this process that we believe to be carried on in the classrooms; it is atleast partly through this process that we think children will learn about themselves and about how to somersault out of the buzzing of the society around them."[1]

Main Components of the Method

The main components of the method of value-orientation are the following three:

1. By having formal or informal dialogue.
2. By giving some written exercises (Value-sheets).
3. By holding individual or group-discussions.

Any strategy we plan under these three methods it should be directly aimed at one or another of the following seven valuing components. According to Louis E. Raths and his associates the term 'value' is a term assigned to those individual beliefs, attitudes, activities or feelings that satisfy the following criteria:

1. It has been freely chosen.
2. It is chosen from one or more available alternatives.
3. It has been chosen after due reflection.
   It is different from impulse or highly emotional choices.
4. It is prized and cherished.
5. It has been affirmed to others.
6. It has been incorporated into actual behaviour.
7. It is repeated in one's life.

Value-clarification is very important task on the part of teachers. It is generally observed that not only children but adults also live by any consistent set of values. Many a time we are guided by others' thoughts and deeds. Moreover, in a number of cases children observe that people do not do what they say and this creates confusion in their minds in respect of certain values. They are not able to decide in what to believe. The more vital responsibility of teachers is to provide necessary guidance and training to make them able to decide in what to believe. All our efforts should be focussed to this very important direction. All our co-curricular activities, games, sports, excursions, etc. should be so planned and executed that they cater to the need of clarifying the values required to take decisions in different contexts for different purposes. They should be taught how to internalize certain beliefs and faiths having sound base of a set of values. No value is to be imposed on the students.

They should be allowed to react to several situations individually and come to the conclusion. This will give them an opportunity for extra thinking.

Dialogue

Louis E. Raths and his associates have mentioned,[2] thirty clarifying responses, which are noteworthy. In this clarifying approach the responses are open-ended, that is, they lead the student to no specific value but provide him/her ample scope for thinking and reacting to the environment around him/her. The wording of the following responses is suggestive only. Then the teacher may use one or more than one responses befitting to the particular situation. Those thirty responses (headings only) are as follows:

1. Is this something that you prize?
2. Are you glad about that?
3. How did you feel when that happened?
4. Did you consider any alternative?
5. Have you felt this way for a long time?
6. What is that something that you yourself selected or chose?
7. Did you have to choose that? Was it a free choice?
8. Did you do anything about that idea?
9. Can you give me some examples of that idea?
10. What do you mean by............? Can you define that world?
11. Where would that idea lead? What would be its consequences?
12. Would you really do that or are you just talking?
13. Are you saying that............. (repeat)?
14. Did you say that............. (repeat in some distorted way)?
15. Have you thought much about that idea (or behaviour)?
16. What are some good things about that notion?
17. What do we have to assume for things to work out that way?
18. Is what you express consistent with............ (note something the person said or did that may point to an inconsistency)?
19. What other possibilities are there?
20. Is that a personal preference or do you think most people should believe that? (another way to get at this—"Is this idea so good that everyone should go alongwith it."?)
21. How can I help you do something about your idea? What seems to be the difficulty?
22. Is there a purpose behind this activity?

23. Is that very important to you?
24. Do you this often?
25. Would you like to tell others about your idea?
26. Do you have any reasons for saying (or doing) that?
27. Would you do the same thing again?
28. How do you know it is right?
29. Do you value that?
30. Do you think people will always believe that? or "Did people long ago believe that"?

While having a formal dialogue with the students such questions (responses) are found to be very useful in clarifying the value. The wording of the question may be changed as per the age of student, to whom the response is directed. The questions must be of probing and provoking nature. The questions should aid them (individuals) in valuing. *For example* following dialogue may be given:

Teacher: Vivek, are you working very hard for Half Yearly Exam.?
Vivek: It is not good to be lazy, you know.
Teacher: How do you know it is not good?
Vivek: Everybody knows that, my parents always say it.
Teacher: That is nice (walks away).

Through this dialogue we come to know how the student (Vivek) knows that his judgement is correct. From time to time such dialogues, formal as well as informal, should be held on various values like friendship, fellow-feeling, sacrifice, leisure, courage, piety, punctuality, silence, devotion to duty, patriotism, love for nature, protecting nature, peace, truthfulness, etc. In this connection it should be noted that accepting the non-judgmental mood is vital for the valuing process.

This technique of responses may work better if the students come from enlightened families. In our rural backward areas the students are so shy and introvert that it will not be wise to expect frank and free response from them. In fact, this procedure does not seem to be workable in the rural areas. Students of good schools of the big cities may respond to the technique. Our problem is that more than 70 per cent of the student population are in our villages, where no adequate facilities of even traditional nature like *tatpatti*, blackboard, etc., exist. All this has an adverse effect on growth of their personality. Therefore, there is an urgent need to evolve some techniques to cultivate values in the mind of the students living particularly in rural areas.

A Writing Strategy

In this technique some exercises are given in written form, which may be called 'Value Sheets'. A value sheet consists of a provocative statement and a series of questions, which are duplicated on a sheet of paper and distributed to class members. These value sheets may be prepared during the progress of lessons, initially or otherwise as it may be convenient. In social sciences and languages there are sufficient possibilities for preparing value sheets. Our literature particularly Sanskrit literature is highly rich in value components.

Varieties of ideas and objects, events and biographies may work as the base value sheets. They may take different forms according to their contents. "Often they are based on single provocative statement. Sometimes two or more divergent positions open a value sheet. Sometimes the questions and statements are woven together so that value sheet has a dramatic development, with the student becoming increasingly involved in a complex issue. Sometimes value sheets consist of nothing more than a series of probing questions that are keyed to a common reading done from the text, a current events reading, or a piece of literature, or keyed to common assembly programme, a class problem, or a major public event, cartoons, films, recordings, television shows and other stimuli can also be used to begin a value sheet."

In order to make the idea clear a few value sheets are given below as examples—

Value Sheet No. 1
Love for Learning

"Learning of all things, the wise declare to be without a superior, because of its incapability of being taken away, or valued or exhausted."

"Learning, although possessed of a low man, introduces him to a king who is ordinarily inapproachable, just as a river, although flowing through a low region, takes one to the inaccessible sea: sources from which floweth great fortunes."

1. Why learning is said to be the best of all wealths?
2. Do you recall any parallel saying in this regard?
3. Which branch of learning you like the most?
4. What is your ambition in life?
5. How does learning help man to upgrade himself?

Value Sheet No. 2
Knowledge of Arms *vs.* Knowledge of Shastras

"The knowledge of arms and that of *shastras*—these two kinds of lore conduce to glory: but the former exposes one to ridicule in old age while the latter is ever respected."

1. Do you think that the above saying is correct?
2. If so, how would you justify this?
3. Do you recall any saying in your mother-tongue on this core?
4. Do you remember any story reflecting the validity of the above saying?

Value Sheet No. 3
Wickedness *vs.* Altruism

Fable—There is a large fig tree in a forest bordering on the road leading to Ujjaini, upon which lived a goose and a crow. One day in the sultry season, a traveller, being fatigued, slept under the tree having placed a bow and arrow on his side. After a short while the shadow of the tree moved away from his face. Then seeing that his face was covered with the sun the swan, that lived on the tree, through mercy, spread his wings and shaded his face again. Thereafter the traveller, happy in the enjoyment of sound sleep, yawned. Now the crow, unable to bear the happiness of others, through the wickedness natural to his species, muted into his mouth and flew away. Thereupon, as soon as the traveller rose and looked up he saw the goose whom he killed with an arrow.

1. In the above story who is said to be good? Why?
2. Why crow is described as bad?
3. If the goose was kind, why did he suffer at last?
4. Can the traveller be called as ungrateful?
5. What lesson do you learn from this fable?

Value Sheet No. 4
National Consciousness
(Preamble)

We the people of India having solemnly resolved to constitute India into a Sovereign Democratic Republic and to secure to all its citizens, Justice—social, economic and political, liberty of thought, expression, belief, faith and worship; Equality of status and of opportunity; and to promote among them all Fraternity; assuring the dignity of the individual and unity of the nation.

In our Constituent Assembly this twenty-sixth day of November 1949 do hereby adopt, enact and give to ourselves this Constitution.

1. What are the three kinds of justice promised to us? Give an example of each.
2. How does a Democratic Republic give equal responsibility to all its citizens?
3. Liberty, Equality, Fraternity—if you had to give up one of these, which would you give up? Why?
4. Write down five things in your own daily life that you can do to make yourself a better citizen of the country.

How to Use Value Sheet?

Value sheets can prove to be very effective tool for valuing. To make the use of value sheets fruitful, it should be borne in mind that valuing is an individual process, which requires very composed and balanced state of mind and quiet atmosphere and as such an application of group-discussion may not deliver the goods. It is very rightly said that character is developed in the flow of the world while thoughts are developed in solitude. Therefore, to elicit private and deliberate responses to the questions may gradually lead to clarification of values of the individuals. For this purpose, personal approach by the teachers is very essential. Value sheets may be given as weekend assignments so that students may get appropriate time for giving unhurried thought based on truly free choice.

For the successful planning and use Rathus, Harmin and Simon have suggested several alternatives. Some of them are as under:

1. Students discuss their written answers in small groups without the teacher's presence. This forces the students to think through issues without looking to the teacher for "the right way".
2. Students turn in their writings and the teacher later reads, without comment or evaluation, selected viewpoints that raise interesting alternatives or illuminate the issue in a special way. This is best done without the teacher identifying the writer, however, with the writer having the opportunity to claim credit for what is read to the class if he or she so wishes. Discussion may follow.
3. Students turn in their writings and the teacher returns them with occasional comments in the margins. The comments should, of course, be in the style of the value theory and should ask further questions that help the students rethink certain aspects of what was written originally. *For example*, asking students if something they wrote came, after considering alternatives, asking them to define a word or an idea, or asking them if they really live in ways consistent with what they write are all valuable comments to use in reacting to what students write for a value sheet. Naturally, teachers do not evaluate the students' values. They may, however, evaluate the language usage, spelling, and so on.
4. Students turn in their writings to a committee which selects representative ones to be read to the class or posted on the bulletin board.
5. Each student completes written answers and then the class has a general discussion about the topic. This is useful inasmuch as it raises new alternatives and ideas for some students. It is harmful inasmuch as pressures for conformity tend to develop. In any case, it is preferable for group discussion to follow individual thought on value sheets and teachers should strive to protect the right of dissent. In fact, they themselves should present alternative arguments if such are not forthcoming from the group. Without individual commitment to a position after full examination of the alternative arguments, no values can be very firm or intelligent.[3]

While using these value sheets the teacher should register high degree of openmindness, and sincerity to the great task of fostering values. Local resources and social conditions should always be kept in mind. Value development requires very open and thoughtful climate. Therefore, it is suggested that it should be mostly given as homework. Introduction, etc. to the proposed value sheet, of course, can be given in classroom situations in a better way.

Keeping in view the significance of value sheets as many as twenty-nine value sheets are given in one of the appendices of this book. While administering these value sheets one should not forget that moralizing has not worked in the past and so it is not going to work in the present. Therefore, these value sheets should not be used for the purpose of moralizing, otherwise our purpose will be defeated. In fact "the purpose of the value-theory, and the strategy of these value sheets, is to help children think through important areas of their lives and eventually to learn to respect their own decision-making abilities." Therefore, the approach should be non-directive, non-defensive and guarded by the concept of 'free choice'. Moreover value-rich and penetrating topics like money, friendship, love and sex, religion and morals, use of leisure time, politics and government, family, maturity, character-traits, etc. should be selected that may touch emotions and provide some intellectual exercise for the individuals concerned.

Subject-Matter Units and Value-Lessons

At times subject-matter can also form the part of value-lesson. Value sheets can be profitably prepared on the basis of some suitable subject-matter units. If the value components based on the one and the same subject-matter units are to be taught to the students of different age-groups, the language of the lesson may be modified suiting to the need of the students. From the following value sheets based on some subject-matter units it will be obvious as to how "subject-matter" questions and "value" questions are interspersed. Here teacher's skill and insight play a very significant role. How he can make one type of learning a reinforcing for the other. Both types of learning-valuing and T-L process may go together, because one may prove supplement for the other. There should not be any controversy on this point.

Raths, Harmin and B. Simon[4] do not believe that the learning of understanding has to precede the valuing process. They usually proceed best when they proceed together. According to them "Valuing is superficial without understanding. Understanding is superficial without valuing. And neither can wait until the other is accomplished." Thus, it is a false notion that maintains that children should learn their subject-matter first and do their valuing later. Knowledge not turned into values has a short half-life in memory and can be almost as easily used destructively as constructively.

Here we are giving some value lessons. Some of them are based on the 'subject-matter' units. These are different from the earlier value sheets in the sense that while teaching these lessons one may adopt discussion method to some extent, whereas in case of earlier value sheets discussion method may prove to be inappropriate, as explained in the foregoing paragraphs.

Fostering of Values through Great Personalities

Biographies of great scientists, social reformers, religious leaders, etc., have very significant value-components. Their character-traits may be quite inspiring, heart-touching and brain-storming. It is rightly said that History is nothing but a collection of biographies of heroes. Life of every great personality leaves behind a repository of knowledge, experience, beliefs and ideas, that may go a long way in integrating attitudes, ideals and beliefs of the individuals and thus, formation of their character. Longfellow's tribute to such great personalities is noteworthy—

Lives of great men all remind us
We can make our lives sumblime,
And departing leave behind us
Footprints on the sands of time,
Footprints that perhaps another,
Sailing over life's solemn mien
A forlorn and shipwrecked brother
Seeing shall take near again.
Let us then be up and doing
With a heart for any fate
Still achieving still pursuing,
Learn to Labour and to wait.

Therefore, knowledge of History is very essential for teachers, may belong to Science stream or Commerce stream. In the proposed Teachers' Training Programmes in the light of the need for value-orientation, knowledge of history, particularly Modern Indian History, has been emphatically recommended—

"Our aim should, therefore, be to provide to teacher trainees a bird's eye view of Indian History and some detailed idea of some of the great movements and events as also of inspiring biographies, not only of Kings and Queens, but also of our great builders of religion and spirituality, of philosophy and ethics, of language and literature, science and technology of art, of music and dance and sculpture and architecture."[5]

As examples we have selected the following six biographical sketches of great men—

1. *Raja Ram Mohun Roy*—A noted social reformer and founder of 'Brahmo Samaj' in India.
2. *Father Damien*—A great Leper saint of Hawaii islands.
3. *Elizabeth Fry*—Pioneer of prison reforms in England and Europe.
4. *Louis Pasteur*—A great discoverer of Disease Germs.
5. *Sarojini Naidu*—A famous poetess, nightingale of India.
6. *Copernicus*—A great ancient scientist.

In order to illustrate the character-traits and intrinsic values involved therein value-questions are also given at the end of each biographical sketch.

1. Raja Ram Mohun Roy

Raja Ram Mohun Roy, a great social reformer and the founder of Brahmo Samaj, was born in Radhanagar (Hooghly) in 1772. Because of his devout mother's teaching, he became a true follower of the *Vaishnav* faith. He secured his early education in his own home, and at the age of nine, was sent to Patna for his higher education in Arabic. With his extraordinary intelligence, he acquired a fair knowledge of Islam as well as of Arabic in a very short time.

At the age of 12, he went to Benaras for education in Sanskrit. Here he studied Hindu Philosophy. The Brahmo knowledge he gained, with the monotheism of the Mohammedan theology, made him disgusted with the use of images. At the age of 16 he wrote an article condemning Hindu idolatry, and this so angered his father that he had to leave home.

He visited many cities of India and finally went to Tibet where he learned a good deal about the Buddhist faith. His outspoken condemnation of Lama-worship so enraged the people that with great difficulty he escaped with his life and returned to India.

He found his country entangled in the various social evils and of these he chose idolatry and *sutee*, the burning of a widow on the funeral pyre of her husband, as the two against which he would fight. He was a brave man, and was sure his views were right. How could he keep silent? He raised a great voice against these evils, and experienced great opposition. Many thought he was the paid agent of the British Government. He had to endure abuse and hardships, but like other men, he paid no attention. He only went on with his work more earnestly.

In 1803, he entered the Bengal Civil Service as a Clerk, and was appointed to work in the Office of the Collector at Rangpur. Soon he rose to the position of a Sheristadar. He began at the age of 22 to study English and because of his amazing ability, picked up a fair knowledge of the language in a short time. During his period of 13 year's service, he saved a small sum of money, and then resigned from his post in order to serve his country more efficiently.

His work was not confined to mere lecturing. He wrote many books in English as well as in Bengali. Some of these were the translation from the Vedanta and the Upanishads. Others were devoted to the exposure of the evils of society. Through his books his ideas were circulated among a great number of people, and many became his followers. He is said to have been the first of the modern students of comparative religion. As a result of his scholarly studies, and at the insistence of his followers, he founded the Brahmo Samaj in 1828. Its principles included the worship of one God, and the abolition of caste-system and animal sacrifice.

In July 1833, the King approved the East India Bill, and the appeal against the abolition of *sutee* was rejected. In a sense the Raja's life-work was accomplished. Two months later he became ill and died on the 27th of September, 1833. He was buried at Bristol, and a monument was erected over his grave by his friend, Dwarkanath Tagore.

The modern social reforms and especially the progress of women in India owes much to this great soul.

Discussion

1. Raja Ram Mohun Roy had to face lot of criticism. Imagine you were one of the critics. Write a paragraph as his critic.
2. Was it possible for him to undertake a great task without scholarly studies? If not, why?
3. In what way did Raja Ram Mohun Roy contribute to India's greatness?
4. Besides scholarship what were other qualities which enabled him to be a noted social reformer?

5. Collect information about contemporary social reformers of India.

2. Father Damien

Father Damien is known as the Leper Saint because he spent his life in caring for lepers and he died a leper himself. Lepers are shunned by all people as leprosy is a very dreadful disease which is highly infectious. Lepers are isolated and generally left uncared for, though recently many efforts have been made in many countries to find settlements for them.

Father Damien was born in Belgium and he became a priest. When he went to work in the Hawaiian Islands, he heard of Molokai, the leper island to which the government sent all the lepers. The plight of the poor lepers and their fearful sufferings touched the lowly heart of Father Damien and he offered to go and live with them and help them. He knew he was running the risk of becoming a leper, but his courage and love for the suffering overcame everything.

The place of the lepers was one of the saddest in the world. There were 700-800 men and women without any hope, waiting only to die. They had no memory of God. The place was a comfortless waste of sand, with no water to wash in and very little food. They had no houses—only rough boards on poles for a roof.

Father Damien set to work and his courage and his bright smiling face were his greatest assets. He acted as their doctor, nurse, teacher, judge, gardener, cook, grave-digger and priest. He went to the city for the boards and with the help of the lepers he built them houses. He discovered a spring high in the mountain and he got pipes from the city and brought water to the houses.

He built a Church and a hospital. He made a large cemetery. He taught the people. He bound up their sores. Some of the lepers had no hands—he fed them with his own hands.

For five years he worked alone, then a priest joined him and later a nurse and a doctor. Ten years after going to Molokai, he made a discovery. He put his feet in boiling water but felt no pain. He went to the doctor and said "Have I leprosy? The doctor replied, "I cannot bear to tell you but what you say is true."

The next Sunday he began a sermon with the words "We lepers." From that time he was one with them in a new sense. He lived with them another six years and during that time he worked with the same unselfishness for the people he lived with. It was his own wish that he should be buried under a certain tree. It was the tree under which he lived when he first came to Molokai.

One great outcome of Father Damien's offering of himself was to make Molokai wellknown. Because of his life and sacrifice money and workers came to Molokai. It was a great comfort to Father Damien to know that the lepers would be cared for and looked after.

He did a great work not only for Molokai but also for India and South Africa. The story of his life led people to take better care of lepers in other countries. It led many young men and women to give their lives to make the condition of lepers happier.

Father Damien's life shines like a star, leading us to be brave and unselfish.

Practical Work

1. Find out what you can do about homes for lepers in India.
2. Find out superstitions prevailing in Indian society due to which lepers suffer more.
3. Find out name of person doing similar work in India. Collect information about him.
4. Consult your physician to know the scientific causes of leprosy.

3. Elizabeth Fry

It is easy to help those who are in want or suffering hardships, but it needs a great deal of moral courage to help those in prison. Those in prison seem so different from us, that it is difficult for us to imagine their hardships. As Pandit Nehru says "High walls and iron gates cut off the little world of prison from the wide world outside. There are no colours, no changes, no movements, no joy for long-term prisoner. Days run into weeks, weeks into months and years till the sands of life run out."

Elizabeth Fry is one of the greatest names in prison reform. She belonged to the Society of Friends. When she was quite young, Elizabeth took a great interest in helping poor people around her. She visited people who were ill and taught the poor children to read and write.

When she went to live in London after her marriage she heard that the prisoners in jail lived very miserable lives and that their living conditions were very bad.

She went to one of the largest prisons in London to see if this was true and when she found it was so, she set about helping those unfortunate people at once. She tried to get better rooms for them. She set apart a room for the children to have lessons. She got together a number of her own friends and organized them into a band to help these miserable people in prison.

Soon there was a thorough change in the lives of these prisoners. They learnt to live useful lives. Children and women were taught to read, write and do other work. The women did a good deal of sewing. In this new atmosphere of work and reform, the prisoners gave up fighting with each other and lived decent lives. The authorities were greatly surprised at the change and everyone spoke with admiration of her work.

Elizabeth Fry's fame became international. France invited her to visit their prison houses and make a report. She went on the same errand to Scotland, Ireland, Belgium, Holland and Copenhagen and helped to bring about many changes in the lives of prisoners.

It was because of Elizabeth Fry that a prison was thought of as a place of reform. People realized that prisoners should be trained and helped. Such prisoners would turn out to be good members of the community in which they live. By the training they received in prison, men and women were given a chance to start life in a new way.

Elizabeth was a good wife and mother. She looked after her home and children well. When Elizabeth Fry died in October 1945, she was mourned by all those who knew her or had heard of her both in England and in Europe.

Discussion

1. Did Elizabeth Fry help to make her country great? How?

4. Louis Pasteur—Discoveries of Disease Germs

Louis Pasteur was born on 27th December 1822. His father, who had been a soldier in Nepoleon's army, was anxious for his son to have the best possible education.

He attended the Elementary School in his own town and when he was 16 he was sent to a Preparatory School at Paris. He passed his B.A. Examination in 1840 and his B.Sc. in 1842. It is interesting to note that he received only 'mediocre' in Chemistry.

In October 1842 he went to study in Paris and applied himself so well that he passed fourth on the list. In 1843 he entered the Normal School where he attended some chemistry lectures that interested him greatly. He spent so much time in the laboratory that he was nicknamed "The Laboratory Pillar." In 1845 he became a laboratory assistant and in 1848 he was awarded the doctorate.

While Pasteur was still a student in the Normal School he started his research in Chemistry. By the time he finished his work for the doctorate, he had discovered a method of transforming tartaric acid into racemic acid. This was a startling discovery and made the young chemist famous. He also discovered that fermentation is caused by bacteria and that bacteria is the cause of disease in wine, beer and milk.

At this time a terrible disease was destroying the silk-worms upon which France depended for her prosperity. The people petitioned the Government and Pasteur was sent to Southern France to study the problem. Thereafter 6 years of careful research he discovered the cause of the disease, the way it spread and the means of prevention. He established the germ theory of disease which up to that time was thought to be a punishment from God.

At the age of forty-five he had a slight stroke of paralysis which left him a cripple for the rest of his life. He continued to carry on his research and his most remarkable discoveries were made after that time. He passed away quietly on September 28, 1895 at the age of seventy-three.

Pasteur remained poor to the end of his days. He freely gave his discoveries to the world and his own country profited greatly. It is said that by wiping out the silk-worm disease he saved France enough money to pay the war indemnity to Germany in 1879.

He was a merciful man who loved all life. He said "I have never killed even a bird for sport; but when it is a question of saving human life I have no scruples about sacrificing life." He was a man of iron-will, rare ability and restless energy. He was a great philanthropist who believed in simple living, high thinking and helping others.

Discussion

1. Discuss Pasteur's great patience and perseverance.
2. How did Pasteur serve his country?

5. Sarojini Naidu—The Nightingale of India

Sarojini Naidu, the great poet, a leader of the struggle for India's independence, the first woman-governor of a province and an ideal wife and mother has served India in many ways and set a noble example for all of us.

She was a Bengali but born and brought up in the Deccan. She was a Brahman married to a non-Brahman. Her life measured almost the whole of the British rule in India for she was born soon after the Mutiny and died four years after our freedom. She represents the best in these two very different cultures. She was a music-maker, a dreamer of dreams so beautiful that they held all mankind under a spell.

She led the *Satyagraha* movement in 1930 and then acted as President of the Indian National Congress. By her courage and self-confidence she brought the promise of hope to millions of her sisters who for centuries had been afraid of men, afraid of society and afraid of life itself. She gave noble and unforgettable utterance to our triumphs and failures and our desire for freedom and the respect of our nation.

She is indeed the nightingale of India and interpreted our country—its beauty and its ideals—to the world. Because she wrote in English, people all over the world are able to enjoy her poetry. In the music of her poetry we feel the sway of our palms, in her rhythms the dance of many feet. She sings of the ebb and flow of our daily life. She says:

> "To priests and to prophets
> The joy of their creeds
> To kings and to cohorts
> The glory of deeds. . .
> For me, O my master, the rapture of song."

Sarojini can touch the ordinary things of life and turn them to gold. Who but she could write enduring of anything so humble and brittle as a glass bangle? She makes us see it as a "delicate bright rainbow tinted circle of light," and she linked it with every stage in the life of a woman. The young girl chooses silver and blue as the mountain mist, the bride chooses the colour of sunlit corn or the flame of her marriage fire. And there are less bright colour for the older matron, purple spotted with grey for her who has cradled fair sons on her faithful breast.

A poet makes us see more clearly, feel more keenly and live more truly and warmly. She has passed away, but her work and life have cast a light upon our land—that shall not pass away. She had no fear of Death for she wrote:

> "Say, shall I heed the dull presages of doom
> Or dread the rumoured loneliness and gloom
> The mute and mythic terror of the tomb?
> For my glad heart is drunk and drenched with thee
> O intimate essence of Eternity."

Practical Work

1. Make a list of Sarojini Naidu's wellknown poems.
2. Write your favourite poem and say what thought the poem gives you.

6. Copernicus

Some 400 years ago, a mathematician named Copernicus studied the earth and the heavens and concluded that the conception of the earth as the centre of the universe was incorrect. Calculations showed him that it was more reasonable to see the sun as the centre and the earth as rotating around it. The German mathematician Johann Kepler confirmed and refined the findings of Copernicus; but this new idea was too revolutionary to be considered dispassionately, on its scientific merits.

"Because man is conservative, a creature of habit, and convinced of his own importance, the new theory was decidedly unwelcome. Moreover, the vested interests of well entrenched scholars and religious leaders caused them to oppose it", writes Morris Kline in his Mathematics in Western Culture.

Martin Luther called Copernicus an "upstart astrologer" and a "fool who wishes to reverse the entire science of astronomy." Calvin thundered: "Who will venture to place the authority of Copernicus above that of the Holy Spirit?" Do not the scriptures say that Joshua commanded the sun and not the earth to stand still? The inquisition condemned the new theory as "that false Pythagorean doctrine utterly contrary to the Holy Scriptures," and in 1616 the Index of Prohibited Books banned all publications dealing with the idea.

Galileo was thought to believe the new theory to have some merit, and was called by the Roman Inquisition and compelled on the threat of torture to declare: "The falsity of the Copernican system cannot be doubted, especially by us Catholics. . . ." On hearing of Galileo's persecution, Descartes, a nervous and timid individual, actually destroyed one of his own works on it.

Writes Kline: "Indeed, if the fury and high office of the opposition are a good indication of the importance of an idea no more valuable one was ever advanced."

1. Can you understand how people of good will might react violently to new ideas that they see as threatening some of their values?

2. Has there been another situation in history that you can recall in which the advance of knowledge was resisted by partisans with similar vigour?
3. Can you imagine something like that happening in the future in the United States if some new idea, say in sociology or some other discipline, were to seriously challenge the *status quo*?
4. What methods do you think might be used to fight new ideas?
5. What methods might be used to fight for the right to consider new ideas?
6. How receptive are you to new ideas, and how resistant are you? Can you think of conditions under which you would try to repress truth?[6]

In order to foster values through the analysis of character traits of great personalities the individuals should be exposed to those problems, which great men have faced in their lives. The presentation of the personality should be balanced one. Alongwith the merits and virtues, errors and weaknesses of men and women should also be exposed. In this connection the following suggestions may prove to be very useful:

1. The real qualities of men and women who have contributed to civilization may be offered as ideals for youth.
2. Values may be taught through providing opportunities for students to identify with men and women, who have suffered in history.
3. Values may be taught by a study of the resources of our industrial civilization and the achievements of many men in many fields.
4. Values may be taught through controversy—whether analysis of past historical problem "solved" by events or a study of current controversial issues.
5. Exploration of other ways of life, of other faiths and cultures, deep enough to place our students in empathetic understanding of other peoples in other times and places, will broaden values.
6. Values may be taught by an honest exposition of the errors man has made.
7. Values may be taught through an honest appraisal of actions and viewpoints revised after experience.[7]

HOLDING INDIVIDUAL OR GROUP DISCUSSIONS

Freedom of Worship

"Man is essentially a religious being—whether he worships on the banks of the Ganges, prays with his face upturned to the sun, kneels towards Mecca or regarding all space as a temple, communes with the Heavenly Father, according to the Christian Creed, man is essentially devout." There is something deep in us that responds to the call for worship. "Unto thee lift up mine eyes O thou that dwellest in the heavens," sang the Jewish Shepherd-King many hundreds of years ago. So this desire to worship a Supreme Being is inherent in man at all times and in all places.

"Forms of worship and methods of approach to God vary according to the age, country and other circumstances. Each man must be free to worship according to his light. God has created man with free-will, *i.e.*, freedom to think and act in his own right. So is the most important matter of all he should have complete freedom. Man holds this freedom dearer than all. Wise Kings and Conquerors have always allowed this to their subjects and gained their loyalty and allegiance."

Our home, our environment and the community in which we live, decide to a certain extent our form of worship. We must be sure what we believe in and how and why we worship in a certain manner to be fully alive to our inheritance of religious freedom. Whatever form our worship takes, we must understand it intelligently and do it with all our heart and mind. Then we can try and understand other people's way of worship and not tease them nor think they are inferior merely because it is different. If individuals are tolerant, then it is easy for the state to extend religious freedom because the whole attitude and atmosphere in the country will be one of tolerance.

Discussion Questions

1. Carlyle says "What greater calamity can fall upon a nation than the loss of worship." What did he mean by this? What does a nation gain by worship?
2. Get the children of different religions in your class to write their method of worshipping God and what inspires them most.
3. Find out all facts about examples in History where men and women sacrificed everything for the sake of religious freedom—The Pilgrim Fathers, The Parsees, etc.

4. A group of girls and boys on the way to their place of worship, pass by a place of worship other than their own and spit at it as being heathen. What advice would you give them? How would you make it clear to them that they are wrong?
5. Let the class discuss the above questions in groups and give their answers; and in the light of their discussion draw up 5 Rules for Freedom of Worship in a country.

Discussion on Situations and Solutions

Let the class discuss the situation and divide the class into squads and then pool their findings.

1. You are going to the cinema with a party of friends. On the way you meet an old school friend who is stranded in your place because of a bus breakdown. What would you do? Why?
2. While at a shop you see two foreigners come in and notice that they are being cheated over prices, because they do not know the language. When you try to put them wise, the Shopman is very angry and calls you a traitor to the Motherland. How would you convince him that he is wrong?
3. Kamala and her father feel that she should only read story books during the holidays, but her mother insists on her doing some kitchen work. Kamala refuses on the plea:
   (*a*) that she is a High School girl.
   (*b*) she needs rest during the holidays. Is Kamala right or wrong? Why?
4. Some evacuees from Burma have come to your village and there is a feeling that they have helped to raise the cost of living with the ready money in their hands. How would you help the village folk to have a more tolerant and friendly attitude towards the Evacuees?
5. Leela complains that her mother is partial to her sons and gives them advantages which Leela herself is denied. How would you help Leela? Her mother?

Discussion on India's Religions

Each religion has something to give to the world and in no other country do we find so many different religions as in our own. It is partly because ours is such a vast country. We must remember that every fifth man in the world is an Indian. But the significant fact is that this diversity shows the spiritual tolerance that India has always had. There is a breadth of vision like our wide plains, which gives us a very tolerant attitude in religious matters. Many have found a haven of refuge in India from other lands where they have been persecuted for their religion. The Parsees came to India in an open boat with their sacred fire, driven by the Muslim invader. They are a very important and enlightened minority in India now.

It is not easy to put in a nutshell what each religion has contributed to the community as a whole. But we can take some of the most important religions in India. Hinduism lays special emphasis on courtesy and kindness and respect for all life and tolerance to all men. They are also pioneers in *Bhaktimarga* as it is called. The religion of Islam lays special emphasis on the Brotherhood of man. The Mohammedan faith has bound all its members in a close bond of brotherhood, and they are ready to help each other at all times. The Buddhist religion has taught us to respect and love all God's creatures and to hold fast to the doctrine of *ahimsa.* The Christian religion has taught us that God is a loving Father and that he loves us individually and cares for each one of us. This fatherhood of God implies the brotherhood of man. Each one of us has a religion—we are born into a family which follows some religion or other. It is our duty to find what beliefs our religion holds and to cling to it and fashion our conduct accordingly. Beliefs must be put into action to become real and action is the basis of all beliefs.

Assignment

Divide the class into squads and give to each a set of questions to do and let them pool their answers and discuss their findings.

1. Who was Guru Nanak?
2. Why did he try to unite the Hindu and Mohammedan religions?
3. Where can you find all the Sikh faith written about? Which town is their most sacred place?
4. What is the Koran?
5. What did Mohammed teach his people?
6. Where do you find the Mohammedan religion now?
7. What did Shintoism teach?
8. Why is it discredited now?
9. How did this religion make for the unity and power of the Japanese people?

10. What are the three religions you find in Palestine today? Why?
11. Who was the law-giver of the Jews? What did he teach them?
12. What is the most important thing that Jews believe in?
13. Why did Buddha go to the forest? What truth did he find there?
14. What is the difference between Buddhism and Jainism?
15. Why are these two religions difficult for people to practise?
16. What did Confucius teach the Chinese people?
17. What is the holy book of the Christians? How many books are there in it? What do they tell you?
18. What did Christ teach his disciples?
19. What is the reason for the very good organisation of Christianity?
20. Who are the Parsees? What religion do they follow?

HINDU SCRIPTURE

A Devotee of God

A devotee of the Lord is always fearless because to him the whole universe is an image, a manifestation of his beloved Lord, and he is always anxious to embrace Him.

A devotee of God is free from hypocrisy because he beholds Him seated in every heart. How can there be any difference between his inner and outer life?

A devotee of God is never angry because he finds his own soul, the soul of his soul. Pervading the whole universe; how then, can he afford to be angry?

A devotee of God is never proud, for he has already surrendered all his pride and vanity at the feet of the Lord. There is no vanity left in him.

A devotee of God has no desires because he has attained the Supreme Soul and hence, all his desires are already fulfilled.

A devotee of God has no avarice because to him there is nothing worth coveting except the Lord.

A devotee of God is ever happy because he has perfectly merged himself in the Lord, the embodiment of the highest joy and bliss.

A devotee of God is without any egoism because he has lost his 'Ego' in the bigger Ego of the Lord.

A devotee of God is the greatest lover as he has imbibed the all-loving nature of the Lord.

'Pearls of Truth'

Islam

None save Glorious Allah serve;
Never from His precepts swerve;
Honour teacher, father, mother;
Unto him who is thy brother,
Unto kindred, friends also,
Orphans, suppliants, sad ones, show
Gentleness and help; to each
Speak with kind and courteous speech.
Give in alms that thou may'st spare.
And be constant in thy prayer.

The Bible

The Lord is my Shepherd; I shall not want.

He maketh me to lie down in green pastures; he leadeth me beside the still waters.

He restoreth my soul; he leadeth me in the paths of righteousness for his name's sake.

Yea, though I walk through the valley of the shadow of death, I will fear no evil; for thou art with me; thy rod and thy staff they comfort me.

Thou preparest a table before me in the presence of mine enemies; thou anointest my head with oil; my cup runneth over.

Surely goodness and mercy shall follow me all the days of my life; and I will dwell in the house of the Lord for ever.

Jesus said "I am the good Shepherd."

Read the above passage from the different scriptures and write in five sentences the gist of each.

Whatever methods or techniques are adopted for fostering of values or clarification of values it should be made a point that values should be consistent with one's culture, tradition, level of growth of science and technology, global peace, etc. As far as Value Education in Indian perspective is concerned, it should invariably be governed by our value-tenets. Already elaborated in Chapter 3 and conditioned by main components of Indian culture. In America (USA) recently the public schools have been accused of teaching (or preaching as its critics claim) a brand of religion known as secular humanism. According to the accusations, this religion denies the existence of absolute moral principles, rules out the existence of God, and places man at the centre of the universe. Through value clarification and moral education strategies, through inquiry techniques in science and social studies lessons critics claim that students are being taught that man's values and beliefs stem from environmental pressures, not God's laws.

Whatever, the fact and ideology may be involved in the above statement, this tone and trend should be totally discarded as the very spirit reflected in the system mentioned above does not suit to Indian tradition and culture. It is not so because to rule out the existence of God is an atheistic gesture. There may be good many atheists in India, who may not be believing in the existence of God. The main objection to such so called secular humanism is that it is contrary to our value-tenets and thus does not suit to our cultural phenomena.

Teaching of Some Natural Values

1. *Teaching of Truth as a Value Component*

Contents
- — Indian heritage pertaining to Truth.
- — All religions of the world; Hinduism, Buddhism, Jainism, Islam, Christianity, Taoism, Confucianism, etc.
- — The contents of all religions based on truth in the form of prayers, *strotras*, hymns, stories and messages.

Teaching Devices
- — Memorization, group-singing, story-telling, showing concerned charts and pictures, biographies of great leaders, visit to the places of historical importance.

Teaching Outcomes
- — Students will acquire skill and knowledge.
- — They will learn to respect their own and that of others' religion and culture.
- — They will show better tolerance for other faiths.
- — They will understand unity of faiths and religions.
- — They will feel brotherhood and one father as God.

2. *Teaching of Non-violence as a Value Component*

Contents
- — Non-injury at body and mental level, seeing oneself in others, extension and expression of love to all human beings, loving God

through all his creation, universal love all-pervasive, a way to moral and spiritual perfection.

Teaching Devices — Above content matters can be imparted to children through following ways:
Loving flowers, birds and animals, helping plants to grow, practising tolerance in daily activity, reading stories and poems on Man and God, drawing pictures regarding God's creation.

Teaching Outcomes — Feeling of oneness with nature and man.
— Will appreciate God's creation.
— Will express their feeling through poetry, songs, dramas, etc.
— They will follow non-violence in attitude and action.

3. *Teaching of Right Conduct as a Value Component*

Contents — Students need to develop ethical skills, self-help, and social skills.
— Above three skills can be achieved by some activities and by their behaviours.

Teaching Devices — These skills are as follows: Group-action, Mono acting, Dramatisation, Story telling, service activities, attitudes test.

Teaching Outcomes — A boy of balanced, dutiful, disciplined personality.
— A boy of an effective leadership in society.
— An efficient follower in society.

4. *Teaching of Love as a Value Component*

Contents — Love for parents, family members, neighbours, creation and love for All and serve for All as **'Motto'**.
— Love will lead towards faith and that will be the spiritual love.

Teaching Devices — The spiritual love can be achieved or can be taught to the pupils by the following devices:
— Story telling, Dramatisation, Historical and

spiritual trips of worship places, showing pictures and films, etc.

Teaching Outcomes — Students will appreciate truth, feeling of oneness, love of God and his creation and attitude of service to others.

5. *Teaching of Peace as a Value Component*

Contents — Peace means the peace of body, peace of mind and peace of soul.

— This can be achieved or gained through the practices and inculcating the habit of simple living, uproot of evil tendencies, to develop truthfulness, to preserve self-respect, respect others' rights, to be true in thought, words and deed. To see good, do good and be good.

Teaching Devices — Group activities, social services, organising cultural programmes, excursions, exhibitions, etc.

Teaching Outcomes — Students will develop leadership.

— Self-confidence, socialization, recognition from parents and acceptance from his friends.

6. *Teaching of 'Democratic Sense' as a Value Component*

Contents — Liberty, equality, fraternity civic sense, concern for public property, regard for the system of the government.

Teaching Devices — Comparison of different forms of governments, exposing the students to different functions of the governments, engaging them in team-work, dramatization, guidance and training for conducting 'Mock Parliament', making them to have regard for 'National Anthem' and 'National Flag', etc.

Teaching Outcomes — Good citizenship, patriotism, leadership, consciousness for duties as well as for rights, team-spirit, concern for fellow-beings, etc.

7. *Teaching of 'Humanism' as a Value Component*

Contents — Concern for all living beings—human beings, animals and plants.

Teaching Devices — Story-telling, memorization of good poems, etc., dialogues, discussion, exhibition of good pictures, reading of inspiring biographies, writing of articles, short stories, etc. visit to historical and religious places, explaining several facets of our composite culture.

Teaching Outcomes — Self-respect, self-reliance, love for nature, love for animals and plants, conservation of natural environment, politeness, concern for others, dignity of labour, team-spirit.

Conclusion

Environment, resources and zeal and sincerity on the part of teachers, these three things are most important for successful implementation of Value-oriented Education. Over and above exemplary behaviour of parents, teachers and other concerned are nonetheless important. Lastly we may conclude that:

> "To teach values by any of the means suggested depends upon the use of procedures, techniques and learning experiences which arouse and sustain emotion as well as reason. People must identify with personalities and human beings who have been or are involved in great problems and controversies if they are to see intimately, feel deeply, and understand fully. Appropriate devices for such teaching are identical with appropriate devices for any good teaching— films, pictures, songs, poetry, documents, dramatization, parables, fiction, letters, diaries, interviews, socio-drama, cartoons, posters, field trips, guestspeakers, panel-discussion or debates."[8]

REFERENCES

1. Louis E. Raths, *Values and Teaching*, p. 35.
2. *Ibid.*, pp. 58-64.
3. *Ibid.*, pp. 117-18.
4. Raths, Harmin and B. Simon, *Values and Teaching*, p. 95.
5. Cyclostyled Report of the Working Group to Review Teacher's Training Programmes, Ministry of Education & Culture, Government of India, p. 119.
6. *Values and Teaching*, Second Edition, pp. 104-05.
7. *Teaching the Social Studies: What, Why and How*, edited by Richard E. Gross, Walter E. McPhie and Jack R. Fraenkel, p. 379.
8. *Ibid.*, p. 379.

9

CO-CURRICULAR ACTIVITIES AND VALUE EDUCATION

Co-curricular activities play a very significant role in inculcating different values in the students. For all-round development of personalities of the students co-curricular activities are considered to be very important now-a-days. Previously the term "extra-curricular activities" was used for outdoor activities and other cultural programmes organised in the school. But now-a-days this term has been discarded keeping in view the importance of these activities. In many progressive schools there is an allotment of certain periods for these co-curricular activities in their regular time-table.

Through these activities, many values can be inculcated profitably. Co-curricular activities form an integral part of the modern school curriculum. They should be made more and more purposive and fruitful as well as value oriented with the democratic base and purposeful pursuit. This can be done, provided children have an opportunity of having living experience of moral life through these activities.

In programmes of outdoor activities, the children are taken out of the school to the areas of adventure, appreciation of art and culture and the places of historical values. They can be brought avenues in the training of initiative, team-work, self-discipline and learn much about our cultural heritage and historical details. Besides games and sports, there are several outdoor activities, namely, NCC, ACC, scouting and guiding. Mountaineering. Trekking, Excursion, Field trips, etc., which may serve the purpose of inculcation of desired values among the students and formation of character.

Games and Sports

Various games and sports not only provide the best recreation but they have profound impact on the temperament and outlook of the players.

They help in the sublimation of the personality of the players. It is a fact that players believe in fighting well without the least consideration of victory or defeat, John A.O. Brien rightly observes: "Competitive athletics seek to groove the competitive instinct into the building of strong character which will fight with courage and insight for social good accustomed to opposition on the playing field, such a character will not crumble before organised resistance in the field of social endeavour and civic enterprise."

He develops a tendency to contest in a fair way against all oppositions and contrary situations of life. According to Baron Piere De Coubertin, the founder of Modern Olympic Games, "The important thing in the olympic games is not winning but taking part. The essential thing in life is not conquering but fighting well."

Training in Physical Education develops the high sense of obedience, which leads a person render his services sincerely. While playing, he is supposed to obey captain, observe rules of the games and respect the decision of empires. There are many sports which help to form and necessitate the qualities of courage, hardihood, energetic action, initiative, steadiness of will, rapid decision and action, the perception of what is to be done in an emergency and dexterity in doing it. Another invaluable result of these sports is the growth of the sporting spirit. This includes good humour and tolerance and consideration for all, a right attitude and friendliness to competitors and rivals, self-control and scrupulous observance of the laws of the games, fair play and avoidance of the use of foul means, equal acceptance of victory or defeat without bad humour, and loyal acceptance of the decisions of the appointed judge, umpire or referee. More important still is the custom of discipline, obedience, order and habit of team-work which certain games necessitate.

It is said that tougher is the opposition, the better is the performance of every player. Player is always found to be very keen to offer a tough opposition without the least excitement of winning or losing. Grautland Rice has very aptly depicted the right spirit of a player in his poem "Alumnus Foot Ball"—

When the Last Great Scorer
Comes to write against your name,
He writes not that you won or lost
But how you played the game.

Therefore, it can be emphatically proclaimed that the qualities described above are essential not only for an individual but for the nation also. In the words of Shri Aurobindo, "If they could be made more common not only in the life of the individual but in the national life and in the international level whereof the present day the opposite tendencies have become too rampant, existence in this troubled world of ours would be smoother and might open to a greater chance of concord and amity of which it stands very much in need. The nation which possesses them in the highest degree is likely to be strongest for victory, success and greatness, as also for the contribution it can make towards the bringing about of unity and more harmonious world order towards which we took as our hope for humanity's future."

It may be any cultural programme or some sports events, encouragement is very essential. It should flow from all the corners—the teachers, parents and community. Player should never be demoralized by humiliating him/her in the group for some average or poor academic performance. It will have an adverse impact on the competence of the players. George Mathew Adams says, "There are high spots in all our lives and most of them have come about through encouragement from someone else. I do not care how great, how famous or successful a man or woman may be, each hungers for applause.

"Encouragement is oxygen to the soul. Good work can never be expected from a worker without encouragement. No one ever lived without it."

Scout and Guiding

Scout and Guiding can go a long way in inculcating desired values in the minds of students. If they are carried on proper lines. The aim of the Scout Guide Training is to improve the standard of our future citizenhood. Specially in character and health; to replace self with service, to make the boys and girls individually efficient, morally and physically, with the objective of using that efficiency for service to their fellow men. Therefore, character, health and strength, handicraft and skill and service to others form the four branches of Scout Training.

It is a very helpful co-curricular activity, which admirably cultivates the values like loyalty, concern for others, courage, 'friendship, self-discipline, obedience, bravery, integrity, etc., in the minds of Scouts and Guides. These values have been clearly incorporated very apparently in the following tenets of Scout Law:

1. A Scout's honour is to be trusted.
2. A Scout is loyal.

3. A Scout's duty is to revere God and serve the country and help others.
4. A Scout is a friend to all, and a brother to every other Scout, no matter to what country, class or creed the other may belong.
5. A Scout is courteous.
6. A Scout is a friend to animals.
7. A Scout is disciplined and obeys orders.
8. A Scout is brave and smiles under all difficulties.
9. A Scout is thrifty.
10. A Scout is pure in thought, word and deed.[1]

The above tenets are applicable to guides also. Keeping in view the multitudes of benefits of Scout and Guiding it should be carried out in all the schools at four levels, *i.e.*, cubs, bulbuls, Scouts and Guides. Dean James E. Russell of Teachers' College, Columbia University, New York, has great praise and admiration for scouting. He describes the programme of the Boy Scout as Man's job cut down to the size of the boy. It appeals to the boys not merely because he is a boy; but because he is a man in making. He further adds that it is not the curriculum of scouting that is its most striking feature, but is the method. As a systematic scheme of leading boys to the right thing and to indicate the right habit, it is almost ideal in the doing—he goes on. "two things stand out—the one is, habits are formed, the other is that it affords opportunity for initiative, self-control, self-reliance and self-direction."

The scouting concentrates on character-building, promotes health, encourages handicraft and stimulates the spirit of service. That is why the Boy Scouts International Conference declares that the Boy Scouts Movement is a movement of national, international and universal character, the object of which is to endow each separate nation and the whole world with a youth which is physically, morally and spiritually strong. The Scout Law requires that a Scout shall truly and sincerely practise his religion, and the policy of the movement forbids any kind of sectarian propaganda at mixed gatherings.

From the above discussion, we may easily conclude that for inculcation of the desired values, the following four aims can be profitably attempted:

1. *Character:* Character-building can be brought about through the patrol system—the Scout Law , Scout lore and wood-craft are the responsibility of the Patrol Leader. With reference to Scout and Guiding character-building includes team spirit,

concern for fellow-men, realization of supreme power, the appreciation of beauty in nature, preservation of natural and cultural environment, love for plants and animals, etc.

2. *Health and Strength:* This aim can be realised through several games and regular exercises. Therefore, in the syllabus for Scouts and Guides the knowledge of personal hygiene, first aid, nature and necessity of balanced diet is included.
3. *Handicrafts and Skill:* These are achieved through indoor activities occasionally but more particularly through signalling, bridge-building, camp expeditions, and self-expression through various arts. All these outdoor activities provide good scope to achieve efficiency in handicrafts.
4. *Service to Others:* This may be termed as crux of the Scout Movement. The first three aims mentioned above are preparatory to this as they involve self-building whereas this is for 'others'. Of course, the joy and satisfaction derived from 'service to others' is for self only, which gradually leads to the development of personalities of Scouts and Guides. Under this head various activities can be undertaken. One day service-camp at railway platform, *shramdan* in the neighbouring village for making/renovating approach roads, teaching of three R's to illiterate adults in the vicinity, teaching of awareness to the villagers about the environmental and hygienic problems and suggesting the solution within the resources available, cleaning of slum-areas—these are source of the activities, which can be conveniently undertaken.

Literary and Cultural Activities

Almost in all the schools and colleges various festivals are organized at deterrent levels as per the availability of the resources. These festivals may be classified into three heads:

1. National Festivals
2. Religious Festivals
3. Birth/Death anniversaries of great persons.

Besides these, there are so many occasions like Sports Day, Teachers' Day, Parents' day, Annual Day, UNO Day, etc., when some literary and cultural activities are carried out in the school. Some of these literary and cultural activities may be as under:

Literary Activities

1. Poem Recitation (English, Hindi, Sanskrit or any other regional language)
2. Debate (English & Hindi)
3. Symposium (English & Hindi)
4. Mock-Parliament
5. Essay Competition (English & Hindi)
6. Story-telling (English & Hindi)
7. Elocution (English & Hindi)
8. Chutkula Competition
9. Quiz and Generai Knowledge Test
10. Preparing class/house/school magazines
11. Presenting paper on some subjects
12. Science and Writers' Club Activities
13. Presenting daily thought in the Morning Assembly
14. Poetry-writing
15. Story-writing competition, etc.
16. Calligraphy compctition
17. 'Antyakshari' and 'Paheli' (Riddle) Competition.

Cultural Activities

1. Skits
2. Playlets
3. Melo-drama
4. Mono-acting
5. Music (vocal and instrumental)
6. Solo-dance (folk and classical)
7. Community singing (in all regional languages)
8. Group-dance (folk and classical)
9. Fancy-dress-show competition
10. Flower-show competition
11. Painting and Rangoli Competition
12. On the Spot Drawing Competition.

Through these activities, the qualities of leadership, self-discipline, co-operation, team-work, etc. can be easily developed. Through these activities, new dimension can be given to the personalities of the students. Planning of these activities is very significant, without which these activities may not bear the fruits. "The wise planning and execution of this programme, moreover, can inculcate wholesome and constructive social attitudes among youth, promote emotional security, develop competence in inter-personal and intergroup relationships so important to growing-up, and at the same time provide immediately healthful and beneficial development of the child and society."

While planning these activities, it should be kept in view that the themes selected for various programmes are consistent with our cultural heritage. "In a programme of education like this one, the tendency is to overemphasise the 'moral' aspects. Moral or morals should not be stated or pointed out directly but must be left to the audience to infer and understand. While selecting themes for projecting the values, we have to select interesting, intelligent and witty anecdotes from the lives of not only saints but scientists, politicians, poets, patriots and kings. There should be no distinction of religion or faith. Often we may find one or two themes from the texts prescribed for their study. The dialogue and discussion must abound in wit and humour. The language must be simple. A few examples may be cited. Episodes from the lives of Buddha, Shivaji, Nanak, Kabir, Ramanuja, Tukaram, Jesus, Francis of Assisi, Mohammad."

Individual differences, mental make-up, needs and aspirations of several age-groups must be kept in view while planning these activities, without which they may not render the desired results. As far as school programme is concerned, various classes may be clubbed in the following way:

Group I	—	Classes I and II	Primary classes
Group II	—	Classes III, IV and V	
Group III	—	Classes VI, VII & VIII—Middle classes	
Group IV	—	Classes IX and X—Secondary classes	
Group V	—	Classes XI & XII—Sr. Secondary classes.	

The following literary and cultural activities are suggested to be conducted with or without modification at the school level:

FOR GROUP I

Literary Activities

1. Recitation
2. Nursery Rhymes
3. Story Telling
4. Calligraphy.

Cultural Activities

1. Action song
2. Group song
3. Puppet show
4. Tables based on Nursery Rhymes and fairy-tales
5. Fancy dress
6. Painting
7. College work

FOR GROUP II

Literary Activities

1. Recitation
2. Nursery Rhymes of slightly advanced nature
3. Story telling
4. Story writing
5. Calligraphy
6. Preparing speeches on a given subject
7. Maintenance of class and house display boards.

Cultural Activities

1. Action song
2. Group song
3. Community singing
4. Group dances
5. School orchestra
6. Short plays and playlets
7. Mono-acting
8. Fancy dress
9. Tableaus
10. Painting and college work
11. Rangoli
12. Flower carpeting.

FOR GROUP III

Literary Activities

1. Recitation
2. Elocution contests

3. Debates
4. Quiz
5. Watchword
6. *Antakshari*
7. Story writing and story telling
8. Slide and film shows on educational subjects
9. Students council activities
10. Youth parliament
11. Exhibitions
12. Club activities—Sc. Club, Humanity Club and Writers' Club
13. Maintenance of class and house display boards
14. Preparing class/house/school magazines.

Cultural Activities

1. Group song
2. Community singing
3. Group and folk dances
4. School orchestra
5. School band
6. Ballets and tableaus
7. Painting
8. Rangoli
9. Flower carpet making
10. Dramas and short plays
11. Fetes
12. Organising various social and cultural festivals
13. Celebration of school annual day, parents' day
14. Celebrating anniversaries and important days of national and international importance.

GROUP IV AND V

Literary and Cultural Activities

All above activities meant for Group III children but at advanced level. Besides on the spot essay and poetry writing contests: presenting papers on given subjects, preparing class/house/school magazines, group and panel discussion.

Activities to be Conducted at the Cluster/Regional Level

Some of the inter-school competitions in the following areas can be conducted at the cluster/regional level:

For Primary Classes

Short plays, Action song, Group/Folk dances, Elocution contests, on the spot painting competition.

For Middle and above Classes

Debate and Elocution contests, short plays, folk/group dances, painting, school band, school orchestra.

In fact these literary and cultural activities form a link between the glorious literary and cultural heritage of our nation. If property planned and executed, these activities have great potential for fostering several moral, ethical, social, aesthetic and environmental values. It will not be an exaggeration to say that these activities form the heart of our school programme provided these are planned and executed in the right spirit. Dr. R.C. Sharma, Dy. Commissioner (Acads), Kendriya Vidyalaya Sangathan, New Delhi, in his book entitled 'School Management' has also emphasized this aspect of education when he says "Schools have, therefore, to give cultural and literary activities a place of pride in their curriculum and time-table and have to use them for the development of the creative urges and personality of children. Cultural and literary activities can also be used for imparting value education, for promoting feeling of national integration and for impressing upon children the need for international amity and world peace. Not only this, cultural activities constitute a vary important medium for the teaching/learning of history, language and literature. Students can dramatise a history lesson, can learn folk dances of different regions, can write stories in the form of dialogues and enact them, can learn songs from different parts of the country and can recite poems, etc. All these activities add to and reinforce the curricular knowledge of students. Thus, cultural and literary activities result in many tangible and intangible gains in pupil's learning and personality development and result in several social benefits, such as promotion of better understanding between different religions, regions and races, reduction of crime and violence by sublimating the animal instincts of man, etc."

Morning Assembly

Morning Assembly has been found very good tool for clarification and communication of certain values. If it is conducted properly it may prove to be very purposive and fruitful for fostering social, moral and spiritual values. Per day stress may be given on one or two values only. By rotation contents of short-speeches, story-telling, recitation, thought for the day, etc. may be changed so that stress on one and the same value is not repeated.

Programme for Morning Assembly should not last for more than 20 minutes. Within 20 minutes following programmes can be systematically planned and implemented:

A.	Singing of the prayer	5 mts.
B.	Observance of silence	1 mt.
C.	Students' pledge	3 mts.
D.	Thought for the day	2 mts.
E.	Special programme for the day (by teacher or student/students)	2 mts.
F.	Announcements by Principal and/or teacher	4 mts.
G.	National Anthem	1 mt (53 seconds)

The timings mentioned above are just suggestive. It may differ from day to day and also from institution to institution. True spirit of the Morning Assembly must be maintained and utilised for fostering different values. Under the special programme any one of the following activities may be chosen for the day:

1. A talk by teacher/student on any topic pertaining to environmental studies, religion, morals, values, etc.
2. A talk by teacher/student on any topic related to science, current affairs, etc.
3. Reading of excerpts from biographies or autobiographies of great leaders, saint, literatures, scientists, etc.
4. Group song/Action song on national or patriotic theme.
5. A talk by teacher/student on sports.
6. Recitation of any good poem or story-telling in English, Hindi or Sanskrit.
7. Community-singing.

Out of the items mentioned above one may be scheduled for each school day. The importance of the messages conveyed by song, thought or excerpt from biography/autobiography must be explained to the students so that they may imbibe it. Similarly silence for a minute or two should be practised daily in the Morning Assembly for helping pupils in concentration and introspection. Songs selected for community-singing must be from different Indian languages so that pupils may like each other's language. It will be a step towards inculcation of national outlook among them.

The sanctity and dignity of the Morning Assembly should be maintained both by teachers and students and all must participate in it. While presenting the daily programme due representation should be given to Hindi and English languages, boys and girls, senior and junior students. Looking into psychological differences and different needs of primary and secondary children, it is suggested that it will be in the fitness of things if separate Morning Assemblies for Primary Sections and Secondary Sections are arranged. This will facilitate smooth and fruitful communication between the teachers and students. It may also help to remove dullness to a large extent.

REFERENCE

1. Baden Powel, *Scouting for Boys: Introduction*, p. xi.

—

10

HOW TO MAKE HISTORY-TEACHING VALUE-ORIENTED

> *"The failure of history as a school subject is more, however, than a pedagogical failure; it is a societal failure. Obstinate students, unaccepted purpose, the absence of motivation, unsuitable materials, unprepared teachers, and dreary, dull, catalogic, inconsequential content all join in part history's unpopularity. It is probably, however, that the most serious and determinative reason for its failure is the insincere and fraudulent social purposes that force the subject into curriculum."*

Latest concept regarding teaching of History is that *it should not be treated as course but a resource*. Resource for what? Resource for inculcation of various moral, cultural and spiritual values by exposing the children to various socio-politico-cultural phenomena, various controversies, several stories of success and failure of the rulers, invaders, commanders, etc. After all our ultimate aim is to prepare the student for better living, ideal citizenship and universal brotherhood. In other words we can say that History should not be taught as dictionary or encyclopaedia of incidents and chronology burdened with ready-made data, figures and generalizations but it should be made more interesting, lively, and thought-provoking. Then only it will be more purposive, meaningful and interesting.

Teachers of History have been found to take a stand that unless the syllabus or curriculum in history is changed or revised it is not feasible to do so. In this connection it is felt that the very plea is not very sound and logical. If we go through the textbooks of history of the last few decades, we will find that there is hardly any substantial change in their contents leaving a few exceptions here and there. Even if the changes are brought about in its volume or contents the teaching may not be fruitful unless we change the curricular image of the subject. Using history as a resource more stress should be laid on human-relationship through analysis of several circumstances of the particular victory, defeat or alliance.

In this context we should agree with the observation of Franklin Roosevelt:

> "If civilization is to survive, we must cultivate the science of human relationship—the ability of all peoples, of all kinds, to live together and work together in the same world at peace."

Here we must not forget that science of human relationships depends upon human values, more so on their emotional and rational bases. For the inculcation of values, students should be made to understand our cultural heritage, our social institutions, various religions of the world and their fundamental preachings, customs and problems of various strata of the society.

The culture-epoch theory in this regard has been of great help to the history teacher.

(a) It has greatly helped in the making of syllabus at least for childhood and adulthood.

(b) The theory has further revealed the value of preliminary anthropological background to the study of history.

(c) It has also shown that the study of history should not be merely intellectual. We must not merely concern ourselves with fact-finding but must also appeal to the imagination and the sentiments of the boy.

Teaching of history as a series of biographies of great men of our country and of the world in a strictly chronological order. At the initial stage of 13 to 14 years for a child history is beyond comprehension. Children who understand individuals, particular facts and episodes but not principles and institutions history should be presented to them as concrete and with particulars.

The ideology behind this theory is that the great men represented their time. They initiated or influenced great historical movements. Thus a preliminary study of great men's life equips pupil with sufficient knowledge. The history of what man has accomplished in this world at bottom is the history of great men who had worked there. Following are the objections for the theory:

1. It is undemocratic. It does not recognize collective life or collective aim in the community.

2. The great men of history do not represent their times. Their very greatness shows that they are far above the average humanity of their times.
3. The great men may be great in their own particular spheres. They cannot sum up the manifold life of the community. But it is quite possible to make historical theory acceptable if the precautions suggested below are taken to follow the above biographical theory. Select outstanding events or movements and grouped individual between them. As no person, however, great, can ordinary sum up his age alone. Many persons should be selected to represent different spheres or classes. We must have heroes of peace as well as of war in our history teaching.

Select typical characters if necessary. If we are teaching stories from Maratha history, Shivaji is not enough. His followers like Tanaji Moropant, his rivals like Chandrarao More and saints who fostered nationalism must be there. Perhaps the stories of a common peasant, a soldier of fortune, a trader may be selected on the basis of the historical material available to us.

While selecting stories for children, we should always think what history will this story tell the children. At the initial stage of child biographical method is very useful. It will also be helpful at later stages to supplement and illuminate narrative treatment at middle school stage. Even at university stage biographical study is of immense help in making history real and living.

Accordingly following course is useful for teaching of history to age groups:

Age 7-8 years

1. Stories from the *Ramayana* and *Mahabharata* as the child of this age group accepts the biographical theory.

Age group 9-12 years

2. A preliminary simple course in world history especially ancient history.
3. Stories from provincial history.
4. Stories from ancient Indian history.

Age group 13-16 years

5. Narrative histories of India—*for example*, Freedom Movement of India.
6. An advance course in world history and civics.

Woodrow Wilson defined History as 'past politics'. Crooce contended that History should be written only by philosophers, and philosophy by historians. But History is something more than politics or philosophy. Of course, History needs a breath of philosophy so that it may get the sense of whole. As History relates to various aspects of life like art, religion, economic life, social institutions, etc. it cannot be compared to any single discipline. History should be studied as a whole and taught as a whole.

It is here that History needs a breath of philosophy so that it may give a wholesome picture of the society or nation concerned. It has been aptly remarked that "without philosophy History is mere fact-grubbing, gradegrinding, losing its nose in past for past's sake and without History, philosophy is epistemology or some cobweb castle in the air, irrelevant to creative man."[1] I would like to quote here a sentence of Napoleon's, one of the last he spoke—"*May my son study History for it is the only true philosophy*." It proves undoubtedly that from History, if properly written, we would learn more about real nature of man, than from all the textbooks of psychology and philosophy in the world.

The supreme aim of all education is the training of character to which History as a subject can make a significant contribution. Teachers of History should present the subject-matter in such a way that students develop a right outlook towards the world around them and appreciate the human relationship. Therefore, the teacher of History should not be complacent with mere teaching of the subject-matter, but he should be able to develop social character and scientific temper among the students. Moreover, we should develop the historic sense so that we can view current events in proper perspective and understand their real significance.

Among the social sciences, History has its own role to play. Social science is a study of the society in relation to man. This is very true in respect of History. It is said that History and Geography are inseparables. History is built on the foundation of Geography. "History is the drama for which Geography spreads out the stage." Therefore, while chalking out the curriculum of Social Studies, the integrity of the subjects like History, Geography, Economics and Civics should be maintained to make it more comprehensive and effective.

The cherished aim of teaching of any discipline, may it be Language, Sciences, or Social Sciences, is to develop the personalities of students harmoniously to enable them to participate effectively in the various activities of society and to be useful and responsible citizens of tomorrow. In the child-centred education, the shifting is obviously from contents of subject to the learner and as such the contents should be changed according to the needs, interests of the students so that the needs and aspirations of the society be fulfilled. Any of these three categories of knowledge, *i.e.*, natural sciences, the social sciences, or the humanities should work as an effective instrument for social change.

But the vital aim of teaching History can be achieved when teacher will try to get the students involved in teaching-learning process more and more by making his lesson effective, interesting and lively. This requires lot of extra reading on the part of History teacher. He should keep himself abreast with the recent trends and concepts of the subject. He should know 'what is Structural History?' 'What is the nature and scope of people's history?' He should know various components of social structural organization, *i.e.*, micro-structures (village communities), macro-system (oriental despotism) superstructural institutions, multi-sectoral structure, intra-sectoral proportion, etc.

The Secondary Education Commission has rightly observed: "At present, in most of the schools, teaching is dominated by cramming and there is no determined attempt to check deterioration of standards of expression in speech and writing. The School Programme is dominated by routine in which the teacher talks and dictates notes and students passively listen to the notes in the classroom and memorize at home, in order to pass tests and examinations. There is no opportunity and desire to acquire knowledge either for its own sake or for life; the dominant motive is to scrape through the examination. Teaching of History is no exception to these observations."

When we compare social sciences with natural sciences and humanities in the perspective of recent explosion of knowledge of science and technology, the significance of social sciences seems to enjoy better recognition specially after World War II. It will be more clear if we analyse their comparative significance in terms of human values. According to one of the American authors, "Science was eminent from World War II until the late 1960's, during which it revolutionized the military, transformed industry, and changed man's environment and style of living in ways too numerous to mention. Its promise to man was a better way of life, and in some respects, it made good its promise. But man paid for its benefits with depersonalization, pollution, vocational upset and loss of natural beauty. The result was that science in the late 1960's began to decline—slowly but inexorably. The prestige of the military sank to a new low. Government subsidies to science decreased. Students in Universities protested against secret research and technological abuses. Scientist-heroes lost some of their lustre. And defections in the ranks of scientists increased.[2] These were a few changes in a developed country like America. There is no gain saying the fact that these changes emerged as a few outcomes of an excess of domination by science in the society. Ours is still a developing country, where science is dominating in the society; but the time is not far off when these changes may be observed over here also. With the rapid growth of computer science, genetics and astro-physics we have entered into the era of star-war. There is very likelihood that with the advent of 21st century there may be shift of emphasis from science to social science on our land also. Therefore, greater responsibility rests on the shoulders of teachers of Social Sciences.

While going through the contents of History reference books, we should not forget that each book by any historian is coloured by his own way of thinking and nationality. That is why for many Europeans, India evoked a picture of Maharajas, snake-charmers, and the rope-trick. For ancient Greeks, India was a land of the gold-digging ants, philosophers who lived naked in the forests, and many mystical activities. Some historians "deliberately stressed the non-modern, non-utilitarian aspects of Indian culture, where the existence of a continuity of religion of over three thousand years was acclaimed, and where it was believed that the Indian pattern of life was so concerned with metaphysics and the subtleties of religious belief that there was no time for the mundane things of life. German romanticism was the most vehement in it support of this image of India."[3]

This view has done as much damage to India as Macaulay's rejection of Indian culture. Phillip Howard has rightly observed that "there is no such thing as a neutral or purely objective historian. Without an opinion, a historian would be simply a ticking clock and unreadable besides."[4] But such opinion should be taken as an 'opinion' only and not as an acknowledged truth. It has also been said satirically that "though God cannot alter the past, historians can; it is perhaps because they can be useful to Him in this respect that He tolerates their existence."

It has been very rightly said that 19th century discovered nationalism, and corrupted nearly all the historians. Martin Macaulay, etc. were patriots first and historians afterwards. Students should not be involved in the historical controversies keeping in view our national interest. There are divergences of opinion whether the year 1857 be called as a year of Indian Mutiny or First War of Independence. In such cases, all the facts and figures should be brought to the notice of students with a view to develop their national outlook.

Many a time we come across statements, which have the impact of particular school of thought. We have to understand and interpret them in proper perspective. Statements like the following having a Marxist tone cannot and should not be generalized:

1. Political power sooner or later follows economic power.
2. Successful revolutions are merely the political signatures to preceding economic victories.
3. From of government depends upon the distribution of land:

(a) If most of it is owned by one man, you have *monarchy*.
(b) If it is owned by a few, you have *aristocracy*.
(c) If it is owned by the people, you get *democracy*.

Such statements, though true in a sense, may prove to be very misleading if their suggestive purport is not caught properly.

Dealing with such statements, the teacher should know the events, though similar they tend to produce different results if their historical background is different. "It was Marx who observed that events which were remarkably similar but which occurred in different historical environment tended to produce totally different results. It is easy to understand this when studying each of these evolutions separately and then comparing them, but it is never possible to reach such an understanding by making use of the universal skeleton key of some general historico-philosophical theory."[5]

Dwelling upon this concept, we can explain the differences between several ecological morals. Due to different historical environment, one and the same custom is practised in one part of the country whereas, it is not liked at all in the other. Historical environment and ecology play very significant role in making or not making certain values sociable and acceptable in a society or country at large. While analysing the values on the basis of ecology and historical environment, one has to be very rational and objective. "Perhaps one of the most prolific sources of error in contemporary thinking rises precisely from the popular habit of lifting History out of its proper context and bending it to values of another age and day. In this way, History is never allowed to be itself." This phenomena is also not to be overlooked. In fact the glory of a nation lies neither in its past nor in its future but in drawing inspiration from the past, thinking of a golden future working for the betterment of the present.

It is only through History that we can best explain the relativity of morals. For examples "Orientals cover the head to show respect: Occidentals bare it. A Japanese woman (though this, like so many truths, may be no longer true) pays no attention to the nudity of a workman, and yet she can be as modest as Priscilla Dean. It was 'obscene' (literally on the "stage"—referring to the Aristophanic looseness of ancient comedy) for an Arab woman to show her face, or a Chinese woman her foot, either concealment aroused imagination and desire and served the good of the race. The Melanesians buried alive their sick and their old, and thought it a kindly way of disposing of their waste. In China, says Lubboc, a coffin is (was?) regarded as an appropriate present for an aged relative, especially if he were in poor health."[6]

In Hinduism monogamy is virtue and polygamy is regarded as vice. Our ancient kings (Rajanya) were exception to this common discipline. In an age of war, polygamy may become a virtue, for it is blessed with many children. In certain tribes, monogamy is one of the penalties. In our country, generally speaking, polyandry is not taken as virtue.[7]

But in certain territories like Jaunsar Bawar Pargana in Dehradun, in Tehri and in Khasi tribes of Jaunpur Pargana polyandry is in vogue even these days. Because of many socio-economic factors these people could not part with it. It is still continuing with them as necessary evil in their social system. Near Nilgiri in Toda an Kota tribes also polyandry prevailed till last century. In one of his proclamations in 1788 Tipu Sultan condemned this custom then prevalent among Nairs.

In our country pre-marital liberty and relations are restricted but in West Counsel years of promiscuity are taken as preparation for a happy marriage. They have socially accepted it as their life-style. That is why we come across factual stories like 'Milk of New York'. In this way we can gather hundreds of instances in which the 'immoral' of our time and place is the 'moral' of other ages or other lands.

The scope of History is very vast. It includes total experiences of man from the remotest period, all achievements and discoveries that have been made in this field of Social Sciences. With the explosion of knowledge that has taken place and has been taking place still, the scope of Social Sciences has become more widened. It is still growing wider and deeper. The student has to learn about his country and about other countries as well in order to live a successful life in the international (world) society. Formerly, History of the country had attained to a status of all importance but now the History of the world has gained importance. The impact of colonialism, liberation movements and the first and

Second World Wars have further necessitated the study of the History of other nations. The developments that are taking place in other countries, the achievements, discoveries and research studies—all have a bearing on the life of our children. Thus, the scope is growing and it continues to grow further. Children must be taught to adjust themselves to all these developments.

History is a subject to be taught with illustrations and as such there is a great scope for character-building and inculcation of values like justice, liberty, fraternity, co-operation, team-spirit, national consciousness, patriotism, coexistence, etc. Human values emerge from definite socio-economic, historical and cultural contexts and are very much related to the class to which a certain group of people belong. Through History, the values like hardwork, courage, concern for others, devotion to duty, etc. can be inculcated profitably. In this connection, I must tell you that in the realm of social sciences, by and large, the absolutist view of values has been given up. It has been relegated to the arena of metaphysics. But in connection with human behaviour, it has been propounded that due to impact of several ecological morals on the social system, the values are at times found to be relative. This relativity is not, of course, applicable to the values like truth, non-violence, peace, kindness, etc.

So teaching of history should depend upon unification of child psychology and useful matter. The facts must be useful for understanding the present-day world, by whom and how the modern world developed. It is possible to prepare a simple and interesting teaching of history and how all the nations have contributed to the making of useful discoveries.

Examples:

1. How irrigation was devised by the Sumerians.
2. Arithmetics by the Indians, Geometry by the Egyptians.
3. Script by the Assyrians.
4. Silk, gun powder, examination system and mariners' compass by the Chinese.
5. Architecture and sculpture by the Greeks.
6. Roads by the Romans.
7. Printing by the Germans and steam power by the English and wireless by the Italians.

Such a course in world history will serve as good contribution to narrow-minded nationalism and will provide a good lesson on universal brotherhood.

Today the responsibility of a History Teacher has increased manifold as the disintegrating forces such as communalism, regionalism, linguism and racialism/casteism, etc. are very active with the help of some foreign elements to destroy the very fabric of national unity and thus, our national integration, freedom and secularism is at stake. A History teacher recalling the unique and basic unity in diversity existing in this country can arouse the consciousness and sentiments of nationhood and patriotism among the students. The study of Indian History provides special opportunities for overplaying the unity and underplaying the disunity. History teachers should rise to the time and they must accept this challenge and foil the malicious design of the external as well as internal enemies of national unity by fostering national integration as a main aim of studying History in our schools and colleges.

To achieve this aim every History teacher should follow the following advice of Edgar Bruce Wesley:

"History is wonderful compilation, it abounds with useful facts, information, knowledge, and wisdom, it is society's memory, the fulcrum of the progress, the sovereign's guide. It is nearly impossible to overtake its social utility, its guidance function, its dramatic appeal, its value as entertainment and its service as a moulder of citizens and soldiers—every teacher and every student should see, utilize, and appreciate this fund of human achievement, this colossal store house, the communicable heritage. No teacher at any grade level, however, should teach a course in History as content—To do so is as confusing, unnecessary, frustrating, futile, pointless and as illogical as to teach a course in the World Almanac, the dictionary, or the encyclopaedia. The content of history is to be utilized and exploited—not studied, learned, or memorized."[8]

REFERENCES

1. Will Durant, *The Mansions of Philosophy, Meaning of History*, p. 309.
2. Gall M. Inlow, *Value in Transition*, p. 104.
3. Romila Thapar, *A History of India*, p. 16.
4. Phillip Howard, *The Times*, Review of Barbara Tuchman's Practising History, 4 Feb. 1982.
5. V.I. Pavlov, *Historical Premises for India's Transition to Capitalism*, p. 9.
6. *Origin of Civilization*, p. 24.
7. एकस्य बह्वयो विदिता महिष्यः कुरूनन्दन।
   नैकस्या बहवः पुंसो विधीयन्ते कदाचन।।
   —महाभारत
8. *Teaching the Social Studies*, Edited by Gross, McPhie, and Fraenkel, Let's Abolish History Courses (Edgar Bruce Wesley), pp. 517-18.

11

EDUCATION IN VALUES THROUGH LANGUAGE TEACHING

Language and literature hold a significant place in the whole system of values. From times immemorial good literature which may belong to any language of the world has both nurtured and sustained high ideals and acted as the guardian and sentient of the moral and social values of mankind. Through portraying real or fictitious characters and situations literature inspires, encourages and exhorts us to strive for and achieve those goals by adopting a set of values that have stood the test of time. By constantly projecting the victory of good over evil, of truth over falsehood, of a Rama over a demon King, Ravana, of a truthful Prahalad over a conceited father Hiranyakashyap, literature upholds the fundamental values of truth, love, peace and right conduct, etc.

It is this unique quality of literature which confers immortality upon it. The political world of Humu is dead but his song of Illiad is still alive, the fantasies of Kalidas still move us like the cry of a living voice when Ujjaini, whose brightest star he was, now lives only in his works. Ravindra *sangeet* and Ravindra poetry still sway us when the Gurudev and his contemporaries are no more. Literature holds mirror to the society. It reflects the aspirations, struggles and achievements of the people. It also analyses the causes of their failures and successes. "Literature like art," in the words of Scott James, "systematises the impulses, desires and propensities of an individual."

Literature is a very vital source of History, specially social history where we come across various characters from different strata of the society. Their characterization and phenomena around them furnish us with very enriched and varied social data of the time and place concerned. Thus, literature incorporates a very useful treasure of values, which can be profitably utilized by the language teacher. Rene Wellek has rightly remarked:

"Used as a social document, Literature can be made to yield the outlines of social history. Chaucer and Langland preserve two views of fourteenth-century society. The prologue to the Canterbury Tales was earlier seen to offer an almost complete survey of social types. Shakespeare in the 'Merry Wives of Windsor', Ben Jhonson in several plays and Thomas Deloney seem to tell us something about the Elizabethan middle class. Addison, Fielding and Smollett depict the new bourgeoisie of the eighteenth century; Jane Austen the country gentry and country persons early in the nineteenth century; and Trollope, Thackeray and Dickens, the Victorian world. At the turn of the century, Galsworthy shows us the English upper middle classes; Wells, the lower middle classes; Benett, the provincial towns."[1]

Thus, a language teacher has an endless store of material for inculcating moral values among his students. In fact he has traditionally been known as the character-builder of a nation. The great headmasters of English Public Schools such as Thomas Arnold produced a galaxy of great men. Today, not only India but the whole world is facing a crisis of moral, ethical and social values. It is, therefore, for the language teacher to rise to the occasion and bring about a virtual renaissance of values. He has to have a greater awareness of his duty. He has to re-equip himself for the task, redouble his efforts and meet the challenge. Dr. S. Radhakrishnan truly pointed out, "A civilization is not built with brick and mortar or steel and machinery, it is built with men, their quality and character.

Confucius valued the arts tremendously. A simple piece of music once cost such a spell over him that for three months he was unable to distinguish the taste of meat. If there is anyone who is totally immune to the power of art, he thought that such a one has no place in human society. Nevertheless Confucius was not on the whole an advocate of "art for art's sake." He cherished it primarily as an instrument for moral education.

By poetry the mind is aroused; from music the finish is received.

The odes stimulate the mind. They induce self-contemplation. They teach the art of sensibility. They help to regulate resentment. They bring home the duty of serving one's father and one's prince.[2]

A language teacher holds the powerful magic of words in his hands. With the added charm of rhyme and rhythm he can vibrate the very soul of a child which no other subject teacher can. As Vivekananda said: Life is only a vibration. That which vibrates this ocean of others vibrates you." A teacher of language can go deeper to appeal of a child's intellect, mind or body. He can reach his 'real self' which is one with the self of goodness, truth and beauty. And, no amount of dissertations and lectures can mould a child's character as well as an emotional experience delivered with the help of creative imagination and sensory images. A good poem is an encoding of a precious experience, a good teacher of poetry does not explain the poem word by word for it will destroy its beauty but decodes the experience and shares its emotional impact with his students. The sudden thrills, the disturbing emotions, the flashes of insight—it is through these that a child's character is moulded, his personality is developed. A character thus, moulded is far superior to any other creation—

> "A builder built a temple,
> He fashioned it with care,
> Each little nook and cranny
> Each little stair,
> A teacher built a temple
> She fashioned it with care
> She filled it with love and kindness
> She shut out all the snare.
> As time went by as you know it must
> The builder's temple crumbled and
> ended up in dust.
> The teacher's temple, tender moulded
> by love and self-control
> Shone with beauty and grace for it
> was child's immortal soul."

A language teacher opens for his students the wonderful world of books. He leads them from the study of textbooks to reading books for pleasure and profit. He guides them in the right choice of books. A few timely hints dropped subtly bring alive the whole biography of a great man and helps the students inculcate those qualities of head and heart which these great men cherished.

Not only that, books should build bridges between our past and present, they preserve our rich heritage and point to their relevance in modern times. The glory of a nation lies neither in its past nor in its future but in drawing inspiration from betterment of the present.

Generally three languages are taught, namely, Hindi, Sanskrit and English. Mother tongue, *i.e.*, Hindi is the most apt medium to reach to the heart of a child, and to motivate the springs of his thought and vitality. Therefore, it is the most pious duty of a Hindi teacher to shape a child's character, to mould his personality, to inculcate in him the fundamental values of life. The text material of Hindi as it stands today is extremely rich in propounding values not only of moral and ethical nature but also of social and political kind. The teacher has just to focus attention of the students to draw and imbibe the various values. So, instead of reframing a value-oriented course the need is to guide the teacher in his task appropriately and this can be done easily through revising Teacher's Handbook or Guidebook or holding a short duration workshop at school for this purpose. At the end of each lesson a number of exercises are given for vocabulary learning, comprehension, evaluation and appreciation of the thought content. To the same one more area may be added, *i.e.*, evaluating the impact of the lesson on a child's personality.

Inspiring stories can be used profitably for inculcation of desired values. Stories like 'The Parrot's Training' (R.N. Tagore), 'The Gift of Magi' (O'Henry), 'The Life of Socrates (Will Durant), 'Kafan' (Prem Chand), 'Usne Kaha Tha' (Chakradhar Sharma Guleri), 'The Life of Gautam' (H. G. Wells), etc. are found to be very effective for fostering desired values. But the use of stories should be made very methodically so that it registers desired results. For this the following criteria should be kept in mind:

1. The story should be written in beautiful and chaste language;
2. It should be of deep human interest but avoid parables or extolling any particular religion;
3. It should not contain plots of cunning and cheating;
4. The general atmosphere of the story should be such as to glorify truth, beauty and goodness.

Story-telling is an art. It will not serve the purpose if it is not followed by question-answer session. It is also significant to point out how the story has a bearing on the child's everyday life.

"It is not as though one injects the qualities of purity, goodness, truth and love into the children when one narrates stories to them. These qualities are a part of the real nature of children. The stories do not put them into the children from outside. The narrated stories have to bring about the blossoming of these qualities, already latent in them, into their behaviour. Story-telling is never complete without a question and answer session. After telling each story, the teacher has to ask questions to test the children's comprehension. The questions asked by the teacher can be of four types: 1. factual, 2. referential, 3. inferential, 4. evaluative.

The first two types test only comprehension. The last two test the child's intelligent understanding and evaluative power. Instead of the teacher telling the moral of the story, the children should be able to infer and appreciate."[3]

Our Sanskrit literature, which is the product of an idealistic society, is replete with petty sayings and epigrammatic wisdom. Capitalising on the immense capacity of a child for memorising at young stage, the Sanskrit teacher should encourage his students to learn by heart useful *shlokas* and *stotras*, which will serve as beacon lights in stormy weather and succour and support their drawing spirits.

Coming to English language, in comparison to Hindi and Sanskrit I find it a less effective tool in providing value education because it is a foreign language. In early stages of learning there exists a barrier of communication and unless there is a spontaneous interaction between the teacher and the taught, it is difficult to impart abstract conception. This does not, however, mean that no useful work can be done in the field of moral education by an English teacher. All languages essentially serve the same purpose. So, with imagination and guidance a teacher of English can strive for and achieve the same objects as Hindi and Sanskrit teachers.

Besides the text material, there are other effective tools in the bag of language teachers. Stories and articles may be written bringing out the significance of certain values and the same may be included in the school magazine or manuscript magazine of individual classes. The topics selected for literary activities such as debates, discussions, quiz competition should be such as would promote consciousness for value inculcation.

The last though not the least important fact is that the language teacher through his own exemplary moral conduct must uphold the system to values he is trying to put across and deserve the right to expound it. Without that, he cannot deliver the goods.

REFERENCES

1. Rene Wellek and Austin Warren, *Theory of Literature*, p. 105.
2. *The Religions of Man*, pp. 173-74.
3. *Teacher's Handbook for The Course in Human Values*, p. 68.

12

NATIONAL GOALS AND VALUE EDUCATION*

> "The good life is the ultimate aim of education, and for each pupil this means to determine himself, realize himself and integrate himself through the habits of acquiring, using and enjoying the truth. The good life makes a claim upon the individual. Everything depends on whether the school can persuade him to acknowledge this as a moral claim, as a demand that he judges that he ought to satisfy."
>
> —Harry S. Broudy (*Building a Philosophy of Education*, pp. 241-42)

Due to misconceptual notion of modernity and violent strides of science and technology speedy erosion of our moral, social, cultural and spiritual values has been causing concern and attracting the attention of various authorities. Right from the dawn of independence of our country the authorities appointed various commissions and committees to prepare action-plans to bring about desired improvement in the existing system of education, a sub-system of our entire social system which include Radhakrishnan Commission (1948), Mudaliar Commission (1954), Shri Prakash Committee on Moral Education (1959), Kothari Commission (1966), Ramamurthy Committee (1990), etc. Each committee or commission has advocated and underlined the express need for Value-oriented Education in our educational institutions particularly in our schools, which number more than 5 lakhs all over the country.

The anxiety and concern reflected in the concluding paragraph of the report of Religious and Moral Education Committee, which was submitted in December 1959, is still more pertinent and relevant as far as the need of 'Value Education' is concerned in the present system of education. A part of the paragraph is as under:

* This paper was read in the Orientation Programme on VE for the Principals of KVS in 1994.

"*We are bound to say that the many ills that our world of education and our society as a whole is suffering today, resulting in widespread disturbance and dislocation of life, are mainly due to the gradual disappearance of the hold of the basic principles of religion on the hearts of the people. The old bonds that kept men together are fast loosening, and the various new ideologies that are coming to us, and which we are outwardly accepting without inwardly digesting their meanings, are increasingly worsening the situation. The only cure, it seems to us, is in the deliberate inculcation of moral and spiritual values from the earliest years of our lives. If we lose these, we shall be a nation without a soul, and our attempts to imitate the outer forms of other lands without understanding their inner meaning, or psychologically attuning ourselves to them, would only result in chaos and confusion, the first signs of which are already very distinctly visible on the horizon.*"

In this series there was a high level Seminar on 'Value Education' held at Shimla on 27-28 May 1981. The Seminar put forth many revolutionary recommendations. One of them is that there is a need for producing literature especially designed for the value-orientation of education. The Seminar further recommended special teacher-orientation programmes to train teachers in the effective methods of development of values among students and teachers. Perhaps in pursuance of this recommendation, many workshops on 'Value Education' were organized by Kendriya Vidyalaya Sangathan, New Delhi. But further followup is yet to be taken up, which is more important. All the teachers of the Education Department of States should also be made acquainted with the concept of 'Value Education'. Further practical programmes based on value-orientation should be designed by the group of experts at Central/State level. The programmes thus, designed should be psychologically sound and well-experimented before they are enforced into practice.

In 1986 Union Government published a mimeographed two-volume document entitled "Challenge of Education—A Policy Perspective," which was under debate. In the draft proposal it has been aptly visualized that the new policy should be instrumental in rejuvenating and updating the existing national system and design of education so as to make it respond more fully to the needs and aspirations of the people and to enable the country to meet the difficult and demanding challenges of the 21st century. The new NEP should make its own real contribution to bring about a social transformation, integrate and unite the people of India and modernise society, *while preserving what is authentically and abidingly Indian in our cultural heritage* and enhance efficiency and productivity in all sectors, industrial, agricultural as well as the service sector.

In the new NEP, the following four national goals are set:

1. A United, Secular India,
2. A Modern Nation,
3. A Productive People, and
4. A Humane and Caring Society

If judiciously planned and successfully implemented, Value Education can prove to be very vital and effective in realizing these goals. Therefore, the Commission has rightly recommended that Value Education should find important place in the school curriculum. In the policy statement, it has been suggested that *"The basic and essential values underlying our Constitution (preamble) as well as those contained in the four national goals referred to above should form the basic syllabus for value education, which should find an important place in the school curriculum and be given the necessary attention and time."*

Responding to the clarion call of the nation Kendriya Vidyalaya Sangathan has taken up a long-term project on Value Education. In consonance with the four national goals mentioned above the following four areas, corresponding respectively to each national goal, have been selected for various ethical, moral, social and cultural values:

1. Area of communication (Goal—A United Secular India)
2. Area of work (Goal—A Modern Nation)
3. Area of service (Goal—A Productive People)
4. Area of citizenship (Goal—A Humane and Caring Society)

Communication

Through the values covered under the area of communication our aim should be to build a united and secular nation. The area of communication has very broad perspective, which may be indicated mainly by the following types of communication:

(a) Verbal communication
(b) Non-verbal communication

The latter is conveyed through body language, sign language and other types of non-verbal communication.

In elevating one's personality art of communication has a major role to play. Therefore, one should try to master skills of communication, whatever language is used. While dealing with others one should observe courtesy, moderation and charity. No doubt to be a good speaker is important, but to be a good listener is equally, if not more, important. Generally we listen to the speaker's words only. We fail to observe airs on his face while speaking, various modulations of his voice, movement of different parts of his body and so on. Whatever is conveyed is the sum-total of all the three components, *i.e.*, words, modulation of his voice and movements of the parts of speaker's body. It is said that the contribution of words in conveying the purport is only 25 per cent, of modulation 15 per cent and 60 per cent of the movement of the body. Therefore, to observe and understand the language of the body is very important. That is why we relish listening to the noted speakers more than going through their scripts. Similarly conversation would not be that much enjoyable in dark as it is in the light.

For internalization of various values among the students the following points are of utmost importance and pertinence:

1. What to communicate
2. What not to communicate
3. Where to communicate
4. Where not to communicate
5. How to communicate
6. When to communicate
7. When not to communicate

The students are expected to be *respectful*, polite and courteous while talking to their elders. They should observe *patience, tolerance* and *good manners* while talking/listening to others and learn *to respect others' views*. Similarly they should be careful of proximity of other persons (desired or undesired, seniors or juniors, etc.) In order to achieve the goal of national integration and maintain the secular character of our nation as enshrined in the preamble of our Constitution, balanced, decent, patient communication leading to better understanding is a must.

Good communication begets good understanding, free from fear or favour, and good understanding generates gradually fibres of good behaviour with peer group, fellow-beings and everybody at large. That is why Confucian tradition of education was primarily concerned with *learning how to behave*. As an indicator of good behaviour Confucius mentioned five values—*courtesy, generosity, good faith, diligence* and *kindness*. He further suggested—

1. If you behave with courtesy, then you will not be insulted;
2. If you are generous, then you will win the multitude;
3. If you are of good faith, then other men will put their trust in you;
4. If you are diligent, then you will have success; and
5. If you are kind then you will be able to command others.

Confucius laid a great emphasis on the purity and sanctity of the communication. One should actually mean it, whatever is communicated. Our identity will be quite doubtful and controversial if our words contradict with our intentions and deeds. Double dealings are bound to be exposed sooner or later, because one cannot befool all the persons at all the times. In this regard the following Confucian saying must always be borne in mind:

> "Clever talk and domineering manner have little to do with being man-at-his-best."

Therefore, it will be misleading to say that all courteous persons are good or righteous. Any sort of piety of heart or holiness is not necessary in so called courteous persons. Artificial mannerism has nothing to do with good character or personal piety. These days, on the contrary, it is observed that persons with ambiguous and controversial character are more refined in manners. Hilaire Belloc has rightly remarked on this point:

> "Of courtesy, it is much less
> Than courage of Heart of Holiness.
> Yet in my walks it seems to me.
> That the grace of God is in Courtesy."

To the poet God's grace appears in courtesy. But it is found there only, where it is coupled with piety of heart and righteousness of the character.

National integration is a national goal towards which all communities should strive. Of late, it has been the subject of ongoing debates for many years. During the last few years due to riots in various parts of the country on one point or the other the subject has caused express concern for the countrymen regardless of their caste and creed. Through inculcation of various values related to the area of communication the true spirit of secularism can be inculcated and thereby national integration can be strengthened. Thus, the concept of separation and compartmentalization would disappear making way for a general atmosphere of unity.

Work

Carlyle has rightly said that if you get some meaningful and useful work to do, don't ask for any other boon. Work is worship. In fact, everyone has got his work-ethos. These ethos are originated from his own culture and cultural values. That is why work-culture differs from nation to nation and from time to time. *Work* itself is a great value. But, this great value never stands alone. It has its associates which include devotion, honesty, sincerity, scientific temper, team spirit, sense of social responsibility, humaneness, discipline, etc.

In the context of school environment for smooth and proper functioning of school punctuality and regularity are essential. On the part of teachers coverage of courses in time, attending various school programmes with zeal and interest and lastly a sense of belongingness will go a long way in making the school atmosphere more congenial for inculcation of various values among the students.

Modernity comes to the nation through diligent and sincere work of the people of the country concerned. Because of sincerity, devotion and dedication of work only Japan could reach at the peak of modern nations even after total disaster in World War II. When Japanese show their resentment to the management they put more work, when they have any grievance against the Government they become more sincere in their work. Work and only work is key to success, be it of a man or a nation. Calvin Vollidge has aptly remarked, "All growth depends upon activity. There is no development physically or intellectually without effort, and effort means work. Work is not a curse it is preprogative of intelligence, the only means to manhood, and the measure of civilization." It is a measure of civilization as the civilization can be known by the work-habits of the inhabitants.

By the virtue of meticulous planning we could build Bhakra Nangal, Bhilai, Durgapur and Rourkela plants, which were rightly called the places of pilgrimage of modern India by Pt. Jawaharlal Nehru, the builder of modern India.

One should take his work as pleasure if he wants to enjoy life as Maxim Gorky says, "When work is pleasure life is a joy! When work is a duty, life is a slavery." The true concept of modernity enjoins that education should be taken in such a way which may not tax and vex one's mind. "Play-way Method" in education itself indicates that taxing the brain of the child is not desirable. The soul of modernity does not lie in the outward appearance but in the original, divergent and rational but humane approach towards various subjects and problems confronted by the society. With this outlook in life we will be able to modernize the society. These days the trend towards modernity is misinterpreted to mean removal or negation of values. Very often we observe total disregard towards values. Today very few people care for or have respect for the age-old values like freedom, belief, sincerity and self-respect, the right to work and express one's views freely. We cherish these values for ourselves; but show total disregard for similar values of others. Such double standards create a sort of hollowness in the society. Such a society devoid of sound value base cannot be called a modern society in the real sense of the term.

In order to modernize the society we should not neglect totally our traditional values. It will be in the fitness of things if we would strive to imbibe our national values giving due regard to our age-old and tested traditional values. Then only we would be able to modernize the society in the real sense by adopting an appropriate work-culture.

Service

By the term 'service' here we mean personal service as well as welfare activity carried on by the state because our aim is to produce productive people. People can be made productive through idealized socio-economic institutions cherishing higher human values like truth, non-violence, love, altruism, concern for others' cultural values, charity, goodness, humanity, etc. But, the limitation of time is always there. Such institutions have great deal of time-lag. Personal service, may be partial or localized, always gives immediate aid or relief to the needy ones. The poor and needy persons cannot wait for the policy-decisions of the government or directives of the party. Service is itself a great value. Vivekananda said, "to serve human being is to serve God." To go on doing something good for the members of the society will go a long way in making the people productive.

The area of service includes values like dedication, hardwork, sincerity, dignity of labour, concern for others, kindness, compassion, love, friendship, etc. By cherishing these values we may serve better the society and nation at large. In addition to this awareness of ecology, environmental protection, population stabilization are other important components under the purview of area of service. If these values are adopted people will be able to utilise their leisure time in more productive manner.

Citizenship

Only good citizens can form a good society. Hence, a training in good citizenship is essential for the student. A good society can be the one which claims to have an active and express concern for its people, which can share sorrows and joy, loss and gain, victory and defeat of its people. In order to form a humane society these values must be inculcated among the students—benevolence, love, equality, compassion, concern for others, kindness, magnanimity, humaneness, responsibility, care for civic and national property, etc.

A good citizen should try to develop his own personality and the social environment together, as the personal ethics and state ethics rise and fall together—it is a universally acknowledged truth. Har Dayal puts it like this:

> "*These two sections of ethics are inseparable and inter-dependent like a pair of scissors. Personal ethics rises and falls with state ethics, and state ethics also varies with personal ethics. Virtuous individuals create and maintain good political and economic institutions; and good institutions produce virtuous citizens. Personal ethics cannot flourish under evil institutions; and noble institutions cannot exist among a corrupt and degraded people.*"

Enlightened citizens can only form a rational government and humane administration which is able to look after the welfare of common man. "Man is the measure of everything" has been said rightly by Karl Marx. The administration ensures happiness of the citizens, then only caring and sharing society will come into existence.

The society which tends to caring and sharing of its people can be called humane. The society, where man to man relationship is cordial and harmonious, where humanism prevails in and outside the administration, where people respect each other irrespective of their caste, creed and colour, where there are no barriers of sect, language, and region can be termed as humane society. Good citizenship expects that the individuals should imbibe a great value of humanity or humanism, which is threshold of all the religions of the world.

"Humanism is a system of view based on respect for the dignity and rights of man, his value as a personality, concern for his welfare, his all-round development, and the creation of favourable conditions for social life. Humanism is the opposite of fanaticism, rigourism, intolerance, and disrespect for the view and knowledge of others . . . some of the most prominent humanists of the renaissance, such as Petrarch, Dante, Boccaccio, Leonardo da Vinci, Erasmus Desiderious Bruno, F. Rabelais, Montaigne, Copernicus, Shakespeare, F. Bacon and others, helped to mould mundane views." In India there is a galaxy of humanistic thinkers which include many personalities of modern times—from Raja Ram Mohun Roy to Mother Teresa.

In sum, we can say that communication, work, service and citizenship are not only values but areas of various values having a broad spectrum and can be mentioned as indicators for fulfilment of four national goals—*United India, Modern Nation, Productive People and Humane Society*—to some extent, if not to a considerable extent.

13

TOWARDS UNITED AND SECULAR INDIA

A united and secular India is one of the four national goals as stated in the New Education Policy. 1605 mother tongues, more than 400 recognised languages, 15 scheduled languages, each one having its own history and literature dating back many centuries. This is the language statistics of our country in a nutshell. In a multilingual, multiracial country like India with variegated culture, national integration is of paramount importance in every aspect of people's private or public life. That is why Gandhi used to say, "I do not want any house to be walled in from all sides, and windows to be closed. I want the cultures of all lands blow in my house but I do not wish to be blown off my feet by any."

If we ponder over, it will not take much time for us to come to the dismal conclusion that throughout the history of the country, never dire necessity of national integration was felt more essential than it is today. Forces of disintegration are lurking everywhere, threatening the very secularity of the republic. Religious obscurantism, linguistic Chauvinism, irrational ethnocentrism and regionalism fragmented and compartmentalised by narrow domestic walls have eaten into the country's unity.

At present the conditions prevailing in the country are not conducive for national integration. Some regions are suffering from fragmentation and parochial feelings on grounds of religion, boundary, river waters, and demand for separate statehood. A critical and careful analysis of the currents and cross-currents of the happenings in various states clearly foretells that divisive forces are active everywhere and unifying forces are inert and ineffective, seen nowhere. The New Education Policy (1986) formulated by the Government of India also stresses this point while it propagates value education. It is very aptly observed, "in our culturally plural society, education should fortify universal eternal values oriented towards unity and integration of people. These values should help eliminate obscurantism, religious fanaticism, violence, superstition and fatalism."

The children in their early formative years are all united and one and easily forget their differences as depicted in the story of Leo Tolstoy "Children are wiser than their elders." It is the environment around them in the late years that goes on dividing them sowing in the fertile soil of their mind seeds of separation. Schools have a responsibility of fortifying the values in students' minds so that the vicious environment is not able to have free play, even though the exclusive responsibility of inculcating national integration and higher values cannot be vested only with educational institutions, where a child spends only 5-6 hours a day. But it is found in practice that major preoccupation at schools, at present, is their systematic and unidirectional transaction of curriculum so that a high level of academic performance as evident from the examination results is discernible. It is easily forgotten that school is one of the many social institutions that has a great bearing on the child's personality, attitudes and his conduct. As far as Kendriya Vidyalayas are concerned among the four important aims and objectives of these Vidyalayas promulgated by KVS the fourth-one explicitly states the importance of national integration. The fourth aim of Kendriya Vidyalayas is, "To develop the spirit of national integration and create a sense of Indianness among children."

The Central Board of Secondary Education in their publication entitled "National Integration through schools" has given the following broad guidelines for schools for developing their own strategy for imparting training and promoting national integration. The main points are:

1. A proper format for the morning assembly.
2. Correct teaching methodology in various subjects.
3. Nationalistic and humanistic attitudes and behaviours of teachers.
4. Respect for national symbols, heroes, leaders, etc.
5. Balanced celebration of national days and festivals.
6. Community and patriotic singing.
7. Participation in community programme, social service, relief work, Jamboories, etc.
8. Excursions, visits and exchange of students.

As already pointed out infusing national integration among children is one of the four proclaimed aims of Kendriya Vidyalayas. A Kendriya Vidyalaya, in reality, is a miniature India. As such they reflect the composite culture of the country. Students hailing from different linguistic and cultural groups, following different religions, mix themselves freely unfettered by any prejudice, differences of caste, colour, creed wane into insignificance in these institutions. Students belonging to the rich and the poor, the low and the high, the civil and defence, the backward and the elite find a common meeting place there. The teaching and learning process are unaffected by difference in mother tongue.

The students, alongwith their parents and the staff in a Kendriya Vidyalaya are constantly moving due to all-India transfer liability of parents and teachers. The physical mobility and consequent chances for interaction of people of one region with another region are impossible and impractical anywhere else. Compulsory attendance in seminars, inservice courses and induction courses also bring staff of different schools belonging to different states into forced contact with one another.

Kendriya Vidyalayas aim at creating a value system which will help children to inculcate the right attitudes of tolerance, existence and sharing. Whether it be the devastation due to cyclone in Andhra Pradesh, the floods of Kosi and the Ganges bringing untold havocs in Bihar, drought of Rajasthan, gas tragedy of Bhopal, accidental fire and death at Jamshedpur, spurious liquor tragedy of Baroda, all feel these are the calamities of their own village intimately involving them. An objective, more conveniently perfected by Kendriya Vidyalayas, because of the inherent advantages in the organisation, is to enlarge the number of students who honestly count themselves as Indians first, keeping away group, regional or caste affiliations very much in the rear. National unity can never be achieved unless we produce more Indians and less number of Maharashtrians, Punjabis, Bengalees or Malayalees.

Pedagogy in Kendriya Vidyalayas plays a considerable role in inculcating integration. In Kendriya Vidyalayas the curriculum contains, besides other subjects, languages, history and geography. Study of geography develops sense of pride in the geographical features of one's country. The mountains, valleys, rivers and their flow and murmur and plains will naturally have a romantic appeal to a student. Instruction in geography aims at promoting accurate and wise thinking about the land and the people of our country, an appreciation of the interdependence of units within it, confidence in the country's capacity to grow into a strong economic and political power, pride in the richness of her resources and a tendency to see things first and foremost in the context of the country as a whole. As such, instruction in and through the content matter of geography, which is a compulsory subject up to class X in Kendriya Vidyalayas, leads to well-poised sense of belongingness, the quintessense of national integration.

Teaching of history, if not done in proper perspective, will lead to serve consciously or unconsciously narrow sectarian and chauvinistic ends. Many prejudices and beliefs that have hampered the unity of the Indian people are not in a small measure due to the distortions of historical facts. Past institutions and events shall not be presented as models of perfection because every institution is transformed into one, more suited to the needs of society. The capacity to differentiate between the emerging and progressive, and dying and regressive is essential to develop attitudes conducive to national integration. While teaching history, attempts should not be made to transfer present prejudices to past political conflicts, or seek their justification therefrom. The fact that in the 40 years rule of Shivaji of Maharashtra and 40 years' rule of Ranjit Singh not a single communal riot took place, there were no forced conversions, there were no second rate citizens and minorities were treated well should be emphasized so that the children can imbibe the appropriate and unifying principles in their life.

Exemplary actions worthy of mention of great rulers, leaders and teachers which are models to be emulated should be emphasized and brought to the attention of students. Accounts of events that fostered communal harmony should be highlighted by history teachers. Stories exemplifying generosity, secularity and tolerance of the past rulers like that of a Muslim calligraphist knocking the doors of Maharaja Ranjit Singh's palace at Lahore, entreating the king to pay Rs. one lakh for a calligraphed copy of the Holy Quran, should be told to the students highlighting their values in correct perspective. The calligraphist submitted to the emperor that he had been to the courts of almost all Muslim princes and Nawabs at Rampur, Lucknow and Hyderabad but nobody could pay him the high cost. He came to Lahore, with high hopes, having heard of the generosity and secularity of the Sikh ruler. Maharaja listened to him, got up from his silver chair, kissed the holy book and asked his finance minister to pay the high price the calligraphist demanded. The foreign minister of the Sikh ruler, Fakeer Azizuddin, who was an eyewitness to this asked his master why he agreed to this huge payment for a book that did not have any relation with his religion. Maharaja's only eye twinkled and quipped:

"God had ordained that I should look upon all the religions with the same eye. That is why he took the light from the other."

In all Kendriya Vidyalayas morning assembly is organised on secular lines with clear emphasis on national integration. A secular prayer in the form of invocation, reading of important news by children with humanistic interpretation by teachers or senior students, patriotic singing and short and sweet discourses on a topic of moral value or on a personality who contributed a lot to the human welfare are the essence of programmes in a Vidyalaya morning assembly. Religious festivals and important days are celebrated in Vidyalayas helping the children to imbibe the different facts of our culture and to appreciate unity in diversity.

Co-curricular activities in Kendriya Vidyalayas are the most effective means of inculcating national integration. The scope of such activities is very wide. Inter-house programmes like declamation contests, quiz competitions, debates and cultural programmes, educational excursions, scouting, NCC camps, student exchanges, community lunches, etc. are effective ways of moulding the minds of students towards national unity and oneness of the country and develop among children genuine feelings of brotherhood. Taboos and restrictions persist because of religious and caste feeling and rigid habits. These habits must be fought against. Even though most of the Kendriya Vidyalayas are non-residential, scholars usually bring their own lunch packets and eat it in the company of other students. A little care, supervision and planning on the part of school authorities will help the students to free themselves from gathering according to community or socio-economic levels during lunch time and will be an excellent opportunity to clear off young minds of the darkness and narrowness of communalism, and regionalism.

National integration is not something that can be imposed on the people. It unfolds itself spontaneously from the depth of their hearts submerging differences of race, caste, creed and religion for a higher summative cause that is national. The earlier it is sowed in the fertile young minds, and nurtured properly with care and skill, the firmer, the faster and more rooted it will appear spontaneously. Hence, schools have a bigger role to play in fostering national integration. Kendriya Vidyalayas really play a vital role for fulfilling this significant aspect in multifarious ways. National integration is one of the proclaimed aims of KVS. Teachers and students belonging to different regions speaking different languages are allowed to interact. Curriculum includes subjects through which integration can be brought in easily. Directives are given by KVS in general and in particular by individual schools to adopt methods of teaching for each subject suited to fostering the feeling of unity and highlighting the oneness of India. Due importance in Vidyalaya programmes is given to co-curricular activities and vast opportunities are given for intellectual and emotional interaction of children, born and brought up in different places speaking different dialects and following a variety of customs. As such, it is felt that among all sorts of educational institutions in the country Kendriya Vidyalayas play a very dynamic and effective role in nurturing national integration in youths.

14

VALUE EDUCATION AND WOMEN*

There is no gainsaying the fact that there has been general deterioration in the standard and behavioural patterns of the people involved in the educational system, a sub-system of our whole social system. One of the major factors responsible for this deterioration has been general deterioration in our moral, social and spiritual values. In the philosophical context values are those standards or a code for moral behaviour conditioned by one's cultural tenets and guarded by conscience, according to which human being is supposed to conduct himself and shape his life-pattern by integrating his beliefs, ideas and attitudes to realize the cherished ideals and aims of life. In this process the good of many or all is to be taken as the sole criterion.

In the terminology of Indian History of Education, the term 'Value' has not been well set yet, because the theme of 'Value Education' was initially acknowledged in the form of 'Religious Education' or 'Moral Education'. Value Education is more wider, practicable and adptable than the former two, as no specific faith or religion is reflected through ethical, moral, social, cultural or spiritual values. Here each and every faith or religion has a contribution to make without revealing its identity. It is only at comparative level that we may endorse that value-tenets in the USA are influenced by Christianity or Indian value-tenets have their seeds in Hinduism, Buddhism, Jainism, Islam, etc. In this regard the Indian phenomenon is uniquely different as compared to the socio-cultural phenomenon of the advanced countries like the UK or the USA. For anyone it will be a futile endeavour to search Indianness in Hinduism, Islam or Buddhism alone. It is a historically acknowledged truth that 'discovery of India' lies in the continuous analysis and synthesis of various faiths of Indian origin in particular and others also to some extent because the essence of these faiths is deeply rooted in our

* Published in *Journal of Indian Education*, July 1988.

composite culture. In spite of this our Constitution stands for secularism. The arena of education is also covered by the spirit of secularism through articles 28 and 30 of the Constitution. The beauty of our secularism lies not in negation of other faiths but respecting equally other faiths, religions and cultures.

The idea of multi-faith school is being successfully translated into practice in the UK. According to one of the surveys, all high schools in Britain are multi-faith in the sense of being pluralist in beliefs and values. Through value education in our pluralistic society, the theme of multi-faith can also be materialized without specifying the identity of any particular faith or religion.

All cherished aims of any nation have been realized through the classrooms only. The Butler Act of 1944 in the UK had a nice line written on top: "What our schools are, the race shall be." It is but natural to have great expectations from our schools. Our teachers and students very often fall short of our expectations because their personalities are developed mostly intellectually by assimilating and vomiting of the information (knowledge) and not by acquisition of moral and spiritual values. The international Commission on Education has rightly pointed out that our education basically suffers from "the gap between its content and the living experience of its pupils, between the system of values that it preaches and the goals set up by society, between its ancient curricula and the modernity of science."

The changing character of curricula is such that students find themselves grossly involved to cope up with the gradually growing burden of the curriculum. Parental expectations are also found to be very high. The expectations from the individual teacher and the institutions at large are of most idealistic nature. While talking to the teachers or their wards, one may easily find the parent sharing his or her own experiences of school days and ideal character and personality and their teacher. By narrating all these, they expect the same from the teachers of their ward. Perhaps for a while they forget that the present educational system is a sub-system of the prevailing social system, a part of the whole. When their expectations are not fulfilled, they become frustrated and start criticising the teachers and institutions without analysing the whole phenomenon and going to the roots of the problem.

Never before was the job of teachers and parents so challenging as it is today. An educationist has rightly observed:

> "*The erosion of values is now a national phenomenon, so complex and gigantic that a more balanced school curriculum, new learning*

materials and competent teachers alone can do very little. The task of national development is massive and urgent and no worthwhile achievement is possible without an upsurge of ethical values, of cleanliness of public life instead of the prevailing cynicism and corruption, and genuine practice of moral and spiritual values by all sections of our people."

The anxiety and concern reflected in the concluding paragraph of the report of Religious and Moral Education Committee (1959) is still more pertinent and relevant as far as the need of Value Education is concerned in the present system of education. A part of the paragraph is as under:

"*We are bound to say that the many ills that our world of education and our society as a whole is suffering today, resulting in widespread disturbance and dislocation of life, are mainly due to the gradual disappearance of the hold of the basic principles of religion on the hearts of the people. The old bonds that kept men together, are fast loosening, and the various new ideologies that are coming to us, and which we are outwardly accepting without inwardly digesting their meanings, are increasingly worsening the situation. The only cure, it seems to us, is in the deliberate inculcation of moral and spiritual values from the earliest years of our lives. If we lose these, we shall be a nation without a soul; and our attempts to imitate the outer forms of other lands without understanding their inner meaning, or psychologically attuning ourselves to them, would only result in chaos and confusion, the first signs of which are already very distinctly visible on the horizon.*"

Women can play a very important role in inculcation of ethical, moral, aesthetic and social values in the youths. As per one of the surveys in Asia, approximately 90 per cent teachers dealing with primary children are female. The Primary stage is a right time when the desired values can be inculcated very effectively. Moreover, eternal values like truth, love, nonviolence, toleration, etc. can be better expressed and demonstrated and inculcated by female teachers.

According to one of the classifications, values are classified into two groups—traditional values and operational values. The traditional values are those virtues (*Sheel*), which are depicted in our old scriptures. Among these values, there are certain values which are not practicable in the present social set-up such as non-accumulation of things

(*Aparigrih*), austerity, etc. From the historical point of view, these traditional values are of vital significance as they had been found to be a good instrument for changing the individual and society at large. Operational values are those which are practicable in the present social set-up. These are called functional or behavioural values also.

Women can make the best use of both the types of values cited for building the desired character of their students/children specially at the primary age. Character is the sum-total of traits and habits, formed not only at school but also at home. At home female member has a major part to play. In order to identify the causes of indiscipline among students in school situation, a very interesting and useful study was undertaken (NCERT), Project Report No. 6 (1979). An opinionnaire was given to 30 students of a school. On the analysis of the opinionnaire, it was found that 60 per cent of 30 students held the home responsible for indiscipline among them. Further it was found that "lack of healthy atmosphere at home, improper training at home, parental over-indulgence, unhindered freedom and not teaching the rudiments of discipline at home were considered to be the causes for indiscipline among students. It will not be an exaggeration to state that in the present context female members of the home have to share the major responsibility of inculcating the subtle values like self-discipline among the children at home, which is the nucleus of character formation.

In the present set-up of society, working women have to shoulder dual responsibility, *i.e.*, of service and household. At the surface it seems that working women may not get sufficient time for inculcation of values among children at home. But working women, if they are sincere and honest in their jobs, have to internalize the values like co-operation, cleanliness, courage, courtesy, dignity of the individual, duly, discipline, endurance, good manner, hygienic living, integrity, punctuality, etc. in themselves. The very display of these values through their conduct is bound to have a lasting impact on the personalities of the children at home. Working women have to show more tolerance or endurance. It is here that working women lack endurance at times, due to which the children at home are debarred of love and affection which they deserve very much. This apparently results into their broken personalities.

Now women have entered almost all the spheres of society. May it be a teacher or police officer, doctor or nurse, engineer or astronaut, athlete or social worker, everywhere women have made a mark. Women can show excellence in the field of value-oriented education because of certain inherent qualities in them. They can play a very significant role in making the programme of Value Education a success at school/ college level. Our present educational efforts are mainly geared to providing an 'education for knowing' with some emphasis on 'education for doing'. Value Education or more rightly called Value-oriented Education should be regarded as an 'education for becoming' in which women as teachers in schools, colleges and universities can play an extremely significant role.

15

PROSPECTS OF VALUE EDUCATION

Stand up, be bold, be strong
Take the whole responsibility
On our own shoulders
And now that you are the creator
Of your own destiny
All the strength and succour
You want is within yourselves
Therefore, make your own future.

—Swami Vivekanand

The question of Value-oriented Education is not an isolated one, its interlinks being closely associated to other sub-systems of our social set up. Therefore, there cannot be any sure-shot or mechanical solution to the problem of Value-Education, as in its phenomena a cluster of opposites are involved, *i.e.*, emotion and reasoning, traditional curricula and modernity of science and technology, social behaviour patterns and actual learning experiences, etc. But during the present decade our educationists and authorities have started to express their serious concern to the problem of deterioration of moral, social and spiritual values, which have been damaging well-knit fibres of our strong and valuable cultural canvas and creating hurdles in the path of progress of the nation. Therefore, the concern to it, has been expressed from several quarters. Thus, value-oriented education is the crying need for the day, without which all our strategies may not work to fulfil the aspiration of the society for better education.

"It is being increasingly felt that no education can be complete or even worthwhile if it does not provide to the individual not only the knowledge of the history of moral, religious, and spiritual ideas which are a great part of human heritage but also a non-dogmatic but disciplined process by which the individual is enabled to imbibe those values, which seem to our human thought as indispensable to the survival of human race at the present critical juncture of human history and to the eventual development of a greater civilization than we have had hitherto."[1]

During the last four years the government has expressed the urgent need to formulate concrete and practical plans for value-oriented education. The High-level Conference held at Shimla on 27-28th May, 1981 is to be considered as one of the significant events in the history of 'Value Education'. During the two days conference deliberations were mainly centered round the meaning and scope of value-oriented education and formulating practical guidelines for governmental action. The conference recommended, *inter alia*, that value-orientation should be the central focus of education and that teachers should be given the necessary training in the effective methods of development of values among students and teachers. Besides this the conference made many revolutionary recommendations. The following is the summary of those recommendations:

1. Provision for value-oriented education should be made throughout the country with due regard for flexibility of approaches.
2. Value-oriented education should be regarded essentially as an education for becoming and self-exceeding. It should be viewed in the context of the present situation of man and the evolutionary process going on within him and his society.
3. Value-orientation should be the main focus of education.
4. This value-orientation should be not only for the children who are in the schools but also for those who are outside. Even parents should be involved in it. In fact, the whole society has to be involved in the programme of value-oriented education.
5. The learning process itself has a great bearing on the value-orientation of children. All activities in the school—curriculum making, instructional techniques and evaluation, etc. should be so designed that they lead to the spontaneous development of desirable values.
6. There is a need for producing literature especially designed for the value-orientation of education.
7. All teachers in the schools should be regarded as teachers of value education and all subjects including physical education can be used for inculcation of right values.

8. There should be an integrated approach in the value-oriented education programme. Instead of tackling piece meal such areas as awareness of ecology, environmental protection, community development, productivity, population stabilization, aesthetic education, national integration, understanding, etc., they should be handled in a comprehensive manner under the broad spectrum of social responsibility and inner development of human personality. Concerned Ministries of the Government should co-operate with one another in this nation-building task.
9. There should be foundation courses both at the secondary schools and universities aiming at giving the children basic knowledge about India, its people and cultural tradition. The course should also aim at making students feel proud of their country and responsible for its upliftment.
10. Some pilot projects for school improvement should be taken up and the Government of India should constitute a steering committee for this purpose.
11. There is a need for establishing a resource centre for literature on value-oriented education. Besides printed matter this centre should also produce 35 mm films emphasizing desirable values. An effective distribution system for making these materials available in all corners of the country should be developed.
12. Special schools designed for value-oriented education should be established. Every State should have at least one institution which may impart value-oriented education from nursery to the postgraduate level.
13. Special teacher-orientation programmes should be taken up at the state level to train teachers in the effective methods of development of values among students and teachers.
14. Some case-studies of schools, where value education is being imparted successfully, should be taken up.
15. There should be a national council for discipline consisting of people who would have moral authority in their own right, and who could guide development of value-education programmes. Members of this council could be invited by state educational authorities and other agencies concerned with education for guidance and advice.
16. There should be an education for the enforcement of law. A code of conduct for every class of persons should be developed and value-education programme for the whole society should

be so designed that everybody learns to respect the social order.

In order to undertake a review of the Teachers' Training Programme, particularly with a view to inculcate moral and social values in students, an informal Working Group was constituted under the chairmanship of Shri Kireet Joshi, then Educational Advisor (later on Special Secretary), Ministry of Education and Culture, in May 1981 with the following terms of reference:

(i) To suggest the necessary changes in the present content and scope of value-orientation in education with special reference to the need to ensure development and promotion among students and teachers not only of the highest values of physical, emotional, mental, aesthetic, moral and spiritual culture but also of those values which are uniquely Indian, and which would promote secularism, pride in heritage and composite culture;

(ii) To suggest a programme of the study of the national freedom struggle.

(iii) To suggest the curriculum content for teacher trainees to achieve the desired value-orientation;

(iv) To suggest special techniques of pedagogy for training in value orientation;

(v) To suggest strategies for reorienting serving teachers through inservice programmes;

(vi) To suggest ways of promoting participation of voluntary organisations in organising training courses for teachers;

(vii) To assess dimensions of effort required as also to indicate the extent of governmental inputs;

(viii) To make suggestions which would be relevant to the determination of the new roles of teachers as counsellors and guides instead of as mere lecturers; and

(ix) To determine the important tasks that teachers will need to undertake towards preparing the new educational materials keeping in view the challenges of our times.

The National Council of Educational Research and Training, New Delhi served as nodal agency for the purpose of the Working Group.

According to Prof. Venishankar Jha, a noted educationist, "The imperative need of the present time in our country is to create conditions necessary for cultivation of refined professional personality and life style for the teacher worthy of his personality and dignity as an inspirer and, to no small extent, as a fashioner of human destiny." For the proper professional growth of the teachers, the elevation of their social status is very essential. For this purpose, the working group has recommended establishment of a National Council of Teacher Education, very different in scope and purpose from the existing one. Besides this the working group has made many practical recommendations, which are as under:

(1) The curriculum relating to value education and to the study of Indian culture should be immediately implemented in all the teachers training institutions.

(2) Until the training institutions are remodelled on new lines as suggested in the report, an interim measure is recommended under which the teachers' training institutions should offer three new papers related to (i) and (ii) philosophy and psychology of value-oriented education and (iii) India and Indian values as optional papers in place of any other three papers which are at present prescribed in the teachers' training programme. In addition, teachers' training institutions may be recommended to incorporate in their total programme of teachers' education as many elements as possible from amongst all the various suggestions that have been made in this report in regard to value-orientation.

(3) Simultaneously, efforts should be initiated without delay, to introduce two streams of teacher training programmes (i) five-year teacher-education programme, after Senior Secondary, leading to master's degree in education and (ii) two-year teacher-education programme after the first three-year graduation or five-year post-graduation, leading to master's degree in education. These programmes would be designed on the basis of the pedagogical ideas, and value-oriented curricula suggested in this report.

(4) A provision may also be made on an optional basis for the two-year teacher-training programme in such a way that a teacher trainee could complete the full programme in two phases, the first phase being of one-year duration, and the second phase of not more than five-year duration during which the second-year programme could be covered, through summer-courses or other short-term courses. Those who have completed the first year

programme could have the possibility of appointment as teachers on probation.

(5) Pioneering and pace-setting value oriented institutions should be established, preferably one in each State, which should be utilised as centres for training teachers on the basis of the new ideas and values recommended in the report.

(6) A few national institutes of teacher education should be designed and established specially to educate the staff of the colleges of teacher education in India.

(7) An All India Public Examination for the evaluation of teacher trainees should be instituted which would have novel features such as the combination of the written test with oral test and submission of a project report; all of which would have a special thrust towards the promotion of excellence, value-education and a sound acquaintance with India and Indian values.

(8) Measures should be taken to eliminate various evils and deficiencies which are growing alarmingly in teacher training institutions.

(9) The above recommendations can be effectively implemented if a further proposal is implemented. The proposal is that the Central Government should by the exercise of its power under concurrency, create a national organisation which would have the following objectives:

 (a) To keep under review the institutions and programmes of teacher education in the country at all levels and to maintain high standards of teaching, research and examination in the field of teacher education with a view to developing attitudes, skills and personality which would reflect the image of the teacher embodied in this report.

 (b) To establish and to maintain: (i) Institute of Teacher Education—designed especially to educate the staff of the colleges of teacher education in India, and (ii) pace-setting model institutions of teacher education, preferably one in each State which should be utilised as centres for training and radiating new ideas and values in the region on the lines recommended in this report.

 (c) To provide aid, financial, material and human, and advice necessary for co-ordination and maintenance of high standards of teaching, examination and research and to stimulate thinking on problems of teacher education.

(d) To function as an accrediting authority with powers to recognise or derecognise teacher training institutions and degree awarded by them.

(e) To conceive of and implement programmes or strategies for bringing the existing teacher education institutions to conform to the aims and objects laid down by the Council.

(f) To organise, preparation and publication of variety of resource material including material for audio-visual aids and use of educational technology necessary for promoting high standards of work in teacher training institutions.

(g) To organise or support seminars, conferences, symposia as also to set up committees and panels for the promotion of the objectives, functions and activities of the Council.

(h) To perform such other functions as may be conducive to the realisation of the aims and objectives of teacher education visualised by the Council on the lines recommended in this report.

(10) It is further recommended that the present National Council of Teacher Education may itself be constituted as the above-mentioned national organisation with this difference in its constitution that it should have, in addition to present composition which consists of Union Minister of Education as President and 40 other members, an executive body consisting of a full-time Chairman and five full-time members to be appointed by the Central Government, which should have the power to appoint standing committees and other committees for carrying out various functions and responsibilities. The Member-Secretary of the Council will also be the Member-Secretary of the executive body. The Chairman and members should be eminent educationists, teachers and educational administrators.

On the recommendations of this Working Group follow-up action has already been started by Kendriya Vidyalaya Sangathan, New Delhi. In this regard KVS had issued directive to all its Regional Offices to conduct workshop on Value Education. In pursuance of the directive, three-day workshops were conducted in May-June 1985 by regional offices of KVS in order to acquaint the teachers with different aspects of value-oriented education and to prepare workable action plan. The objectives of the workshop were as follows:

1. To list the values to be inculcated among the students for each stage.
2. To list appropriate steps for inculcating the above values.
3. To specify the role of teachers and principals in the inculcation of proposed values.
4. To prepare minimum programme to be followed by the Region and KVS.

The author of these lines had an opportunity to direct one of such workshops on 'Value Education' in May 1985 at Pachmarhi and to present a working paper entitled "Value Education—Theory, Practice and Prospect." Each school of the Region was asked to sponsor two teachers for the workshop. The consolidated report based on the reports of Workshops of Value Education compiled by the Regions is expected to be published soon.

Value-orientation should be arch-theme of our education. Value-Oriented Education is indispensable in shaping the future of the society and country at large. For this purpose, the wholehearted co-operation of all formal and non-formal agencies of education is needed very much. In China proverbially it is said that you cannot prevent the birds of sorrow from flying over your head, but you can prevent them from building nests in your hair. Similarly if we cannot further strengthen the moral, ethical, social and professional values, at least, we can and we should stop further deterioration of these values in the wider interest of mankind. There is a great deal that most of us can individually do to check the deterioration and to enhance further strengthening of these values. Lastly one can but pray—

> "O, Lord! Grant me the serenity to accept the things I cannot change, courage to change the things I can and wisdom to know the difference."

REFERENCE

1. Prof. Kireet Joshi, Cyclostyled report of the Ministry of Education and Culture on the Working Group to Review Teachers' Training Programmes (In the light of the need for Value-orientation), p. 28.

APPENDICES

APPENDIX-I

Value Sheets

- — Brotherhood
- — Concern for others
- — Coexistence
- — Cleanliness
- — Discipline
- — Devotion
- — Devotion to Duty
- — Emotional balance
- — Equanimity
- — Endurance
- — Efficiency
- — Friendship
- — Freedom
- — Gratitude
- — Honesty
- — Humanism
- — Justice
- — Kindness
- — Leadership
- — Obedience
- — Purity
- — Peace
- — Punctuality
- — Quest for knowledge
- — Self-control
- — Self-help
- — Success *vs.* Reputation
- — To appreciate good work
- — Unity of faiths

Value Sheet 1

Brotherhood

God hath made of one blood all nations of men.

—New Testament

Of a truth men are mystically united; a mystic bond of brotherhood makes all men one.

—Carlyle

Until you have become really, in actual fact, as brother of everyone, brotherhood will not come to you.

—Fyodor Dostoyevski

What room for doubt and what for sorrow can there be in him who knows that all spiritual beings are the same in kind differing only in degree.

—Sri Krishna

1. What do you mean by 'brotherhood'?
2. How caste, creed and colour really become obstacles in the way of brotherhood?
3. Liberty, equality and fraternity—these are three important values. Of these which one you consider to be the most important?
4. How does the value of brotherhood help to maintain peace and harmony in the society?

Value Sheet 2

Concern for Others

Teach me to feel another's woe.
To hide the fault I see;
That mercy to others show
That mercy show to me.

—Pope

To feel much for others, and little for ourselves; to restrain our selfish and exercise our benevolent affections, constitutes the perfection of human nature.

—Adam Smith

1. What an individual will be called who does not have any concern for others?
2. While showing concern for your friend, what precautions you will take?
3. What concern you show to those—

(i) who keep your surroundings clean,
(ii) who produce cereals for you?

Value Sheet 3

Coexistence

We have put forward the Panchsheel of the Five Principles and spoken of peaceful coexistence. All this has no meaning if the hydrogen bomb pursues its triumphant and malevolent career. The principles and considerations which govern our mutual relations and the approach of the two countries to each other are as follows:

1. Mutual respect for each other's territorial integrity and sovereignty.
2. Mutual non-aggression.
3. Mutual non-interference in each other's internal affairs.
4. Equality and mutual benefit.
5. Peaceful coexistence.

—J.L. Nehru

1. Is there any particular nomenclature for five principles of co-existence? If so, what do you know about that?
2. How will you compare these five principles with the objectives of U.N.O.?
3. Out of these five principles, if you have to delete two which would you like to delete?
4. Collect details of Bandung Conference held in Jakarta in 1954. How is it significant with global peace point of view?

Value Sheet 4

Cleanliness

So great is the effect of cleanliness, that it extends even to his moral character. Virtue never dwelt long with filth; nor do I believe there ever was a person scrupulously attentive to cleanliness who was consummate villain.

—Rumford

Cleanliness is next to Godliness.

—John Wesley

1. What do we mean when we say that records of Mr. 'A' have been very clean?
2. Is there any relationship between cleanliness and character?
3. If you have to prefer one of these two—outward cleanliness and inward cleanliness, which one will you prefer?
4. What should we do to keep our environment clean?

Value Sheet 5

Discipline

Historically, those people that did not discipline themselves had discipline thrust upon them from the outside.

—Alistair Cooke, America

A stern discipline pervades all nature, which is a little cruel that it may be very kind.

—Edmund Spenser

(A) In one section of Class VII there is no teacher, but the students are doing their work quietly.

(B) In another section of the same Class students are making lot of noise and not maintaining order in the absence of the teacher. But as soon as the teacher arrives they become perfectly silent.

1. These are two models of discipline. Which one is better? Endorse reasons for each..
2. What do you do to maintain discipline on the play-ground or during functions and celebrations?

Value Sheet 6

Devotion

A man who perfects himself in devotion finds springing up in the progress of time this spiritual knowledge which is superior to and comprehends every action without exception.

—Shri Krishna

The mother, the father and the preceptor should be lovingly served with body, mind and money.

—Swami Dayanand

1. In our *Upanishad* it is said—

   "मातृदेवो भव, पितृदेवो भव, अतिथिदेवो भव।"

   (Be one to whom Mother is as God, be one to whom Father is as God, be one to whom a Guest is as God.)

   In the light of these dictums list your duties towards mother, father and other elderly persons in the family.
2. Give some examples of devotees.
3. How did Gandhiji perform his duties towards his parents?

Value Sheet 7

Devotion to Duty

No personal consideration should stand in the way of performing a public duty.

—Ulysses S. Grant

Duty determines destiny.

—William Mackinley

The reward of one duty done is the power to fulfil another.

—George Eliot

The habit of one's duty drives away fear.

—Charles Baudelaire

Only duty is thy concern and not the fruit. Let not the fruit of action be your object, nor let your attachment be to inaction.

—*The Bhagavadgita*, 2.47

1. Should duty be supreme concern of an individual? If so, why?
2. How far you agree with the saying that "duty determines destiny"? Give reasons.
3. Duty and destiny—are both essential for one's success in life?
4. Have you come across such situation where emotion has played its role while performing duty? What was the outcome?
5. Enumerate your own duties as a student.

Value Sheet 8

Emotional Balance

Let the people praise you or blame you, let fortune smile or frown upon you, let your body fall today or after a *Yuga*, see that you do not deviate from the path of truth. How much of tempests and waves one had to weather, before one reaches the heaven of Peace. The greater a man has become, the fiercer ordeal he has had to pass through.

—Swami Vivekanand (VII.126)

Only those are the great who do not move even in the presence of movable moments.

—Kalidas

O to be self- balance for contingencies!
O to confront night, storms, hunger, ridicule, accidents, rebuffs as the trees and animals do.

—Walt Whitman

1. Give very simple example of emotional balance.
2. Have you ever come across a scene of emotional imbalance in a classroom or playground? What was your reaction thereupon?
3. How is emotional balance helpful to the individual?
4. Reeta wanted a pen from Lata. Lata asked Reeta to wait just for a while. In spite of waiting Reeta snatched away the pen from Lata. Was Lata wrong? Why?

Value Sheet 9

Equanimity
(Evenness of mind or temper)

If you can talk with crowds and keep your virtue, or walk with kings—nor lose the common touch, if neither foes nor loving friends can hurt you, if all men count with you, but none too much, if you can fill the unforgiving minute with sixty seconds worth of distance run, yours is the earth and everything that's in it, and—which is more—you will be a man, my son.

—R. Kipling

1. What is the point in the above poem titled 'if' by R. Kipling.
2. Do you feel any difference while talking to your poor friend and rich friend?
3. How many close friends you have? Are they very close to you? Justify your own statements.

Value Sheet 10

Endurance

The manner in which one endures what must be endured is more important than the thing that must be endured.

—Dean Acheson, Quoted
Merle Miller, Plain Speaking: An Oral Biography Harry S. Truman

Not in the achievement, but in the endurance of the human soul, does it show its divine grandeur and its alliance with the infinite God.

—E.H. Chapin

1. What are the other synonyms of the word 'endurance'?
2. How will you observe this virtue at home?
3. Give some examples of great persons who excelled in this virtue.
4. Narrate some anecdote from Gandhi's biography, which may depict this virtue.

Value Sheet 11

Efficiency

Efficiency means learning to do things in the best, easiest and quickest way to achieve not only material accomplishments but your other goals of life as well.

Therefore, efficiency is purpose, practice, patience, the ability to use your passions and emotions, likes and dislikes, habits and experience.

It is alertness, presence of mind, readiness to adjust yourself to the unexpected, impinging the ego against negative events and situations until they give way.

Efficiency means controlling yourself, your family and your work instead of being controlled by them. It means making use of your time and talent so that you live to the full at the important fields of your life, work, play, love and service.

'Efficiency', writes John Gillin, 'is another ideal value, sometimes, of course, not followed. In line with the mechanistic worldview it is held that all things should operate to the full extent of their inherent capacities and at the lowest cost in whatever terms. This applies not only to machines, but also to social organisations and personalities.'[1]

1. What do you mean by an efficient student?
2. Mention a few suggestions you would like to give to your friend to win efficiency?
3. Explain the phrase "making use of time and talent."
4. Efficiency is not money-making—discuss this with your friends.
5. "Perfectionism is the enemy of efficiency"—What is the point in saying so?

Value Sheet 12

Friendship

A friend is one before whom I may think aloud.

—R.W. Emerson

The firmest friendships have been formed in mutual adversity. Iron is most strongly united in the fiercest flame.

—C.C. Colton

Let friendship creep gently to a height. If it rushes to it, it may soon run itself out of breath.

—Thomas Fuller

Tirelessly benevolent,
Save a friend on evil bent,
This is sainthood's perfect song,
Every substitute is wrong.

—*Panchatantra*

The friendships which last are those wherein each friend respects the other's dignity to the point of not really wanting anything from him.

—Cyril Connolly,
The Unquiet Grave, 1945

Comprehension must be the soil in which grow all the fruits of friendship.

—Woodrow Wilson, Speech,
Mobile Alabama, 1913

A friend in power is a friend lost.

—Henry Brooks Adams

1. What does friendship mean to you?
2. How do you befriend the people?

3. Narrate some story to justify the saying that a friend in power is a friend lost. Recall the story of Drona and Drupad (*Mahabharata*).
4. It is said that the firmest friendships have been formed in mutual adversity. Do you have any experience, which may testify this saying?
5. How important do you think it is to develop and maintain friendship?

Value Sheet 13

Freedom

Freedom is the gift of God—the right of every nation—you may claim it. But if you claim it by any means that are repugnant to God, it will not be blessing for you.

—Mahatma Gandhi (From a speech), October 1928

There will be no freedom in this country or in the world so long as a single human being is unfree.

—Jawaharlal Nehru

Freedom exists only where people take care of the Government.

—Woodrow Wilson
Speech, New York, 22 Sep. 1912

Christianity promises to make men free, it now promises to make them independent.

—W.R. Inge, The Philosophy of Plotinus, 1929

A society in which men recognize no check upon their freedom soon becomes a society where freedom is a possession of only a savage few.

—Judge Learned Hand,
Life Magazine, 1 July 1944

1. Is there any relationship between freedom and prosperity of an individual? If yes, explain how?
2. Why it is said that freedom exists only where people take care of the Government?
3. Equality, liberty and fraternity—these are 3 virtues. Rearrange these words in order of importance.
4. India attained freedom through non-violence. Quote other 2 examples from the World History.

Value Sheet 14

Gratitude

Gratitude is a fruit of great cultivation, you do not find it among gross people.

—Samuel Johnson

He who receives a good turn should never forget it, he who does one should never remember it.

—Charron

The obligation of gratitude may easily become a trap, and the young are often caught and maimed in it.

—Eric Gill, Autobiography

1. **If someone has done something good to us, should we forget it? If not, why?**
2. **If you have done some good to somebody, will it be wise to remember the same?**
3. **Sometimes obligation of gratitude may become a trap for the individual. Narrate some incident to justify the statement.**
4. **How do you feel, if you do not express gratitude at the occasion for the good done to you by him/her?**

Value Sheet 15

Honesty

No legacy is so rich as honesty.

—Shakespeare

A straight line is shortest in morals as well as in Geometry.

—Rahel

1. **What do you mean by 'honesty' as a student?**
2. **How do you observe honesty at home while behaving with your elder/younger brothers and sisters?**
3. **What will/will not you do to observe honesty—**
   - **(a) At the dining table**
   - **(b) While doing homework**
   - **(c) While writing your Unit Test/Examination Paper**
   - **(d) While playing with younger friends.**

Value Sheet 16

Humanism

If you cannot believe in God, humanism is next best thing.

—Lord Longford, Diary of A Year

To serve humanity is to serve God.

—Anon

1. **There are famous Urdu couplets—**

   सभी कुछ हो रहा है इस तरक्की के जमाने में।
   मगर यह क्या गजब है आदमी इन्सां नहीं होता।।
   जब कि दुश्वार है काम का आसान होना।
   आदमी को भी मयस्सर नहीं इन्सां होना।।

   What is the point in the above couplets? How will you explain it.
2. **List all those qualities you would like to incorporate under 'humanism'?**

Value Sheet 17

Justice

The sentiment of justice is so natural and so universally accepted by all mankind, that it seems to be independent of all law, all party, all religions.

—Fancois Marie Voltaire

I have always held that social justice, even to the least and the lowliest, is impossible of attainment by force.

—Mahatma Gandhi

Justice discards party, friendship and kindred and is, therefore, represented as blind.

—Joseph Addison

We love justice greatly, and just men but little.

—Joseph Roux

Justice is itself the great standing policy of civil society and any departure from it, under any circumstances, lies under the suspicions of being no policy at all.

—Edmund Burke

1. What is social justice? Can it be attained by force?
2. Do you love justice? Why?
3. Someone has done justice to his job, but that caused harm to you. Will you hate that person. If not, why?

Value Sheet 18

Kindness

Kindness has the effect of balm; it soothes suffering, softens pride, dissipates selfishness and exorcises bad temper.

—B. Hedley

Kindness is the golden chain by which society is bound together.

—Goethe

Little deeds of kindness, little words of love. Help to make earth happy like the heaven above.

—Julia A.F. Carney

A kind heart is a fountain of gladness, making everything in its vicinity freshen into smiles.

—Washington Irving

The cheapest of all things is kindness, its exercise requiring least possible trouble and self-sacrifice.

—S. Smiles

Ask thyself daily to how many ill-minded persons thou hast shown a kind disposition.

—Marcus Antoninus

1. Enumerate those deeds of kindness, which you can exercise in your routine life.
2. How will you observe kindness towards birds and animals?
3. Narrate some incident of kindness which impressed you much.
4. What are the advantages of kindness in one's life?

Value Sheet 19

Leadership

Courage, endurance, fearlessness and above all self-sacrifice are the qualities required for our leaders. A person exhibiting these qualities in their fullness would certainly be able to lead the nation; whereas the most finished orator, if he has not these qualities, must fail.

—Mahatma Gandhi

One of the tests of leadership is the ability to recognize a problem before it becomes an emergency.

—Arnold Glasgo

The most important quality in a leader is to be acknowledged as such. All leaders whose fitness is questioned are clearly lacking in force.

—Andra Maurois, The Art of Living

All of the great leaders have had one characteristic in common; it was the willingness to confront unequivocally the major anxiety of their people in their time. This, and not much else, is the essence of leadership.

—J.K. Galbraith, The Age of Uncertainty, 1977

The art of leadership consists in consolidating the attention of people against a single adversary and taking care that nothing will split that attention.

—Adolf Hitler, Mein Kamph, 1924

1. What are 4 essential qualities for leadership?
2. What is the most important quality of a leader?
3. List a few names of great leaders of various fields, *i.e.*, Social leaders, Political leaders, Religious leaders, etc.
4. What qualities of leadership you will try to exhibit as a School Captain or Secretary of Students' Union?

Value Sheet 20

Obedience

Wicked men obey from fear, good men from love.

—Aristotle

Whoever strives to withdraw from obedience, withdraws from grace.

—Thomas A. Kempis

Obedience is mother of success and is wedded to safety.

—Aeschylus

The way of obedience at last brings him to the door of salvation.

—Guru Nanak

But head and roof of the law and the launch and the hump is—obey!

—R. Kipling

1. What do you mean by 'obedience'?
2. How do you practise it at school or college?
3. Write a paragraph on "obedience is mother of success."
4. If you have to make a choice between obedience from fear and obedience from love—which one you will prefer?

Value Sheet 21

Purity

Blessed are the pure in heart; for they shall see God.

—*New Testament*

Through the practising of Benevolence, Tenderness, Complacency, and Disregard for objects of happiness, grief, virtue and vice, the mind becomes purified.

—Patanjali

Purity is the ability to contemplate defilement.

—Simone Weil, Gravity and Grace, 1914

1. Raghu keeps himself very neat and clean by taking bath, etc. daily. But he is in habit of telling a lie and befooling others. Would you say that he has purity? If yes, how? If not, why?
2. Outwardly purity is better or inner purity?
3. If you have to select one of these two, what one will you prefer? Why?
4. You might have heard the name of cobbler saint Raidas. He used to say—*Man changa to kathauti men Ganga* (if cobbler is pure in heart and mind water in his wooden bowl is as pure as that of Ganges).
   What is the point in this saying?

Value Sheet 22

Peace

Where there is no peace, there is no limit of sufferings.

—Swami Dayanand

Men of true discernment, first
Try reconciliation;
For victories of peace
Suffer no frustration.

—*Panchatantra*

Peace cannot be kept by force. It can only be achieved by understanding.

—Albert Einstein
Notes on Pacifism

It is far easier to make war than to make peace.

—Georges Clemenceau,
Verdum, 14 July 1919

The mere absence of war is not peace.

—John F. Kennedy

Peace is not only better than wars but infinitely more arduous.

—George Bernard Shaw,
Heartbreak House, Preface, 1920

1. Why it is said that mere absence of war is not peace?
2. Can peace be kept by force? If not, why?
3. Why peace is necessary in society and in the nation at large?
4. Do you envisage any sort of relationship between peace and prosperity or discord and suffering?

Value Sheet 23

Punctuality

Punctuality is a form of self-indulgence.

—Robert Lynd

Punctuality is the stern virtue of men of business and the graceful courtesy of princes.

—Lytton

1. What do you mean by punctuality?
2. What is the difference between regularity and punctuality?
3. Can one be regular without being punctual? If so, how? Explain.
4. Punctuality and regularity are two components of 'self-discipline'. Mention other main components of 'self-discipline'.

Value Sheet 24

Quest for Knowledge

There is no purifier like knowledge. He,.who has attained purity of heart through practice of *Karmayoga*, automatically realizes it in the self in course of time.

—*The Bhagavadgita*

That jewel of knowledge is great riches, which is not plundered by kinsmen, not carried off by thieves, nor decreased by giving.

—Bhartrihari

Real knowledge, like everything else of the highest value, is not to be obtained easily. It must be worked for, studied for, thought for; and more than all, it must be prayed for.

—Arnold

Science is organized knowledge.

—Spencer

Learn to live, and live to learn,
Ignorance like a fire doth burn,
Little tasks make large return.

—Taylor

The word knowledge strictly employed, implies three things, *viz.*, truth, proof and conviction.
Knowledge is like money, the more a man gets, the more he craves.

—Shaw

All wish to possess knowledge, but few, comparatively speaking, are willing to pay the price.

—Juvenal

Learning without thought is labour lost; Thought without learning is perilous.

—Confucius

I had six honest serving men, they taught me all I knew; their names were where and what and when—and why and how and who.

—R. Kipling

Learning is wealth to the poor, an honour to the rich, an aid to the young and support and comfort to the aged.

—Lavater

1. Why knowledge is said to be one of the riches? What is its peculiarity?
2. How knowledge is support and comfort to the aged and aid to the young?
3. In what respect knowledge is compared to money?
4. What is the point in saying that learning without thought is labour lost?

Value Sheet 25

Self-Control

There is nothing in our society today which would conduce to self-control. Our very upbringing is against it.

—Mahatma Gandhi

The highest object of man's life is to free himself entirely from all three classes of pain, etc., the ills arising from other creatures, and the suffering caused by natural forces such as excessive indiscipline of mind and senses.

—Swami Dayanand

It is the whole history of mankind that power lacking the inner strength of self-restraint will be eventually cast down.

—Adlai Stevenson

1. What is the highest aim of life?
2. Why self-discipline is said to be necessary?
3. What do you mean by control of mind?
4. What do you mean by control of senses?
5. Is control of senses possible without control of mind? If yes, how? If no, why?
6. Narrate some story reflecting a series of troubles, for the individual for want of self-control.

Value Sheet 26

Self-Help

"One should lift oneself up by one's own efforts and should not degrade oneself; for one's own self is one's friend and one's own self is one's enemy."

—*The Bhagavadgita,* VI/5

Every man is the author of his own fortune.

—Sallust

It is vain to ask of the Gods what a man is capable of supplying for himself.

—Epicurus

1. What do you mean by 'self-help'?
2. How do you practise it at home?
3. "One should never degrade oneself"—what is the point in this saying?
4. There is a famous couplet in Urdu:

   इन्सां ही मुकम्मल है जमीं पे जन्नत लाने को।
   तू खुदा की आरजू न कर, जुश्तजू न कर।।

   How will you compare this couplet with the saying of 'Epicurus' cited above?

Value Sheet 27

Success *vs.* Reputation

"Chuan-sun Shih inquired under what conditions a gentleman could be said to have succeeded."

"What do you mean by success?"

"To have good reputation both in the state and within one's own home."

"This is reputation, it is not success. The one who has succeeded is upright in his very substance and fond of justice. While watching his every word and facial expression, he is concerned with placing himself below others. Then both in the state and within his own home he is considered to have succeeded. The man with merely a reputation assumes the attitude of manhood-at-its-best, but his every action belies it. Nevertheless, within himself he never doubts but that he is man-at-its-best. Thus, he has a good reputation both in the state and within his own home."

—The Sayings of Confucius, James R. Ware, p. 80

1. How important do you think it is to have good reputation both in the state and within his own home.
2. Can a man be called successful who does not have reputation at his own home? If no, why?

3. Write a paragraph on a Man-at-his-best.
4. Narrate a few personal qualities of a man, who has achieved success in real sense?

Value Sheet 28

To Appreciate Good Work

People have been known to resort to every artifice to find out what their friends and admirers think and say of them.

More than fame and more than money.
It is the comment kind and sunny,
And the hearty, warm approval of a friend;
For it gives to life a savour,
And it makes us stronger, braver,
Yes, it gives us heart and courage to the end.
If he earns your praise, bestow it!
If you like him, like him now!
Let the words of true encouragement be said,
Do not wait till life is over,
And he's underneath the clover,
For he cannot read the tombstone when he's dead!

—Berton Brayley

Be quick to praise and slow to censure, and you will be surprised at the change in your home, office or in the factory.[2]

1. Why one should be quick in praising good work?
2. Why one should be slow to censure?
3. Have you ever tried to find out what your friends think of you? Write your personal experiences thereupon.
4. Have you ever realised the effects of good and kind comments? Narrate your personal experiences.

Value Sheet 29

Unity of Faiths

If God be within the mosque, then to whom does this world belong? If Rama be within the image, then who is there to know what happens without?

Hari is in the east, Allah in the west. Look within your heart, for there you will find both Karim and Rama.
All the men and women of the world are His living forms.
Kabir is the Child of Allah and Rama. He is my Guru.
He is my *pir*.
Vain, too, are the distinctions of caste.
All shades of colour are but broken arcs of light.
All varieties in human nature are but fragments of humanity.
The right to approach God is not the monopoly of Brahmans, but belongs to all who are sincere of heart.

—(based on the works of Kabirdas)[3]

1. Are Hari and Allah one and the same? If yes, how will you convince your friend of this speculation?
2. If there God is mosque or temple? Collect some couplets of Kabir on this very theme.
3. Why Kabir has mentioned himself as Child of Rama and Allah?
4. According to Kabir what is the right approach to God?

REFERENCES

1. J. Maurus, *How to Win Personal Efficiency*, pp. 15-16.
2. *Ibid.*, p. 40.
3. A.L. Shrivastava, *Medieval Indian Culture*, p. 47.

APPENDIX-II

Code of Conduct for Students in Different Situations and Occasions*

Formation of Healthy Habits and Right Attitudes

In the Vidyalaya campus:

1. General

(a) They should wish the teachers whenever they come across any teacher of the Vidyalaya.

(b) They should walk properly while going into or coming out of the classrooms. They should avoid running and rushing.

(c) They should avoid walking and talking and assembling in front of the Principal's office or classrooms.

(d) They should not loiter in the Vidyalaya campus.

(e) When they need to go out of the classroom, they should walk gently without causing disturbance to the other classes.

(f) They should not walk in groups or with their hands on the shoulders of the other students.

(g) They should walk gently in a line while going to library, playground or for SUPW classes.

(h) They should not leave the Vidyalaya campus without permission of the class teacher or subject teachers.

(i) They should not cause any damage to the plants or trees of the school campus.

(j) They should not write on the walls or doors.

2. Inside the Classroom

(a) They should not disturb the seating arrangement of the class.

(b) They should take care of their chair and desk.

(c) They should sit in the chair allotted to them and should never sit in the chair of the teacher in his/her absence.

(d) In the absence of the teacher they should study some subject or do some reading. In no case they should make a noise or indulge in quarrels and other undesirable activities.

---

* Evolved in the workshop on 'Value Education' held at Pachmarhi in May 1985 under the directorship of the author.

(e) They should not write on the blackboard, but keep it clean for the next period.

(f) They should keep their classroom neat and clean.

3. During Interval

(a) They should not loiter without purpose inside the building.

(b) They should eat their lunch in the place assigned for them sitting properly in a group and pick up the residuals or bits and leave the place neat and clean.

(c) They should wait patiently for their turn standing in a line for drinking water at the tap.

(d) They should go into their classes well in time when the interval is over.

(e) They should wash their hands clean before and after taking their lunch.

4. Inside the Library

(a) They should read silently without causing any damage to the books, magazines and newspapers.

(b) They should put the books/magazines in their proper place when the period is over.

(c) They should make no mark at the pages of the books and should not write anything in them.

(d) They should not tear off anything from the books or magazines.

5. While coming from Home to School

(1) Students should be dressed up in well-groomed uniform. They should feel proud of their uniform.

(2) They should keep left while walking or cycling along the road.

(3) They should bring their books and notebooks strictly as per their time-table of the day.

(4) They should not stop on the way for roadside stones, if any, and avoid talking to the strangers.

(5) They should not be tempted to ask for a lift from the strangers.

(6) On reaching the school they should straightway go to their classrooms.

6. When School is Over

(1) Students should come out of their classes one by one gently and silently.

(2) They should switch off the fan and shut the window before leaving the classroom.
(3) They should set the furniture in order before they leave the room.
(4) They should walk up to the bus patiently and get into the bus one by one according to their turn giving priority to small children.
(5) Inside the bus, they should sit properly without indulging in boisterous laughter, making noise, passing comments and struggling for seats.
(6) They should be courteous to the bus drivers and conductors.
(7) They should not take out any limb of the body while the bus is running.
(8) Avoid jumping from the bus in motion while getting down.
(9) On reaching home give a gentle knock or push to the door. Avoid shouting for the opening of the door.
(10) Give a gentle smile to the parents, brothers and sisters on reaching home.

7. During Functions and Celebrations

(1) They should perform the tasks earnestly and sincerely assigned to them.
(2) They should sit properly only in their seats or at the place assigned to them.
(3) They should give due honour to the audience by sitting silently and behaving courteously and respectfully.
(4) They should extend full co-operation to the organizers of the function.
(5) They should take active part in the success of the programme in the best way and perform the duties assigned to them willingly.
(6) They should not crowd around the stage and leave their place in the middle of the programme.

8. While conversing with the Teachers, Principals and Elders

(1) They should talk to their elders politely and with due respect to them.
(2) They should not stand with their hands in their pockets.
(3) They should not have chewing gums in their mouth while talking to the elders.

(4) They should not interfere when they are talking to somebody else or is busy with his work.

(5) 'Thank you', 'sorry' and 'beg your pardon' should be amply used when the occasion demands.

APPENDIX-III

Code of Ethics for Teachers*

We, the members of the National Education Association of the United States, hold these truths to be self-evident:

— that the primary purpose of education in the United States is to develop citizens who will safeguard, strengthen and improve the democracy obtained through a representative government;

— that the achievement of effective democracy in all aspects of American life and the maintenance of our national ideals depend upon making acceptable educational opportunities available to all;

— that the quality of education reflects the ideals, motives, preparation and conduct of the members of the teaching profession; and

— that whoever chooses teaching as a career assumes the obligation to conduct himself in accordance with the ideals of the profession.

As a guide for the teaching profession, the members of the National Education Association have adopted this code of professional ethics. Since all teachers should be members of a united profession, the basic principles herein enumerated apply to all persons engaged in 'the professional aspects of education—elementary, secondary and collegiate.

First Principle: *The primary obligation of the teaching profession is to guide children, youth and adults in the pursuit of knowledge and skills, to prepare them in the ways of democracy and to help them to become happy, useful, self-supporting citizens. The ultimate strength of the nation lies in the social responsibility, economic competence and moral strength of the individual American.*

In fulfilling the obligations of this first principle the teacher will—

1. Deal justly and impartially with students regardless of their physical, mental, emotional, political, economic, social, racial or religious characteristics.
2. Recognize the differences among students and seek to meet their individual needs.

---

* Adopted in 1952 by the National Education Association, U.S.A., p. 392.

3. Encourage students to formulate and work for high individual goals in the development of their physical, intellectual, creative and spiritual endowments.
4. Aid students to develop an understanding and appreciation not only of the opportunities and benefits of American democracy but also of their obligations to it.
5. Respect the right of every student to have confidential information about himself withheld except when its release is to authorized agencies or is required by law.
6. Accept no remuneration for tutoring except in accordance with approved policies of the governing board.

Second Principle: *The member of the teaching profession shares with parents the task of shaping each student's purposes and acts towards socially acceptable ends. The effectiveness of many methods of teaching is dependent upon co-operative relationship with the home.*

In fulfilling the obligations of this second principle the teacher will—

1. Respect the basic responsibility of parents for their children.
2. Seek to establish friendly and co-operative relationship with the home.
3. Help to increase the student's confidence in his own home and avoid disparaging remarks which might undermine that confidence.
4. Provide parents with information that will serve the best interests of their children, and be discrete with information received from parents.
5. Keep parents informed about the progress of their children as interpreted in terms of the purposes of the school.

Third Principle: *The teaching profession occupies a position of public trust involving not only the individual teacher's personal conduct but also the interaction of the school and the community. Education is most effective when these many relationships operate in a friendly, co-operative and constructive manner.*

In fulfilling the obligations of the third principle the teacher will—

1. Adhere to any reasonable pattern of behaviour accepted by the community for professional person.

2. Perform the duties of citizenship and participate in community activities with due consideration for his obligation to his students, his family and himself.
3. Discuss controversial issues from an objective point of view, thereby keeping his class free from partisan opinions.
4. Recognise that the public schools belong to the people of the community, encourage lay participation in shaping the purposes of the school, and strive to keep the public informed of the educational programme which is being provided.
5. Respect the community in which he is employed and be loyal to the school system, community, state and nation.
6. Work to improve education in the community and to strengthen the community's moral, spiritual and intellectual life.

Fourth Principle: *The members of the teaching profession have inescapable obligations with respect to employment. These obligations are nearly always shared employee responsibilities based upon mutual respect and good faith.*

In fulfilling the obligations of this fourth principle the teacher will—

1. Conduct professional business through the proper channels.
2. Refrain from discussing confidential and official information with unauthorized persons.
3. Apply for employment on the basis of competence only, and avoid asking for a specific position known to be filled by another teacher.
4. Seek employment in a professional manner, avoiding such practices as the indiscriminate distribution of applications.
5. Refuse to accept a position when the vacancy has been created through unprofessional activity or pending controversy over professional policy or the application of unjust personnel practices and procedures.
6. Adhere to the conditions of a contract until service thereunder has been performed, the contract has been terminated by mutual consent or the contract has otherwise been legally terminated.
7. Give and expect due notice before a change of position is to be made.
8. Be fair in all recommendations that are given concerning the work of other teachers.

9. Accept no compensation from producers of instructional supplies when one's recommendations affect the local purchase or use of such teaching aids.
10. Engage in no gainful employment outside of his contract where the employment affects adversely his professional status or impairs his standing with students, associates and the community.
11. Co-operate in the development of school policies and assume one's professional obligations thereby incurred.
12. Accept one's obligation to the employing board for maintaining a professional level of service.

Fifth Principle: *The teaching profession is distinguished from many other occupations by the uniqueness and quality of the professional relationships among all other teachers. Community support and respect are influenced by the standards of teachers and their attitude towards teaching and other teachers.*

In fulfilling the obligations of this fifth principle the teacher will—

1. Deal with other members of the profession in the same manner as he himself wishes to be treated.
2. Stand by other teachers who have acted on his behalf and at his request.
3. Speak constructively of other teachers but report honestly to responsible persons in matters involving the welfare of students, the school system and the profession.
4. Maintain active membership in professional organizations and through participation, strive to attain the objectives that justify such organised groups.
5. Seek to make professional growth continuous by such procedures as study, research, travel, conferences and attendance at professional meetings.
6. Make the teaching profession so attractive in ideals and practices that sincere and able young people will want to enter it.

APPENDIX-IV

Inculcation of Value Through Stories

Exposition of various ethical, moral, social and spiritual values through stories has been a pet device with our ancient seers. This very device has been found to be so effective and fruitful that in the medieval and modern times also it has been adopted for the purpose.

Here in this appendix six such stories are given. The values and value-tenets implied in these stories are as follows:

1. **How Much Land does a Man Need**—In this famous Russian story Tolstoy narrates the tragic fate of a man who sought to find his enduring happiness in the amassing of great riches. To seek happiness in amassing of wealth is not a right path—is the suggestive sense of the story. Further it proves that *a man's life doth not consist in the abundance of things which he possesseth*. Though dead, Pakkom, main character of the story, will live in the world's literature as a reminder of the folly of seeking enduring happiness in piled-up riches and even more riches. A moment comes when the fingers finally clutch the object of their long pursuit, death intervenes to release their grip. The very folly causes worry and anxiety to a man and fills him with vexation of spirit.
2. **Gargi**—It describes the nature of Atman (a great soul) as well as the existence of *Brahman* (Universal Creator). The aim of the story is to acquaint the readers with these two basic value-tenets of Indian culture. It also establishes that it is spiritualism and constant quest for it our ancestors stood for and not materialism.
3. **Sudama**—This is a very popular story found to be in Hindu scriptures. Friendship is an important value component visualized in this story. Friendship between Lord Krishna and Sudama was an ideal one. This is an excellent example of ideal friendship.
4. **Booker Washington**—This is the story of a Negro in America who was born a slave, but who became free and attained covetous position in the society through his hard work, sincerity and righteousness. The aim of the story is to help the students

to grasp Booker Washington's vision of what education really means and to inspire them with admiration for his courage. If presented properly the story will definitely bear the desired fruits.

5. **Helen Keller**—This is a story about a girl who, although she was both blind and deaf, managed to get a college education. The aim of the story is to realize how much they learn through what they see and hear. It will also inspire them with admiration for Helen Keller's magnificent courage, and help them to realise the great difficulties under which the blind and deaf get their education. The purpose of the story will be deemed to be served if the readers are inspired to show concern for the physically handicapped children and help them whenever and wherever they find an occasion to do so.
6. **Rabindranath Tagore**—This is the story of Rabindranath Tagore, a great poet of India, who won Nobel Prize for literature in 1913. Progressive thinkers of education are not complacent with the idea of having a garden in the school, but they propose to have a school in the garden. Rabindranath Tagore can be called a pioneer of this very progressive idea. In India he successfully tried to translate his dream of "school in garden" by establishing "Shantiniketan." The aim of the story is to help the children to realise their responsibility for beautifying their school. By this, they will be able to imbibe certain environmental values also, *i.e.*, love for plants, concern towards pollution, etc. They will also develop the sense of appreciation of fine arts and other objects of natural beauty.

How Much Land does a Man Need?

Pakkom, a peasant, was not rich, but had enough for himself and family. He was quite satisfied until one day he visited a richer relative in the city. Then envy consumed him and made him feel dissatisfied with his few acres. By selling a colt and half his bees, putting his son out as a labourer, and borrowing from his friends he was able, alongwith the few hundred rubles he had saved, to buy more acres. He ploughed fields, reaped his crops and was happy. Now he knew how much land a man needed to be perfectly happy.

Soon, however, the rumour reached him that people were migrating to new lands along the Volga, where rich fertile acres could be had for the asking. Selling his farm, Pakkom moved down into the Volga region where he staked out a still larger farm and prospered even more than before. Now Pakkom knew how many acres a man needed to find happiness.

Once again his contentment was disturbed by glowing accounts of land still more fertile in the territory of the Bashkirs where it could be purchased for a song. The prospects fascinated Pakkom, who thought that now he would have an estate second to none in the kingdom. Selling his farm and taking the proceeds, he travelled miles to the province of the Bashkirs.

Here he was told that for 1000 rubles he could have all the land which he could go around in a single day. The only stipulation was that if he did not return to the starting place within the day, his money would be forfeited. Here surely, thought Pakkom, was a bargain made to order for him. He was exultant. With his sturdy peasant legs, he knew that he could traverse an enormous tract of land—all the land which a man would need to make him happy.

As the first faint ray of the sun broke through the Eastern sky, Pakkom set out resolutely on his mission. It was a curious interest, thought Pakkom, with which the assembled Bashkirs watched his departure. Walking about a mile, he halted, scooped out some turf and piled it up to show which way he had passed, and then proceeded. On and on he plodded, quickening his pace and digging more pits. The sun was now high in the heavens. Perspiring under its rays, he still plodded on, convinced that it was too early to turn around.

Beautiful black soil with lush green grass stretched out before him. No, he could not forgo that. Pressing forward, he found that with each step the soil grew richer. Beginning now to grow weary, he was tempted to turn about, but still richer fields lured him on. "Just one hour more of hardship," he thought to himself, "and I shall be the richest in the kingdom and enjoy my riches for a life time." At last he noticed that the sun was already in the west, and so he turned sharply to the left to tramp on many miles in that direction, still more fertile land beyond, seemed as he pushed on and on.

Warned by the lengthening shadows he turned the second and the third corner, He now realized that he must quicken his pace, for the starting point was far away. His body ached, he was panting. His legs grew unsteady. Every nerve and muscle screamed for rest, but still he dared not stop. All his fortune was now at stake as he saw the sun sink lower in the darkening sky.

Walking would not get him there in time, so he began to run. He threw away his blouse, his boots, his flask. Weary and exhausted, he stumbled on. His mouth was parched, his throat was burning, his heart was pounding like the prancing hoofs of race horses. Perhaps he would fall dead. Yet he knew he could not stop now. He ran and ran. He could see now the top of the hill from which he started. Sure enough, there were the Bashkirs waiting.

Summoning all his remaining strength, Pakkom dragged himself up the hill, and reaching the summit threw himself forward that with outstretched hands he might reach the starting point. A stream of blood gushed from his mouth. He had reached the starting point. All the land he had covered was his. But he could not take it with him. He was dead. A Bashkir put an appraising eye upon his stature and dug a grave. Seven feet it measured from head to foot—just enough for the giant muzik they placed therein. Seven feet—that was all the land that Pakkom needed now.

GARGI

This famous story from a *Upanishad* brings out two important value-tenets—transmigration of *Atman* (the Great Soul) and existence of *Brahman* (the Universal Creator). Through these two value-tenets the story visualizes the style of thinking of our ancestors and thereby shaping their own life-patterns.

Janaka, King of the Videha Desa, once performed a Vedic sacrifice. At the end of it, he organised a philosophical competition among the seers who had gathered there. For the successful competitor he announced a prize of a thousand milch cows with precious gold coins tied in a bundle to the horns of every one of these animals.

The contest began. No one in the gathering had the courage to claim the prize, because they all had misgivings about their ability to hold their ground and worst the others in the philosophical tests. One sage, however, felt that he could defeat all others in the contest. His name was Yajnyavalkya. He threw the gauntlet by asking one of his disciples to drive the cattle home. Then started the opposition. One of the sages in the audience took up the challenge and started questioning Yajnyavalkya. The name of this bold challenger was Aswala. He was the high-priest in King Janaka's court. He asked Yajnyavalkya to define *Brahman*. The latter simply parried the question by giving the negative reply that he would bow to whomsoever *Brahman* had been revealed. Aswala next asked Yajnyavalkya to describe the manner in which a *Grihastha* (or householder) would conquer death. The latter's reply was that conquest over death could come to one through the worship of *Agni*, the God of

Fire. Aswala plied poor Yajnyavalkya with a number of other questions relating to the details of the various Vedic sacrificial rituals. Undaunted by the challenge Yajnyavalkya answered all these questions calmly and correctly. Not finding his own knowledge sufficient to floor the brave and erudite Yajnyavalkya, Aswala had to accept defeat. In the meantime, however, Aswala's attempt at defeating Yajnyavalkya had filled others in the assemblage with courage and, hence, the challenge continued. A few of the questions asked and replied given were as under:

Question: "Where is King Parikshit?"

Answer: "In the particular place in Heaven set apart for those who perform the great '*Aswamedayaga*' or the Horse-sacrifice of Kings.

Question: "What is *Atman* (the Great Soul)?"

Answer: "*Atman* or the Great Soul could not be known by questions and answers. It is omnipresent. It has neither a beginning nor an end. It could be reached only through meditation. One has to realise it oneself."

Thus, the questioning went on. Yajnyavalkya was unperturbed and answered all the questions correctly and with cool composure. Then emerged from those gathered there a woman-challenger. Her name was Gargi Vachaknavi. Her examination was of a far higher level than all the previous questioning and the following were the verbal duels between the two.

Question: "By what substance is the elementary matter pervading all the concrete things of the universe, itself pervaded?"

Answer: "By ether."

Question: "By what is that ether itself pervaded?"

Answer: "By *Brahmaloka*, the land of *Brahma*, the Universal Creator."

Question: "By what is that *Brahmaloka* pervaded?"

This was the limit of sage Yajnyavalkya's patience. It was obvious to him that there was more mischief than a genuine search for Truth in Gargi's questioning. The sage merely asked her to stop questioning for the mere sake of questioning. At this rebuff Gargi withdrew from the contest. This was, however, only temporary. She again came forward with her questions, but this time she was sincere. She said that she had only two final questions to put and stated them as under:

Question 1: "What is it that is both beyond and between the Heavens and the Earth and that is the past, the present as well as the future?"

Answer: "That which is Omnipresent through *Akasa* or ether is also the past, the present and the future."

Question 2: "What is that subtle substance which pervades through *Akasa* itself?"

Answer: "It is the Supreme Soul or Spirit which transcends everything else. It is without a beginning and has no end. It is all-pervading. It is present in every human being and experiences neither pain nor old age."

Gargi, the challenger from the fair sex, was completely satisfied with Yajnyavalkya's answers. The learned assembly acknowledged not only his superiority over all the others, but also admired the depth of Gargi's learning.

SUDAMA

During Lord Krishna's boyhood days he had a classmate whose name was Sudama. Both of them studied together as resident scholars under their teacher, Sandipani, at Ujjain.

Returning home on completion of his course of studies, Sudama married and commenced life as *grihasta* or householder, true to the teaching of the Hindu scriptural injunction. *Acharyaya priam dhanam ahrityam praja tantum mavyavatchetsihi* (an Upanishadic saying which means 'your studies having ended, pay your teacher his fees as per his heart's desire, go home, take a wife for a progeny and lead the life of a dutiful householder'). In course of time his partner in life bore him a large contingent of twenty-seven children. It is said that, not knowing how to name such a large number of young ones, he gave them the names of the twenty-seven stars of the Hindu Almanac.

Needless to say that, with so many mouths to feed, the poor man, not having been a person of any means even otherwise, was reduced to an extreme state of destitution. He did not have sufficient clothes to wear. Hence, his garments were always in tatters. On that score people had nicknamed him Kuchela (meaning 'the man in rags').

The unattached *Yogi* that he was, Kuchela was not in the least affected by the state of poverty he and his family were continually in. His poor wife was all skin and bones, she frequently not having had a square meal for several days on end. The drudgery in the house was a severe strain on her poor physique. Still she proved herself to be a fitting companion to her enlightened husband. She never uttered a word of complaint to him about their pitiable plight.

Sudama had fond memories of his stay in the household of his Guru, Sandipani, at Ujjain and of his intimacy during those days with his fellow-companion, the young Lord Krishna. He was never tired of regaling to his wife his memories of those happy and never-to-return days. On many an occasion he would speak to her about those boyhood days in terms somewhat as follows:

> "Young Krishna was beauty personified. His face, his gait, his talk, his smile, everything about him, in short, had a peculiar charm of its own. He was the idol of the other inmates of the Ashram. Long before we actually came to know of his royal parentage, we had all concluded that he must be a prince. Such were his noble qualities. It seems that he and his people have now moved from their native land of Mathura to a distant island called Dwaraka in the western seas, where he rules as king. Gone, alas! are those happy days I spent in his company, never, indeed! to return."

One day when Sudama was in one such reminiscent mood, his wife told him, "My dear, you speak so often so highly of your juvenile friend, Krishna, now a monarch, why not pay a visit to him, so that, taking pity on us in our present predicament, he might be moved to bestow on us some sort of wealth and relieve us of at least part of our misery. It is so hard, as you must yourself have noticed, to keep the wolf from the door."

Sudama's first reaction to this advice was to turn it down with an indifference, if not with contempt. His wife, however, kept on prodding him about it, so that, at last, he agreed to try it out. It was customary to take a present and offer it when one visited a king. What could poor Sudama carry with him? Not having anything of value in their own house, his wife somehow managed to obtain a loan from an obliging neighbour of a few handfuls of beaten rice and gave it to him to be taken as present to his friend. With that wonderful present tied into a small bundle with a piece of torn cloth, Sudama set out on his journey to Dwaraka to meet his old friend, Krishna.

From his place of residence it was a considerable distance to Dwaraka and the poor man had to trudge the whole of it. At long last he reached the city. With its lofty and beautiful buildings Dwaraka was a place of wonder which struck him dumb. Ujjain, the only other city he had seen in his life, paled into insignificance before the grandeur of this city.

His appearance in rags acted as a great handicap to him in his attempt to gain entrance into the king's palace. Somehow he managed it, thanks to the help given by a group of Brahmins who were also going in. Finally he found himself standing before his friend, Krishna, now Dwaraka's king. The latter was then sitting on his throne in his audience chamber alongwith his queen consort, Rukmini. On seeing his old friend, the king jumped down from his seat and welcomed him not only with a warm embrace, but also with all honours due to a visiting dignitary. Rukmini joined her royal husband in the reception accorded to Sudama, a poor Brahmin clad in tatters. The sight of the hospitality showered on the miserably-dressed and poor-looking Brahmin visitor by both their king and queen filled the entire royal household with wonder.

Sudama was then offered sumptuous and delicious refreshments. While he was munching these Krishna began to talk of their old days at Ujjain in Sandipani's school. He lovingly recalled many incidents that had occurred then. For example, he mentioned in some degree of detail of the incident in which himself and Sudama, having stayed away one day into the forests to get fuel for their preceptor's wife and, missing their way, spent the whole night in the dark jungle much to the dismay of the teacher and his wife.

The two friends spent a good deal of time in their reminiscent moods. Then, in the midst of those talks, as though remembering something suddenly, Krishna asked Sudama whether the latter had brought with him any present. Poor Sudama was really ashamed to untie the knot in the dirty, ragged piece of cloth of the bundle, which he had so far been hiding in his upper garments, and expose the 'precious' beaten rice he had brought. Krishna guessed the discomfiture of his companion and, saying, "Come, Come, dear man! don't be shy. Out with it. Let's see what it is" pulled it out from its hiding place.

Out came the beaten rice from Sudama's cloth bundle and Krishna, putting into his mouth a handful of it, ate it with such relish that one who saw it would think that it was a delicacy.

Sudama was with Krishna for a few happy days. To him it looked as though he were in heaven itself. Then the time became for his leaving the palace and returning home. Krishna's leave-taking was as affectionate as had been his reception, he this time actually walking some distance escorting his friend before parting company with him.

While wending his way home it struck Sudama that he had completely forgotten about the object of his visit. No doubt his royal friend had made affectionate and kind enquiries about Sudama's marriage, wife, children and his life in general as a *grihasta* (or householder), and all this had pleased him. But these mere enquiries did not cut the ice of his poverty. How was he to face his wife, who would surely be expecting her husband to come back laden with some riches to relieve them of their penury? For a fraction of a second he even wondered how his friend, Krishna, who must have surely noticed his miserable condition, had, of his (Krishna's) own accord, offered him no relief.

Then he consoled himself with the thought that Krishna had left him how he was, probably because of the natural corrupting influence of wealth. On that score he even felt happy that nothing had been done to better his lot.

With these thoughts running alternately in his mind he reached his village home. When he entered what he thought was the street in which his house stood, imagine his wonder on seeing in the place of that old hut from which he had commenced his journey to Dwaraka, a beautiful palace with garden testefully laid out all round it. Had he come to the wrong place?--He stood for a split second completely dazed and struck with wonder. It was only when his wife and children, all dressed in rich garments, came out of that gorgeous house and greeted him that he realised what had happened. He now knew that he had made no mistake about the place he had to return to. It was also clear to him now that the transformation in his absence had been the work of Krishna. "How gracious of him to repay me with all these riches in return for a humble gift of just a handful of beaten rice from me! Verily he is a God on Earth, to shower his blessings just when one is in need of these, unlike the cloud in the skies which pours its rain indiscriminately both when the farmer wants it and when he would even like to be without, as, in the latter case, the rain would prove destructive to his crops"—so saying, he reverted to his calm and quiet life of humility and devotion both to his duties and God. He also took care to see that his new-found riches did not puff him up with pride.

BOOKER WASHINGTON

(The Boy who struggled for an Education)

Booker Washington's mother was a Negro slave. His father was a white man, but Booker had never seen him. He lived with his mother and two younger children in a broken down hut. He was given no schooling and had to work very hard for their master. Every night his mother prayed that Lincoln would win in the Civil War then going on in America, so that she and her children might be free. When Booker was seven years old that prayer was answered. The Washington family went away to another part of the country where Booker worked for 12 hours a day in a salt-mine. He realised that if he wanted education he would have to get it for himself. So every night he stayed up late and taught himself to read and write.

One day he heard of Hampton, a school for ex-slaves. He made up his mind to get there somehow. He went as a house servant and worked so hard and well that his mistress helped him with his lessons. At last he had saved up a little money so he started off on the journey of 500 miles to Hampton. His money paid his fare on the coach for only 40 miles. For the rest he walked, earning a little money for food here and there. Three weeks later he reached Hampton. After many persuasions he obtained employment as a porter and was thus, able to earn money to pay for his board and fees, but it meant working many hours apart from his lessons. When he was 17, and had been there only 3 years he passed out of school. Four years later he was appointed House master. Then came his great opportunity. His Principal recommended him as Principal of a new school to be opened at Tuskegee for Negro ex-slaves.

When Booker got to Tuskegee he found many Negroes anxious to become students, but there were no buildings. Booker got permission to use a tumble down shed, and enrolled 30 students. He discovered that they all wanted 'book learning' that would enable them to live without having to work—or so they thought! Booker realised that he must change their ideas of education if they were to become useful citizens, able to earn a living. He bought an old plantation with dilapidated buildings and taught the students to repair them. He then wanted to clear the ground and grow food. Some students refused. When they saw Booker himself taking an axe to cut down trees, however, they followed his example. He taught his students that manual and brain work go together, and to illustrate this followed the principle of one day's work and one day's study for all students. The students learnt to grow food, make clothes, boots and shoes, brooms and carts, printing, metal work, gardening and other practical jobs.

He was very successful. He has written the story of his struggles and difficulties and of all that he tried to do. Many people who heard of what he was doing gave gifts. He was given animals for his farm, wood for building and money by both negroes and white men. Many times, however, the money came when he was desperately in need. And all this happened in a place where 16 years before no negro could be taught from books without the teacher being punished.

One other great thing that Booker did was to help to break down the barriers between black and white. He saw that some white people despised the black and some black people hated the White. Booker treated all man alike. One day he had a great opportunity. He was asked to speak at a great public meeting on the same platform as white men. The man who had been born a slave was to speak to the people who had been his masters. He made a wonderful speech, pleading for friendship and understanding.

HELEN KELLER

(The Blind and Deaf Girl who went to College)

Helen Keller was born both seeing and hearing, but at the age of 19 months, she had an illness which deprived her of both sight and hearing. She was unable to learn to speak. She would try to make people understand what she wanted by signs and when they could not understand she would go into outbursts of temper. Her parents took her to different doctors but no one was able to cure her. At last when she was nearly seven a teacher was found for her—Miss Anne Sullivan. She herself had been blind as a child so she understood what it was like.

She taught Helen the names of things by making her feel them and then spelling into her hand by signs the names of the different things. At first Helen did not see the connection between the objects and the strange signs her teacher made in her hand, but suddenly, one wonderful day she realised that everything had a name and from that time learnt very rapidly. After learning to understand the signs Helen began to learn to read. Her teacher gave her words in raised letters on strips of cardboard and she arranged them in sentences. She learnt geography from raised maps made by her teacher, and nature study by feeling the plants.

When she was 10 years old Helen learned to speak. She learned by placing her finger-tips lightly on the lips of a person who was speaking and by feeling the muscles and vibrations in his throat. She then practised until her lips and throat produced the same shape and vibrations. This meant very hardwork and much practice, but Miss Sullivan helped her with great patience.

When she was 13 she began to learn foreign languages, French and Latin. When she was 14 she went to a special school for the Deaf and Dumb where she could get the best methods of lip-reading. After that she went to an ordinary school so that she might prepare for college. Miss Sullivan had to go with her to pass on the teaching by the sign alphabet. Since, naturally, Helen could not hear the teachers. There she learnt German also. The Head of the school learnt the sign alphabet so as to be able to help her. Helen had learned to type and did all her homework on a typewriter. When the time came for Helen to write her examination the Head was very kind. She did her examination in a separate room. The Head read through the questions in the sign alphabet. Helen typed the answer, then the Head read to her what she had written and made any corrections she asked him to. She passed her examination well with honours in two subjects! Remember that this was an examination taken by boys and girls who could both see and hear. The next year Helen studied Mathematics and Science. She did not like Mathematics and found the subject difficult as she could not see the diagrams on the board and follow the teacher's explanations. Miss Sullivan made figures for her out of bent wire. She found it too difficult to study in school so her mother took her out of school and let her study privately. At last, however, she had passed all her subjects and was allowed to go to college.

At college her difficulties continued. So few of the books that she had to read had been printed in Braille (the special raised type for the blind) so Miss Sullivan had to read the set books into her hand. This is a slow business and Helen had to spend many hours with her books while other girls were playing or going to social gatherings, but so keen was Helen on receiving a good education that she was prepared to spend much time studying. Helen, however, was never one for learning by heart without thinking. She felt that the college curriculum did not leave people enough time to think, and was herself always trying to find time to think for herself. She had the right idea of what education should be.

RABINDRANATH TAGORE
(Making a School Beautiful)

As a body Rabindranath Tagore hated his school, the kind of education he received and everything about it. He said that his school-days were like a sentence in the Andamans! He hated all the dry-as-dust learning of textbooks—the lack of joy and freedom. So he determined to make a school that would be very different from those he had been forced to attend.

He started with five pupils and chose a place where his father built a house as a retreat for devotional purposes Shantiniketan. This was far away from any town in a dreary desert place, with little vegetation. It did not seem a very beautiful place! But Rabindranath determined to make it beautiful. He got his boys working, few as they were, and by following scientific methods stopped the soil erosion that was carrying away all the fertile surface soil. Then they began to plant all kinds of trees and plants so that now the place is more like a botanical garden than an ordinary school compound. There are so many different flowers. Nature must always be the first source of beauty.

Then as time went on and the school grew Rabindranath was able to add different departments. Right from the beginning the children had been encouraged to paint and draw, to dance, sign and play, and after some time a special department for this was opened, and the pupils learned other ways in which they could make their school life beautiful.

APPENDIX-V

Co-operative Learning for Value Education

India is passing through a transition period. The age old social fabric is disintegrated. A market oriented system is evolving in every part of our life. Education is also affected by the market economy and value system is eroded because of market forces. At this junction we need a education where the amalgamation of value and knowledge will take place. Answer to this critical problem is probably co-operative learning, through which we can provide mastery learning and value education to our pupils. Co-operative learning is a process of learning where the children learn through co-operation among themselves from different resources.

1. Characteristics of Co-operative Learning

1. It is a co-operative effort among the learner to learn a topic.
2. The teacher plays the role of an organiser.
3. It helps to achieve mastery learning over a particular subject-matter.
4. Through this technique the moral and social values are incorporated among learners.
5. It is a time taking process.

2. Problems in Value Education

Practically, value is imparted in our education through example. Teacher is the model in front of a class. The teacher should behave in front of the whole society in copy book style (idealistic manner) and the students are expected to imbibe the values propagated by teachers. One point is overlooked, that is pupil is more in contact with the society than his teachers. So, the child carries the values of society. It is also not fair to expect a super human behaviour from a teacher in the present society. The students are also exposed to media which has its wide impact on children. In this way value education becomes difficult through school education.

3. Values

The very first step towards the supreme values is moral value. Moral value is very subjective. If it is made more objective, then we expect the following values in the broad spectrum of moral values:

(a) Sincerity
(b) Faithfulness
(c) Obedience
(d) Gratitude
(e) Honesty
(f) Benevolence
(g) Generosity
(h) Cheerfulness
(i) Selflessness
(j) Freedom from egoism
(k) Stoicism (Equality in joy and suffering, honour and dishonour in success and failure.)
(l) Sharing with others
(m) Tolerance
(n) Unity
(o) Mutuality

4. How to Organise the Co-operative Learning

1. Divide the class into small groups. Each group should contain 5 to 7 students.
2. In each group students of different cognitive styles should be there.
3. In each group students of same locality should be there to have post-school correspondence.
4. In every group, a group leader should be there and he/she should be unanimously elected on the basis of his/her qualities.
5. A topic may be given to the students. Same topic may be used for all the groups.
6. Every student will study the topic individually. The students can clarify the doubt amongst themselves and if still it is not clarified the group leader will learn the topic from teacher and then he will communicate it to his friends.
7. Teacher will prepare some thought—provoking questions on the particular topic. Question papers will be given to each

group and then they will discuss the questions among themselves. Question paper will be circulated among the groups. This should be a time bound programme.

8. A written test may be given to the students. Total marks of each group will be calculated. Then position may be given to each group.

5. Role of Teachers

Teachers should have clearcut idea about students to divide groups. Teacher should be able to control the class during discussion. Teacher should be technically sound to prepare the questions. While preparing question paper he should give sufficient stress on value-based question.

Example: Topic-Blood Group

What is blood transfusion? Blood transfusion is not harmful to donor—Explain.

You should donate blood and you should not purchase it from Blood Bank—Explain.

In the whole process the teacher's role is indirect but he should be instrumental to develop certain skills such as communication skill, leadership quality, trust, decision-making ability conflict management skills, tolerance, etc. amongst students to help achieve value education through co-operative learning.

6. Conclusion

It is a time when we should put a check on erosion of values in our society. We are moving towards learner-centred education. These two qualities are essentially present in co-operative learning. The only difficulty with co-operative learning is its slowness. But it is individualised and pupil will have 'mastery learning' over the subject-matter. If we compare the advantage against its disadvantages, we may find it is suitable for school education. Research work on this particular issue may open a scope for its implementation in school education.

BIBLIOGRAPHY

Agrawala, V.S., *Studies in Indian Art*, Varanasi.

Bhattacharya, Vinaytosh, *Cultural Heritage of India*.

Clarke, Jay, *Beginning Values Clarification*, Pennant Press, 1975.

Dewey, John, *Moral Principles in Education*, Philosophical Library, New York, 1959.

————, *Human Nature and Conduct*, New York: Holt, 1922.

————, *Art as Experience*, New York: Miniton, Balch, 1934.

————, *Theory of Valuation*, Chicago: University of Chicago Press, 1939.

Dictionary of Philosophy, Progress Publishers, Moscow.

Encyclopaedia of Religion and Ethic, Edited by James Hastings, T&T Clark, Edinburg, 1965.

Faure, Edgar, Ed., *Learning To Be—The World of Education Today and Tomorrow*, UNESCO Report, Paris, 1972.

Fraenkel, Jack R. "Teaching About Values." In *Values of the American Heritage: Challenges Case Studies, and Teaching Strategies*, Yearbook of the National Council for the Social Studies, 1976.

Friedenberg, Edgar Z., *The Vanishing Adolescent*, Boston: Boston Press, 1959.

Gandhi, M.K., *My Religion*, Navajeevan Publishing House, Ahmedabad.

Gregg, Rechard B., *A Compass for Civilization*, N.P.H., Ahmedabad.

Griffin, Willis H. and Udai Pareek, *Process of Planned Change in Education*, Somaiya Publications Pvt. Ltd., Bombay 1970.

Gupta, N.L., *Current Trends and Problems of Progressive Education*, Krishna Bros., Ajmer, 1985.

————, *A Search for Human Values*, Arya Book Depot, New Delhi, 1992.

————, *Values & Creativity*, Arya Book Depot, New Delhi, 1992.

————, *New Education Policy*, Krishna Bros., Ajmer, 1987.

————, *Neo-Humanism and Human Values*, Mohit Publications, New Delhi, 1999.

————, *Education and Values in Mahabharata*, Concept Publishing Company, New Delhi, 1995.

Har Dayal, *Hints for Self-Culture*, Jaico, 1961.

Harman, S., *Plight of Pupils in Schools*, D.L. Publications, London, p. 70.

Harmin, M., H. Kirschenbaum, and S.B. Simon. *Clarifying Values Through Subject-Matter*, Minneapolis: Winston Press, 1973.

Inlow, Gail M., *Values in Transition.*

Iyer, Shiv Swamy, *Evolution of Hindu Moral Ideals.*

Kaul, G.N., *Value & Education in Independent India.*

Kirschenbaum, Howard, *Values Clarification: An Advanced Handbook for Trainers and Teachers*, La Jolla, Calif.: University Associates Press, 1977.

Kohlberg, Lawrence, "The Cognitive-Developmental Approach to Moral Education," *Phi Delta Kappan*, June 1975, 56(10), 670-77.

————, "The Relationship of Moral Education to the Broader Field of Values Education: Theory, Practice, Problems and Prospects," *Waterloo*, Ontario: Wilfred Laurier University Press, 1975.

Maitra, S.K., *The Ethics of Hindus*, 2nd Edition.

Maslow, A.H., *Motivation and Personality*, New York, Harper and Row, 1954.

Maurus, J., *How to Use Your Complexes.*

————, *How to Win Personal Efficiency, Better Yourself.*

Metcalf, Lawrence E., ed., *Values Education: Rationale, Strategies, and Procedures*, Washington, D.C.: National Council for the Social Studies, 1971, pp. 1-28.

Mukherjee, R.K., *Ancient Indian Education.*

Pack, Robert F. and Robert J. Havighurst, *The Psychology of Character Development*, New York: John Wiley & Sons, 1960.

Ranganathanand, Swami, *Eternal Values for a Changing Society*, BVB, Bombay, 1971.

Sears, P.S. and V.S. Sherman, *In Pursuit of Self-esteem*, Belmont, Calif.: Wadsworth Publishing, 1964.

Simon, Sidney B., Leland W., Howe, and Howard Kirschenbaum. *Values Clarification: A Handbook of Practical Strategies of Teachers and Students*, New York: Hart Publishing, 1972.

Smith, B.C., "Values Clarification in Drug Education: A Comparative Study," *Journal of Drug Education*, 1973, 3(4), 369-76.

Wallek, Rene. and Austin Warren, *Theory of Literature.*

Westermark, E., *The Origin & Development of Moral Ideas*, Vol. II, Educational Policies Commission, U.S.A.

Whitehead, Alfred North, *Adventures of Ideas*, Penguin Books, 1948.

Whitehead, A.N., *Aims of Education*.

Sanskrit and Hindi

Ashtadash Upanishad, Edited by Limaya and Wadekar, Vedic Samshodhan Mandal, Pune, 1958.

Bharatiya Niti Ka Vikas, Dr. Rajbali Pandey, *Bihara Rastra Bhasha Parishad*, Patna.

Bharatiya Nitishastra Ka Itihas, Dr. Bhikhanlal Atreya.

Charaka Samhita, Chaukhamba Vidya Bhawan, Varanasi.

Jain-Bauddha Shikshan Paddhati, Dr. N.L. Gupta, Hindi.

The Mahabharata, BORI, Pune, Udyogparvan and Shantiparvan.

Mahabharata Kaleen Shiksha, Dr. N.L. Gupta, Chetna Prakashan, New Shukrawari, Nagpur, 1976.

Manav Mulyon Ki Khoj, N.L. Gupta, Vishwa Bharti Prakashan, Nagpur, 1990.

Manu Smriti, Edited by Hargovind Shastri, Chaukhamba, Varanasi, 1970.

Marathi Prakashan, Sitabuldi, Nagpur, 1985.

Mulya Parak Shiksha, N.L. Gupta, Krishna Bros., Ajmer, 1987.

Pracheen Bharat Ke Aacharya Aur Unki Uplabdhiyan, Dr. N.L. Gupta, Chetna Prakashan, Nagpur, 1978.

Sanskriti Ke Char Adhyaya, Ramdhari Singh, 'Dinkar'.

Reports and Periodicals

1. Report of the High Level Seminar on Moral Education (Shimla, May 27-28).
2. Report of the Group to Review Teachers' Training Programme (in the light of the need for Value-orientation), Ministry of Education and Culture, Govt. of India.
3. Towards A New Education Policy (Draft Proposals), CBSE, New Delhi, 1985.
4. National Policy on Education 1986, Programme of Action, Ministry of HRD, August 1986.
5. National Education Commission (Kothari Commission 1964-66), Govt. of India.
6. Some Issues of '*Journal of Indian Education*', NCERT, New Delhi.
7. National Integration Through Schools, CBSE, New Delhi.

INDEX